10/03

OPPOSING VIEWPOINTS®

Suicide

Roman Espejo, *Book Editor*

Daniel Leone, *President*
Bonnie Szumski, *Publisher*
Scott Barbour, *Managing Editor*
Helen Cothran, *Senior Editor*

GREENHAVEN
PRESS®

THOMSON

GALE

San Diego • Detroit • New York • San Francisco • Cleveland
New Haven, Conn. • Waterville, Maine • London • Munich

© 2003 by Greenhaven Press. Greenhaven Press is an imprint of The Gale Group, Inc., a division of Thomson Learning, Inc.

Greenhaven® and Thomson Learning™ are trademarks used herein under license.

For more information, contact
Greenhaven Press
27500 Drake Rd.
Farmington Hills, MI 48331-3535
Or you can visit our Internet site at http://www.gale.com

Cover credit: © PhotoDisc

LIBRARY OF CONGRESS CATALOGING-IN-PUBLICATION DATA

Suicide : opposing viewpoints / Roman Espejo, book editor.
    p. cm. — (Opposing viewpoints series)
    Includes bibliographical references and index.
    ISBN 0-7377-1241-4 (pbk. : alk. paper) — ISBN 0-7377-1242-2 (lib. : alk. paper)
    1. Suicide—Juvenile literature. 2. Teenagers—Suicidal behavior—Juvenile literature. [1. Suicide.] I. Espejo, Roman, 1977– . II. Opposing viewpoints series (Unnumbered)
    HV6545 .S814 2003
    362.28'0835—dc21   2002032214

Printed in the United States of America

"Congress shall make no law...abridging the freedom of speech, or of the press."

First Amendment to the U.S. Constitution

The basic foundation of our democracy is the First Amendment guarantee of freedom of expression. The Opposing Viewpoints Series is dedicated to the concept of this basic freedom and the idea that it is more important to practice it than to enshrine it.

Contents

Why Consider Opposing Viewpoints?

"The only way in which a human being can make some approach to knowing the whole of a subject is by hearing what can be said about it by persons of every variety of opinion and studying all modes in which it can be looked at by every character of mind. No wise man ever acquired his wisdom in any mode but this."

John Stuart Mill

In our media-intensive culture it is not difficult to find differing opinions. Thousands of newspapers and magazines and dozens of radio and television talk shows resound with differing points of view. The difficulty lies in deciding which opinion to agree with and which "experts" seem the most credible. The more inundated we become with differing opinions and claims, the more essential it is to hone critical reading and thinking skills to evaluate these ideas. Opposing Viewpoints books address this problem directly by presenting stimulating debates that can be used to enhance and teach these skills. The varied opinions contained in each book examine many different aspects of a single issue. While examining these conveniently edited opposing views, readers can develop critical thinking skills such as the ability to compare and contrast authors' credibility, facts, argumentation styles, use of persuasive techniques, and other stylistic tools. In short, the Opposing Viewpoints Series is an ideal way to attain the higher-level thinking and reading skills so essential in a culture of diverse and contradictory opinions.

In addition to providing a tool for critical thinking, Opposing Viewpoints books challenge readers to question their own strongly held opinions and assumptions. Most people form their opinions on the basis of upbringing, peer pressure, and personal, cultural, or professional bias. By reading carefully balanced opposing views, readers must directly confront new ideas as well as the opinions of those with whom they disagree. This is not to simplistically argue that everyone who reads opposing views will—or should—change his or her opinion. Instead, the series enhances readers' understanding of their own views by encouraging confrontation with opposing ideas. Careful examination of others' views can lead to the readers' understanding of the logical inconsistencies in their own opinions, perspective on why they hold an opinion, and the consideration of the possibility that their opinion requires further evaluation.

Evaluating Other Opinions

To ensure that this type of examination occurs, Opposing Viewpoints books present all types of opinions. Prominent spokespeople on different sides of each issue as well as well-known professionals from many disciplines challenge the reader. An additional goal of the series is to provide a forum for other, less known, or even unpopular viewpoints. The opinion of an ordinary person who has had to make the decision to cut off life support from a terminally ill relative, for example, may be just as valuable and provide just as much insight as a medical ethicist's professional opinion. The editors have two additional purposes in including these less known views. One, the editors encourage readers to respect others' opinions—even when not enhanced by professional credibility. It is only by reading or listening to and objectively evaluating others' ideas that one can determine whether they are worthy of consideration. Two, the inclusion of such viewpoints encourages the important critical thinking skill of objectively evaluating an author's credentials and bias. This evaluation will illuminate an author's reasons for taking a particular stance on an issue and will aid in readers' evaluation of the author's ideas.

It is our hope that these books will give readers a deeper understanding of the issues debated and an appreciation of the complexity of even seemingly simple issues when good and honest people disagree. This awareness is particularly important in a democratic society such as ours in which people enter into public debate to determine the common good. Those with whom one disagrees should not be regarded as enemies but rather as people whose views deserve careful examination and may shed light on one's own.

Thomas Jefferson once said that "difference of opinion leads to inquiry, and inquiry to truth." Jefferson, a broadly educated man, argued that "if a nation expects to be ignorant and free . . . it expects what never was and never will be." As individuals and as a nation, it is imperative that we consider the opinions of others and examine them with skill and discernment. The Opposing Viewpoints Series is intended to help readers achieve this goal.

David L. Bender and Bruno Leone,
Founders

Greenhaven Press anthologies primarily consist of previously published material taken from a variety of sources, including periodicals, books, scholarly journals, newspapers, government documents, and position papers from private and public organizations. These original sources are often edited for length and to ensure their accessibility for a young adult audience. The anthology editors also change the original titles of these works in order to clearly present the main thesis of each viewpoint and to explicitly indicate the opinion presented in the viewpoint. These alterations are made in consideration of both the reading and comprehension levels of a young adult audience. Every effort is made to ensure that Greenhaven Press accurately reflects the original intent of the authors included in this anthology.

Introduction

"Each individual has . . . the right to exercise some control over the time and manner of one's death."
—*Ronald Dworkin et al.*

"The 'right' to die could become a death sentence for the most vulnerable."
—*Anneke Quinta*

In the United States, suicide is legal, but committing suicide with assistance from a physician, family member, or friend is illegal in nearly every state. As of January 2003, thirty-five states have statutes directly banning physician-assisted suicide (PAS) and nine states criminalize it through common law. The major exception, Oregon, currently allows PAS under its controversial Death with Dignity Act. Although Oregon voters passed the act in November 1994, it was not implemented until October 27, 1997, when the Ninth Circuit Court of Appeals lifted a legal injunction against it. The act allows terminally ill patients to lawfully obtain prescriptions for lethal medications from their physicians in order to commit suicide. At the time of this writing, approximately seventy cases of legal PAS have taken place in Oregon since the law was enacted. The Death with Dignity Act, because it is the first law of its kind to be implemented in the nation, is a milestone. Other key developments in the debate over PAS include the conviction of PAS advocate Jack Kevorkian and two controversial court cases.

Assisted suicide initially appeared on the nation's radar screen years earlier when Jack Kevorkian, a former pathologist from Michigan, publicly helped individuals with terminal or debilitating illness end their lives with his "suicide machines." On June 4, 1990, fifty-four-year-old Janet Adkins, who suffered from Alzheimer's disease, injected herself with a lethal dose of medication with a push of a button on a machine Kevorkian had built. Kevorkian was charged with murder following Adkins's death, but a state judge dismissed the charge against him after ruling that Michigan had no law that banned assisted suicide. In 1991, Kevorkian helped forty-three-year-old Sherry Miller and fifty-eight-year-old Marjorie Wantz commit suicide by using a machine that delivered carbon monoxide. Murder charges were brought against him the following year, but they were once again dismissed by a state judge because of the absence of a prohibitive assisted suicide law in Michigan. In December 1992, then Michigan governor John Engler responded to Kevorkian's activities by signing a temporary ban on assisted suicide. Despite the new ban, the revocation of his medical licenses, and being (unsuccessfully) tried four times for assisted suicide, Kevorkian continued his practice until 1998. In November of that year, a murder charge was brought against Kevorkian after CBS aired a controversial videotape of him aiding the suicide of fifty-two-year-old Thomas Youk, who suffered from Lou Gehrig's disease. Although the case was initially dismissed, Kevorkian was eventually charged with Youk's murder and brought to trial. In March 1999, after reviewing the videotape, a Michigan jury found him guilty of second-degree murder and delivering a controlled substance. He was consequently sentenced to ten to twenty-five years in prison. By this time, Kervorkian had attended at least 130 suicides.

While Kevorkian seemed to draw America's attention to the emotional and moral aspects of assisted suicide, the battle to recognize assisted suicide as a fundamental, constitutional right began with two court cases during the mid-1990s. In the first case, *Washington State vs. Glucksberg* (1994), physician Harold Glucksberg and other doctors challenged Washington State's prohibition on PAS, stating that the right to die is protected under the Due Process Clause of the Fourteenth Amendment. They argued that if it is constitutional to allow terminally ill patients on life support to refuse further treatment with the intent to die, it is also constitutional to permit terminally ill patients not on life support to choose death by requesting lethal medications from their physicians. A federal district court judge ruled that Washington's ban on PAS was unconstitutional. In response, the state of Washington appealed, and the Ninth Circuit Court of Appeals reversed the decision. However, on May 9, 1996, the Ninth Circuit Court of Appeals overturned its previous decision and ruled that Washington's ban on PAS was unconstitutional.

In the second case, *Quill vs. Vacco* (1994), physician Timothy Quill and several of his colleagues disputed New York State's prohibition on allowing physicians to prescribe lethal drugs to terminally ill patients. They based their arguments on the same principles that Glucksberg had used to challenge Washington's ban on PAS. The U.S. District Court for the Southern District of New York upheld the prohibition. However, on April 2, 1996, the Second Circuit Court of Appeals reversed the District Court's decision and ruled that New York's ban on assisted suicide was unconstitutional. Nevertheless, the ruling did not stand because on June 26, 1997, the U.S. Supreme Court ruled that PAS was not a fundamental, constitutional right, which effectively overturned the *Glucksberg* and *Quill* decisions.

The U.S. Supreme Court ruled that assisted suicide was not a constitutional right, but the court did not place restrictions upon the assisted suicide laws that state governments could enact, a decision that, in essence, protected Oregon's Death with Dignity Act. Nonetheless, vigorous opposition to Oregon's law continues to grow. While activists in Oregon and across the nation are working to fight the act, in November 2001, U.S. Attorney General John Ashcroft took action against Oregon's law by enacting a drug enforcement policy that prohibited physicians in that state from giving their patients lethal medications that are federally controlled. But in April 2002, federal judge Robert E. Jones upheld the Death with Dignity Act, stating that under the Controlled Substance Act, the federal government cannot prohibit Oregon physicians from prescribing lethal medications. Jones also took steps to protect physicians who practice PAS under Oregon's law from prosecution.

Although these judicial rulings have protected Oregonians' right to PAS for now, the assisted suicide controversy is not likely to abate any time soon. At the heart of the debate are the issues of individual rights and the sanctity of life. The authors in *Suicide: Opposing Viewpoints* offer varied perspectives on assisted suicide, as well as on the acceptability of suicide in general, in the following chapters: Is Suicide Ever

Acceptable? What Are the Causes of Teen Suicide? Should Assisted Suicide Be Legalized? and How Should Society Address Suicide? The views in this anthology all touch upon the fundamental and unsettling question of whether suicide is ultimately an avoidable tragedy or a solemn solution to human suffering.

CHAPTER 1

Is Suicide Ever Acceptable?

Chapter Preface

Committing suicide for honor is sometimes viewed as a reasonable, permissible, and praiseworthy act. This is clearly demonstrated by acts of terrorism committed by Islamic extremist groups at the beginning of the twenty-first century. International relations teacher Sohail H. Hashmi claims, "Suicide for any reason has been strongly condemned throughout Islamic history and its practice is extremely rare in Islamic societies. In the context of war, however, the line between suicide and combat is often extremely fine and easily crossed." For example, the Islamic hijackers who crashed airliners into the World Trade Center, the Pentagon, and a field in western Pennsylvania on September 11, 2001, allegedly waged *jihad*, or holy war, against America in the name of Allah. Therefore, in the eyes of these men, their suicides were not only justified but, indeed, honorable.

The spate of suicide bombings in Israel in 2002 is more evidence that some followers of Islam make allowances for suicide. In Palestine, where Islamic beliefs dominate, suicide bombers are publicly honored and earn religious approval from a great segment of their community. Cable News Network (CNN) Jerusalem Bureau Chief Mike Hanna contends that those "who carry out the attacks are seen as heroes in the fight against Israel, martyrs for the teachings of Islam, even role models for Palestinian youth." For instance, thousands of mourners attended the funeral of Shadi al-Kahlout, a Palestinian who was shot and killed by Israeli soldiers to prevent him from carrying out a suicide bombing mission. His mother, Subhia al-Kahlout, states, "I was sad to lose him. At the same time, according to our religious teachings, my son is alive in God's company." In addition, Saudi ambassador to Great Britain Ghazi Algosaibi stated that the eighteen-year-old Palestinian woman who blew herself up in front of an Israeli market died "to honor God's word. She embraced death with a smile while the leaders are running away from death. Doors of heaven are opened for her."

The American Association of Suicidology claims that terrorists who carry out suicide missions are not "primarily suicidal," nor are they "necessarily suffering from mental illness." However, those who believe that suicides committed by competent individuals in certain circumstances can be rational, even moral, hold these ideas. In the following chapter, *Is Suicide Ever Acceptable?*, the authors argue whether the circumstances, motivations, and goals of a suicide can make it an acceptable act.

> "*The prevailing hostility to suicide and its infamous reputation have led our society to cruel and immoral policies.*"

Suicide Can Be Morally Acceptable

Ernest van den Haag

Ernest van den Haag is a retired professor of jurisprudence and public policy at Fordham University in New York City. In the following viewpoint, van den Haag refutes the religious and philosophical objections to suicide. In regards to religious objections, van den Haag asserts that they do not apply to individuals with secular beliefs. In addition, he claims that the philosophical argument stating that a person has a duty to live is not persuasive because a person's life belongs to him or her, to do with as he or she sees fit, even if that includes ending it. Moreover, van den Haag claims that making allowances for suicide will not endanger society provided appropriate cautions are put into place.

As you read, consider the following questions:

1. Although the Bible does not condemn suicide, why do individuals with Judeo-Christian beliefs oppose suicide, as stated by van den Haag?
2. How does van den Haag support his claim that assisted suicide is not murder?
3. In the author's opinion, why does suicide have a bad reputation?

Ernest van den Haag, "Why Does Suicide Have a Bad Reputation?" *Chronicles*, August 1998, pp. 20–22. Copyright © 1998 by Ernest van den Haag. Reproduced by permission.

Whether and when we enter this world is decided not by, but for us. Nor is it up to us to decide when to leave it. Most of us would like to stay longer than we are allowed—but our lifespan is ordained by forces beyond our control. We are quite resigned to this; however, when we become greatly impaired and life no longer holds much promise, some of us think of shortening it and of asking others to help if necessary. Is that legitimate? Are there serious moral objections?

In the past, the usual lifespan was brief and illness often ended it abruptly. The old were honored largely because they were so few. We live longer now, and death is likely to approach gradually, depriving us of our abilities one by one, until we sink into incompetence and finally unconsciousness. This has made shortening life more tempting. Yet most people feel that they ought to be no more responsible for their death than they were for their birth. Religion and tradition also tell us that we ought to wait patiently for our end and always try to postpone, never to advance it. The medical profession sees this as its main task, and most non-physicians as well think it presumptuous to engineer death ourselves. It might be premature in any case: unforeseen good things may still be in store. No animal commits suicide, and our animal instincts oppose it. Thus we are resigned to a natural death, the date not chosen by us, or known in advance.

Instinct, Religion, and Tradition

But instinct, religion, and tradition do not always prevail. There would be no problem if they did. Suicides do occur, even though most people look upon them with horror, as an aberration explainable only by madness. Indeed, there frequently is a mental disorder; but not always. And the assumption that mental disorder *ipso facto* must be the cause of suicide conveniently avoids moral problems that ought to be addressed.

The pre-Christian ancients, perhaps with the exception of the Stoics, did not favor suicide. But they opposed it only mildly, thinking it reasonable at least in some situations and obligatory in others. However, the Judeo-Christian religion fervently opposes suicide, although there is no scriptural warrant for this opposition: the Bible nowhere condemns suicide. Yet the traditional opposition seldom is questioned even by those alienated from tradition. It rests on the belief that God created us in His image and endowed us with many abilities, including free will. We are the Creator's creatures. He gave us life—and He alone has the right to take it. We do not. "Thy will be done."

Under certain circumstances, others may lawfully and with divine sanction kill us, but we never are allowed to do so ourselves. Life is a gift from God, and it would be irreverent and impious to throw it away. Above all, our life is not ours to dispose of. We are but stewards entrusted with God's property. In some ways this view makes life appear as though a prison. God holds the key, and we are morally bound to stay until released. In due time He will let us out, to go to heaven or to hell. Meanwhile, attempts to escape by climbing over the walls are illegitimate and sinful and will be punished accordingly. Yet we did not volunteer for life. Whether we can legitimately volunteer for death is the problem—at least for the non-religious.

Philosophical Arguments

Philosophical arguments against suicide are neither cheerful nor persuasive. Aristotle thought that in many ways we are creatures of the communities that reared us and have a duty to live so that we may contribute to them. This is an uncommonly weak argument. It would follow that, should we become a burden on the community, suicide would become legitimate, perhaps even required. (Aristotle does not draw this inference.) Further, whatever the community did for us, we never volunteered to join it and to become obligated to live when we no longer want to. In modern times, involuntary obligations are always questionable, although most people recognize some such obligations, e.g., to their parents. An involuntary natural obligation to live may be analogously constructed. We also may be morally obligated to obey laws for which we did not volunteer. But laws prohibiting such things as murder or fraud protect us from one another, whereas the prohibition of suicide would protect us from ourselves. This does not seem to be called for. It is unclear to whom the obligation to live is owed and how it is justified. Aristotle further thought that suicide violates "right reason" and therefore is "unjust" toward nature and the state. Plato, too, opposed suicide without offering much of an argument. He writes, "A person who kills himself [is] violently robbing what fate has allotted," without bothering to argue the authority of fate. Why must we obey it when we can do otherwise?

[Philosopher] John Locke decided that we own the product of our labor because "every man has a property in his own person" and, therefore, in whatever he produces. It would be a small step to infer that, since we own ourselves, we can dispose of ourselves and decide whether to live or die. Property, after all, is the right to dispose of what one owns. But, being a good Christian, Locke did not take this step. We remain God's creatures and owe a duty to live the life God gave us. "Everyone is bound to preserve himself and not to quit his station willfully." In effect, we don't fully own ourselves (contrary to what libertarians believe) but merely are in (temporary) possession, tenants on God's property.

The Duty to Ourselves

[Philosopher] Immanuel Kant opposed suicide as a violation of the duty to live. He thought we owe this duty to ourselves. But a duty owed by and to ourselves is not very different from a debt owed by and to ourselves—which we can always forgive. Actually, since the debtor and the creditor are the same person, no debt is really owed to anyone by anyone. To say that we owe a debt, or a duty, to ourselves means no more than that we feel we ought to do (or not to do) something. It adds no argument, only emphasis, to that feeling, while suggesting that an independent argument has been added. In the words of [philosopher] Thomas Hobbes: "He that can bind can release; and therefore he that is bound to himself only, is not bound."

The notion of a duty owed to oneself also may envision a split in the self between a part to which the duty is owed and the part owing it. Such internal conflicts do occur (without them psychotherapists could not make a living). Quite possibly, conscience (or our long-term interest) wants one thing and the pleasure-seeking part of the self another. Still, the duty to which conscience calls us is always a duty either to others or to some moral idea which we have accepted. Kant thought that our duty is to reason. (But he did not show that suicide is irrational.) The obligatoriness of the duty depends on the moral weight of its demands, not on its being a duty to oneself. And Kant did not actually offer a convincing argument for the duty to live.

A Double Moral Standard

Some people whose suicides were prevented felt very happy that they were. They felt elated to have the gift of life back. Isn't this sufficient a reason to intervene? Absolutely not. All of us are engaged in making irreversible decisions. For some of these decisions, we are likely to pay very dearly. Is this a reason to stop us from making them? Should the state be allowed to prevent a couple from marrying because of genetic incompatibility? Should an overpopulated country institute forced abortions? Should smoking be banned for the higher risk groups? The answers seem to be clear and negative. There is a double moral standard when it comes to suicide. People are permitted to destroy their lives only in certain prescribed ways.

Sam Vaknin, "The Murder of Oneself," http://samvak.tripod.com, 2000.

[Philosopher] Arthur Schopenhauer did not think highly of life. He was convinced that the suffering it brings exceeds its pleasures. (He did not tell how he measured and compared.) Since desire brings suffering in excess of the pleasure of fulfillment, Schopenhauer felt that we should strive for desirelessness, as he believed Hindus and Buddhists did. Thus, by avoiding life (for to avoid desire is to avoid life), we would avoid suffering. One might think that Schopenhauer would justify suicide, but he actually opposed it as an illegitimate means of achieving desirelessness. Buddhists thought that suicide would only bring reincarnation, not Nirvana. Schopenhauer's arguments seem unusually murky here. But one must remember that, by justifying suicide, philosophers would place themselves in an awkward position: they would have to justify staying alive while arguing in favor of being dead if they argued that suicide is obligatory, or even desirable. Schopenhauer preferred to make it attractive (or to make life unattractive) but futile. Among major philosophers, David Hume was alone in thinking suicide legitimate. He has remained alone.

Our Lives to End or Continue

Few people want to commit suicide and every effort should be made to dissuade them, for their wish may be temporary. However, if they are altogether resolved, they cannot be prevented at length from carrying out their intention, and if they are mentally competent, there is no justification for thwarting them. There is no justification either for denying help to those who, although mentally competent, are physically so disabled that they need and request help to end their life. Their wish for ending their life is more intelligible than that of others. But no excuse is needed from a secular viewpoint. It is your life to end or to continue.

Why do so many people insist that suicide always ought to be prevented even when preventing it prolongs the hopeless suffering of incurably sick persons? Why does suicide horrify people? Chaste persons not only abstain from illicit sex, but also usually think that those who do not are morally wrong (or at least weak) and should be prevented from doing what they want. That is also how people who want to live feel about people who want to die. Could it be, then, that we feel that those who do not act according to the survival instinct we all share are, as it were, traitors to life, quitters who give in to a temptation that must be shunned, even though (or perhaps because) it is felt at times by nearly everyone?

Consensual Homicide

Murdering others is wrong and a crime because it takes the life of those who were entitled to live and did not want to die. But suicide ends the life of a person who no longer wishes to live. He obviously consents to taking his own life, or to having it taken. What makes killing others wrong, what makes homicide murder, is lack of consent. Consensual intercourse is legitimate, but non-consensual intercourse is rape and a crime. The law acknowledges the difference which consent makes with regard to sex (and to property) but ignores it with regard to homicide, including assisted suicide, perhaps because consent cannot be valid if (as religious dogma asserts) we don't own ourselves; more likely because consensual intercourse (or property transfer) is common, whereas consensual homicide certainly is not.

We all have an instinctive wish to continue living. But instincts leave us some choice, allowing reason to direct our actions, sometimes in defiance of our instincts. Unlike animals, we have a choice, and can act according to our moral norms. Yet the prevailing hostility to suicide and its infamous reputation have led our society to cruel and immoral policies. We threaten to punish anyone, including physicians, who helps another to end his life.

There are dangers in legalizing assisted suicide or euthanasia, mainly concerning competent and informed consent. But these dangers can be surmounted by appropriate precautions. Once we discard the presumption (actually a circular definition) that all persons bent on suicide *ipso facto* are insane, we have to make sure that those requesting assistance are mentally competent. Some objectors insist that this can never be reliably ascertained. This seems absurd. Laymen as well as psychiatrists are quite capable of distinguishing persons of sound mind from others who, temporarily or permanently, are not. Were it not so, valid contracts or wills could never be made, and no business could be done. It is bizarre to argue that we can distinguish the sane from the insane except when it comes to people who wish to die. The possibility of abuse which bedevils all human practices can never be eliminated altogether, but safeguards can minimize abuse. To argue that physicians, once they are authorized to help those who request help to end their life, would also shorten the life of people who wanted to live is no better than arguing that once physicians are authorized to amputate diseased limbs, they will amputate healthy ones as well. No slope is that slippery.

Suicide's Bad Reputation

Why does suicide have such a bad reputation? It defies what we instinctively feel and want to believe: that life is always worth living, whatever the circumstances. It seems to reject life itself and thereby to breach the solidarity of the living. Without this solidarity, there can be no society. Human solidarity, cultivated by religious, political, and educational institutions, takes many forms. But those who breach it by suicide are always seen as renegades. They used to be ostracized even in death. Plato urged that they be interred in "isolated" graves. In the Middle Ages, they were denied consecrated ground, and a stake was driven through their hearts. Yet some cultures have made allowances for suicide. It has not endangered their societies. Suicide is not infectious (despite occasional imitations), and it is unlikely ever to become popular enough to endanger any society. Nothing is lost, then, if we stop hindering or prohibiting assistance. Something is gained. We will, at last, allow individuals to control their lifespan within the boundaries set by nature, and we will reduce or eliminate the immense undeserved suffering to which hitherto we have sentenced so many innocent people.

"Those who commit suicide are guilty of murder."

Suicide Is Not Morally Acceptable

Richard Rupnarain

In the following viewpoint, Richard Rupnarain asserts that suicide is immoral for three reasons. First, he claims that suicide is murder, which violates one of God's commandments. Next, Rupnarain claims that it also violates one's obligations to oneself, other people, and God. Finally, he concludes that suicide is not morally permissible because it does not benefit society. Rupnarain is a reverend and writes for Evalis Services, an organization that promotes Biblical values.

As you read, consider the following questions:
1. What Biblical examples does the author use to support his claim that God prohibits murder?
2. How does the author respond to David Hume's argument that suicide may be permissible for a person who is burdensome to society?
3. How does Rupnarain counter the claim that suicide may be an act of self-love?

An article in a recent edition of the *Toronto Star* entitled, "High Suicide Rate Mars Island Paradise," brought back memories of the suicide of one of my colleagues several years ago. While fellow workers blamed themselves or others for her death few dared ask if she had the moral authority to commit suicide. With suicide rates climbing in many countries (according to World Health Organization statistics quoted in the article), the question is still relevant: Do we have the moral authority to take our own lives?

Using the criteria for determining what may or may not be done in particular situations, as outlined by [biblical scholars] Paul and John Feinberg in *Ethics For a Brave New World*, I will argue that suicide is immoral for the following reasons:

1. It is not morally obligatory.
2. It is not morally permissible, and
3. It is not morally supererogatory.

Morally Obligatory

If suicide is morally obligatory it means there is a moral command which either mandates or forbids it. While there is no direct Scriptural mandate to affirm any form of suicide, assisted or otherwise, there is indirect prohibition against taking human life. The Lord punished Cain for the murder of his brother Abel (Gen.4:13), and as if to explain the severity of the punishment, reminded us in the following chapter that Seth was made, like his father and mother (Gen.1:26,27), in the image of God (Gen.5:3). After the Flood, and perhaps with the relics of the dead littering the environment, God once again reminded mankind of the preciousness of human life. He warned Noah's generation that taking life will incur reciprocal punishment and explained the reason for the severity of judgment: "For in the image of God made he man" (Gen.9:6). After the overthrow of the Egyptians, and the defeat of Amalek in the wilderness God once again mandated, "Thou shall not kill" (Ex.20:13). The mandate to desist from taking human life seems to follow instances of either individual killing or mass carnage. It is as if God wanted to remind man that while in His sovereignty and wisdom He has at times chosen to take such actions it is by no means a precedent for man to follow.

It could be argued that in all these prohibitions against murder, the person of the killer is irrelevant. Be it oneself or another, the prohibitive command against killing was clear and universal without any allusion to the relationship of the killer.

This interpretation would mean that those who take their own lives or have others assist them, are in violation of the unconditional divine prohibition. They are guilty of murder, perhaps to an extent even greater than that of the murder of another person. After all, their act was premeditated, and performed by their own hands against themselves. It is beyond self-abuse for they have removed life which belongs to another, even to God, who said, "All souls are mine" (Ezek.18:4).

Hence, while there is no mandate to allow suicide under any circumstances, there are clear prohibitions against murder, and since the person of the murderer is not limited to another outside of the crime, those who commit suicide are guilty of murder and stand in jeopardy of having a place in the lake of fire (Rev.21:8).

Suicide Is Not Morally Permissible

To say that an action is morally permissible means one may or may not do it without incurring any moral guilt. The question then is, Can someone incur moral guilt for an act of suicide? In a sense we may never know since those who committed suicide are dead. But perhaps we can obtain a clue from those whose attempt at suicide either failed or was aborted. Suicide notes left by "victims" seem to indicate that while they felt what they were about to do was not right it was the best solution to their problem. But apart from the individual feelings of guilt and remorse, the moral permissibility of suicide extends beyond the individual.

For [philosopher] David Hume, the crucial issue was whether suicide violates one's obligations to self, to others, and to God. While Hume argues that life and death are natural causes and therefore no one needs to appeal to God on such matters, we should remember that all life comes from God and belongs to Him, and that God has intervened on occasions to protract or prolong life. For instance, the Lord extended the life of Hezekiah by fifteen years while He cut short the lives of Ananias and Sapphira and King Herod. He also indirectly extended the lives of many others, like Naaman the Syrian, by healing them of sicknesses and diseases. In addition God has promised long life to those who honour their parents, a promise which Paul repeats in Eph.6:2. So, contrary to Hume, life is given, controlled, and taken, by God. One is thus obligated to God for his or her life.

A Sin Against God

We need to consider the reasons why suicide is wrong and why it is not the way to avoid painful circumstances. As an act of rebellion, suicide is a sin against God. These are some of the reasons why suicide is wrong:

- It violates the Ten Commandments.
- Nowhere does the Bible condone a person ending life to escape circumstances.
- Life is a gift from God.
- Suicide is an expression of self-hatred, and the Bible says we are to "love our neighbors as ourselves."
- Suicide usurps the power that belongs only to God.
- A person who commits suicide short-circuits God's will for his or her life.
- It is an expression of lack of faith. Philippians 4:19 states, "My God shall supply all your need according to His riches in glory by Christ Jesus."
- This applies to financial needs and emotional and physical needs.
- Suicide is an act of selfishness.
- It hurts the cause of Christ.

Charles Stanley, *The Charles Stanley Handbook for Christian Living: Biblical Answers to Life's Tough Questions*, 2001.

The second argument advanced in justification of suicide concerns one's obligations to others. Hume has used the argument that suicide is the response of someone who has been called by God from his or her station in life. If so, those who commit suicide should not leave notes of regret, failure, sadness, and guilt. Suicide should be surrounded instead by notes of celebration and gaiety. A more credible verdict is noted by William Styron in his book, *Darkness Visible*. An acute sufferer of depression himself, who contemplated suicide on several occasions, Styron believed that to commit suicide is to desert one's position in the universe, or to abandon one's station in life. And that belief kept him from taking the road to what the mother of Kurt Cobain, the late leader of rock band Nirvana, called, "That stupid place."

Clearly Utilitarian

Hume further argued that the act of suicide is being morally responsible to society on the grounds that if someone cannot promote the interests of society or may be burdensome to others and to society, it would be in the interest of others to terminate themselves. This argument is clearly utilitarian in approach. It assumes that unless someone has something to offer they are better off dead. On the basis of this argument society will be better off without the aging and the very young. Both groups are dependent on society. But are they only dependent? Is there no wisdom to be gained from the aged? And are there no lessons to be learnt from the young? Did not Jesus say the faith of the young is worthy of emulation? Can we not emulate their childlike trust and sincerity? Surely there is more to someone than their capacity to contribute tangibly to society. It is the moral strength of individuals and families that determine whether society will stand or fall, and not their material well-being. In this respect, the elderly can and do contribute to that strong moral framework.

Finally, with regards to self-love, or one's responsibility to guard one's life, some have argued that suicide, rather than being seen as deserting one's obligations to oneself, should be seen as one fulfilling the desires of their heart. If such is the case it can be argued that suicide is nothing short of extreme selfishness.

Using David Hume's basis for determining moral responsibility, we see that suicide violates one's obligations to self, to others, and to God. Therefore the act of suicide cannot be deemed morally responsible.

Morally Supererogatory

This third condition of moral rightness refers to deeds, not duties, which are praiseworthy because they produce good which goes beyond what duty demands. It is only relevant to our present discussion if the suicidal person thinks he or she is doing society a favour by taking their lives.

But are we not all a part of society? And if we are, then for whom are we doing a favour but ourselves? Furthermore, since the suicidal will not be around to see the outcome of his "favourable" act, there is no way for them to determine that they are in fact doing something good or something praiseworthy for society. From my experience with individuals who attempted or committed suicide, there is only preoccupation with escape from inner pain, perhaps depression, or revenge, or an incurable disease. It is never to make the world a better place.

In defence of suicide it is often argued that many Biblical characters committed suicide, including Saul (1Sam.31), Samson (Judg.16:28–30), and Judas Iscariot (Mt.27:5). While the acts of Saul and Judas are clearly not morally supererogatory, the question as to whether Samson's last glorious act can be deemed supererogatory is debatable. We do not know for sure whether Samson knew he was going to die. But even if he knew there was a possibility that he might die, it could hardly be deemed suicide to avenge and free his oppressed country from Philistine domination. His actions were no different from that of a warrior in battle for his country. And such was he. He saw an opportunity to defeat his enemy in one fell swoop and seized the moment. He did not premeditate the destruction of the temple of Dagon as a glorious but subtle way of suicide but saw it as a beachhead for freedom. This is not the mindset of the suicidal.

For these reasons suicide cannot be deemed a praiseworthy deed and it cannot qualify as an act that is morally supererogatory.

In summary, we have seen that suicide is not morally obligatory. God does not sanction it under any condition. It is not morally permissible because it violates one's obligations to oneself, to others, and to God. And it is not morally supererogatory because there is nothing praiseworthy in such an act. Using these three criteria to determine moral rightness we can conclude that suicide is morally unacceptable.

"*Why . . . should we deny an earlier death
to someone who rationally understands and
accepts the hopelessness of his situation?*"

Suicide Can Be a Rational Act

Charles F. McKhann

In the following viewpoint, Charles F. McKhann claims that
suicide in particular circumstances may be a rational and
reasonable act. According to McKhann, an individual suffering from a terminal and painful illness may be in the position
of making a rational decision to hasten his or her death.
McKhann asserts that the consideration for rational suicide
must take into account the suffering that is to be avoided,
the process used to make the decision for suicide, and the capacity of the individual to make such a decision. In some
cases, suicide can be a beneficial and sound choice. Mc-
Khann is a professor of surgery at Yale University and author
of *A Time to Die*, from which this viewpoint is excerpted.

As you read, consider the following questions:
1. What are the two major foundations of suicide, as stated
   by McKhann?
2. According to McKhann, what are three components that
   should be included in a rational decision to commit
   suicide?
3. What examples of nonrational and irrational suicide
   does the author give?

The basic definition of suicide includes the intended death of oneself, carried out by oneself, under circumstances free from outside coercion. The question now is whether there are any circumstances when such an act is reasonable, rational, and morally acceptable. Traditional medical and psychiatric thinking considers all suicides to be the product of disturbed mentation, usually depression, and therefore irrational. But the concept of rational suicide, widely held in ancient Greece, is reawakening in our culture. Although it will always apply to only a small minority of all deaths, this concept is rapidly gaining acceptance among patients with terminal illnesses and the physicians who care for them, as well as with medical ethicists and others who concern themselves with end-of-life decisions. The dilemma of a person who is painfully and terminally ill, faced with our current restrictions on suicide, has made it necessary to reevaluate our attitudes toward suicide, as has the plight of those being kept alive, after life has lost all value or meaning, with extreme application of modern technology. These issues underlie the concept of rational suicide. There are indeed people whose dying is so prolonged and whose suffering is so intense that their desire for an earlier and more comfortable death is easily understood by and acceptable to most people.

Many people with fatal or progressive and severely debilitating diseases reach the point where their suffering seems needless and cruel and where they would prefer an earlier and more comfortable death to living out the natural course of their illness. They have well-thought-out reasons to wish to end their lives sooner rather than later. Such a person has a legal and moral right to refuse treatment and even elementary maintenance care. Beyond that, should he have the means at hand, he may take his own life. Legal for several years, the morality of this act is gaining acceptance on the basis that it can be an entirely reasonable and rational wish.

Two Major Foundations

A patient with colon cancer stated, "How and when I'm going to die should be my decision. It would give me great comfort and peace to know that nothing on earth is going to cause me to suffer pain or a nasty death, being totally dependent. There's my escape, right in the palm of my hand. I'd like that. It would give me control over my own life and body that I don't have now, but which I think I'm entitled to." Others have expressed similar thoughts. According to one author on the subject, "It is rationally justified to kill oneself when a reasonable appraisal of the situation reveals that one is really better off dead." Another wrote: "As soon as it is clear, beyond reasonable doubt, not only that death is now preferable to life but also that it will be every day from now until the end, the rational thing to do is to act promptly."

Rational suicide, with or without assistance, has two major foundations: the desire to avoid unnecessary suffering and the desire to exercise one's autonomy and self-determination. Even though these may not be explicitly stated, the first is an essential reason for wishing to have an earlier and more comfortable death, and the second provides the impetus for actually doing it or asking for help. It should be noted that the criteria for rational suicide apply equally to all forms of assisted dying, for all such actions are initiated by the patient and are similar in many ways. The benefits of an earlier death, in the eyes of the patient himself, should exceed or at least be equal to the costs that will be exacted. In general, rational acts produce well-being and reduce harm. This is the essence of electing earlier death over prolonged suffering. The criteria for rationality in the desire to die fall into three categories: the nature of suffering that is to be avoided, the decision-making process, and the decision-making capacity of the individual. We must look at these criteria mostly from the point of view of an objective outsider, because most patients consider themselves to be rational, whether someone else would or not.

Rationality

We have examined many forms of suffering that a person who is seriously ill might wish to avoid. They all result from having a hopeless condition, for which improvement or cure cannot be expected, and they include terminal illness, pain and suffering that are intractable and unbearable, or a progressive debilitating condition. Any of these could reduce the quality of life to an unacceptable level. Imminent death is not a requirement for a rational wish to die. Although their suffering may be great, I do not include people whose reasons for wishing to die are due to primary mental illness or to pain that is purely psychological in origin.

Several components should be included in a sound and rational decision-making process:

1. One should have the ability to understand and assess the illness itself as the cause of the suffering that is to be ended. Closely related is the ability to understand and weigh all of the alternatives to earlier death, including further treatment, comfort care, or hospice.
2. A rational decision should involve some understanding of the impact an elective, earlier death would have on family and close friends.
3. The decision should not be an impulsive one, but should be considered carefully over a period of time.
4. Ideally, the rationality of a decision to die should be tested on an objective listener of one's own choosing. As will be seen, however, until rational suicide and assisted dying are more widely accepted, such a consultation is apt to be avoided by the patient who is truly rational and understands the risks.
5. A decision to end one's life should be compatible with other personal beliefs and values. Religious beliefs are the most obvious, but even strongly held values are sometimes discarded in favor of the desire for relief and autonomy when the stress is severe.

Nonrational and Irrational Decisions

The rationality of an act is often more easily defined by common usage, even through examples, than it is in concrete terms. Because end-of-life decisions can be nonrational, irrational, or rational, we must explore these distinctions. A Jehovah's Witness may refuse blood transfusions, even when they are necessary for survival, because of nonrational religious beliefs. Similarly, a person of strong faith might feel that he has to endure life to its natural end, regardless of suffering. This would also be a nonrational, religious issue; he must do it. Nonrational acts are borne of belief systems, rather than evolving from the world of common experience. They are "matters of faith rather than reason" but are widely recognized in our society as acceptable exceptions to the rational-irrational diathesis.

Suter. © 1997 by David Suter. Reprinted with permission.

The teenager who despairs over a dissolved love affair may consider his options very carefully and conclude that death is the only way to end his misery. Society, however, considers his suicide to be a completely irrational act and feels justified in doing whatever possible to intervene. It knows that he is too young and distraught to understand that he will get over the feeling of despair at his loss and probably live a normal and even happy life, if he can be persuaded not to take such an irreversible step. The admonition of Edwin Shneidman, a scholar of suicidal behavior, applies here: "It is not a thing to do while one is not in one's best mind. Never kill yourself when you are suicidal." Realizing that the entire community would reject his plan, the teenager cannot discuss it or in any way test its "rationality" on other people. A survivor of a leap from the Golden Gate Bridge is said to have defined suicide as a permanent solution to a temporary problem. Although the young person who is temporarily distraught has a legal right to take his own life, society feels otherwise, and most agree that such untimely deaths should be prevented whenever possible. In this sense, the will of society is allowed to override the autonomy of the individual for his own good, precisely because his reasons for wanting to die are probably temporary and are generally considered to be inadequate.

A Completely Different Problem

The seriously ill person who anticipates a bad death but wishes to avoid unnecessary suffering has a completely different problem, and consideration of an earlier death may be totally rational. He may ponder his position very carefully, weighing a few more days or weeks of life against relief from his suffering. He knows that it is not a temporary situation. The illness will get worse, not better, and death is impending, if not imminent. As the end of life draws close, time does become a central issue. Must he wait passively, as some would require, for his disease to overwhelm his body and exhaust his resources, finally producing a living corpse whose meaningful life ended weeks ago? Or should he be free to choose his own hour of departure, to meet his own needs and desires, with the elements of personality and personhood intact and a mind still able to make a final and most important decision, the decision to die on his own terms, when he may indeed be in his "best mind." He may have no strong religious or moral reservations, and no personal or family obligations that will be satisfied by a few additional weeks of life. Indeed, under optimal circumstances, if physician-aided dying were legal, it could be discussed with others, including family members who have the greatest concern and the physician who might be asked to help. The dying person might also realize that his wish for a timely death is rational in the eyes of many people, that a significant majority feel that there are medical circumstances when an earlier death would be acceptable and should be legal. Few would deny a dying person the right to continue his existence, even with futile medical support, in the irrational hope that a cure is just around the corner. Why, then, should we deny an earlier death to someone who rationally understands and accepts the hopelessness of his situation?

A More Complex Example

A more complex example is the person who has a recognized depressive disorder but who also has a devastating terminal disease. Such a person might present his case very rationally and be legally competent to make most medical decisions, most of the time. Should this include rational suicide? In this borderline case I can see where compassion for suffering could outweigh concerns about questionable competence or rationality. A still more difficult example is the person whose only problem is a persistent serious depressive disorder that does not respond to treatment. Severe depression has been accepted as a justifiable reason for assisted dying in Holland, but I do not believe enough is known about this type of disability to consider its inclusion in the United States. People with severe depression are not dying. Indeed they can live normal life spans. More important, remarkable new drugs have become available to treat depression, and more can be expected. The result is that people who are depressed but not dying or suffering from irreversible disorders may very well benefit by waiting for effective treatment to be developed.

Points of Consideration

There are some general but simplistic concepts of rationality that do not apply to rational suicide or assisted dying. Rationality is often construed as being based on common sense and social norms. In a sphere that is so new and controversial, judgment by these criteria will hardly be possible. Similarly, rational acts are thought by some to be those that are convincingly rational to others. Again, the listener may agree or may have entirely different thoughts on the subject. Even mental health professionals can have strong prejudices in this area, casting doubt on their other qualifications as judges of rationality. Instead, the rationality of an individual must be looked at very objectively, based on his own understanding of his own situation.

A rational decision of such magnitude requires that a person has acceptable decision-making capacity. This evaluation includes the most contentious points in any consideration of rational suicide or assisted dying, if only because it is much more difficult to verify than are suffering and other components of the decision-making process.

1. The decision should be an autonomous one, a personal choice made in the absence of outside pressure.
2. The individual should be mentally competent to make a life-and-death decision.
3. The decision should be made in the absence of treatable clinical depression. . . .

Not All Contemplations Are the Same

In a moving article describing his mother's experience with cancer and eventual suicide, Andrew Solomon said that "having been through the whole business, I would put the infrequency of suicide down more to the difficulty of it than to the undesirability of its objectives." The discrepancies among various reports underline the need for much larger and more probing studies of the degree to which serious physical illness can inspire considerations of rational suicide or physician-assisted dying, particularly in the absence of any previous documented mental illness.

Public acceptance of rational suicide requires recognizing that not all contemplations of suicide are the same. It is essential to consider the main reasons for wishing to die to see the difference. The underlying issues remain the autonomous right of the individual to avoid unnecessary suffering.

| *"Rational suicide' is a contradiction in terms—an oxymoron."*

Suicide Is Never a Rational Act

Adina Wrobleski

The late Adina Wrobleski, author of the books *Suicide Survivors: A Guide for Those Left Behind* and *Grief Reactions Among Suicide Survivors*, wrote extensively on suicide grief. In the following viewpoint, Wrobleski rejects the concept that suicide can be rationally chosen. She believes that decades of scientific research have proven that suicides are caused by biological brain diseases and are never a result of rational choice. Wrobleski contends that advocates of the rational suicide theory do not understand the terrible grief experienced by the survivors of those who commit suicide.

As you read, consider the following questions:
1. What is the author's view of suffering?
2. What assumptions are made about suicide survivors, as stated by the author?
3. According to Wrobleski, how is rational suicide a coerced choice?

Adina Wrobleski, "'Rational Suicide': A Contradiction in Terms," *Contemporary Perspectives on Rational Suicide*, edited by James L. Werth Jr. Philadelphia: Brunner/ Mazel, 1999. Copyright © 1999 by Taylor & Francis. Reproduced by permission.

I learned about suicide on August 16, 1979. My 21-year-old daughter, Lynn, got up but did not go to work. In the morning, a neighbor saw her mow the lawn, and around lunch she apparently had some soup. Some time after that, she went down the hall to her bedroom, locked the door, lay down on the floor, and shot herself in the heart. Her husband found her body around 4 P.M.

An Oxymoron

Since that time, I have talked with and heard from hundreds of suicide survivors—people who are grieving a suicide death. We know what *real* suicide is about. I have never met a survivor of a "rational suicide." That is presumed to be a rational person who sorts through the pros and cons of her or his life and decides to "choose" death. It is deeply offensive to most suicide survivors to hear people talk so glibly about how wonderful suicide is. The advocates seem to enjoy their endless discussions about death.

"Rational suicide" is rather like the question of "how many angels can dance on the head of a pin?" It involves earnest discussions, paper presentations, journal publications, and learned conferences. It is an evanescent pyramid upon which careers have been made, but it is time to tell the "rational suicide" emperor he has no clothes on.

I submit that "rational suicide" is a contradiction in terms—an oxymoron. The beliefs of so many people arguing for "rational suicide" obscure the fact it does not exist. But if there is such a thing as "rational suicide" I am opposed to it; actually, I am opposed to its advocacy.

If "rational suicide" is for people in unbearable pain, why do we reserve it only for old people? "Rational suicide" advocates like to argue that we treat our pets with more compassion than we do old and sick people. By their arguments, would it not be an act of compassion to "help" tiny lives out of their pain? [Founder of the Hemlock Society, a right-to-die advocacy group] Derek Humphry says that this is not acceptable "because they are not able to consent." We allow dying children an ordeal we deny our pets. But actually who decides when one dies by "rational suicide?" Who supplies the pressure on the old and sick to die before their time?

Where is the morality in "rational suicide?" The advocates believe it is moral to help people avoid suffering. But suffering is part of life; going through suffering is what makes most of us stronger and kinder people. Whoever expected life to be easy? I believe that life is random, and almost everyone gets some kind of tragedy. For some, it is the agony of heart disease; for others it is diabetes; and for some, suicide death.

In the past it is understandable that such a shocking and human behavior as suicide should have been wrestled with by philosophers and religionists. But science has proved through 39 years of replicated research that suicide is directly related to biological brain diseases whether they are diagnosed or not. When there is so much clinical information available about suicide, it amazes me that a sizable number of people are again discussing suicide as a philosophical and hypothetical issue. It is as if astronomers suddenly reverted to astrology for explanations of the universe.

Superficial and Facile

"Rational suicide" has a superficial and facile sense to it. This is because it is normal for all of us to have thought about our own death and under what circumstances we think we could kill ourselves. Combined with the taboo on suicide, which creates a fascinatingly sinister atmosphere, there is a certain siren song of romance about suicide and death that titillates some people. They enjoy speculating on the hypothetical circumstances under which they might kill themselves. This speculation is most enjoyable when one is healthy, and death years away.

The prototypical "rational suicides" are the deaths of Jo Roman, Jean Humphry, and Janet Adkins. All their husbands had parts in their wives' deaths. For example, Janet Adkins never talked to nor met Dr. Jack Kevorkian until she got to Michigan; her husband made all the arrangements. Derek Humphry mixed the lethal cup his wife drank, and Mel Roman (a physician) apparently secured the seconal his wife took.

The survivors have appeared on national television shows, describing the "nobility and dignity" with which their loved ones died. They quietly discussed their parts in the death.

Real suicide survivors are too shocked and anguished to even know their names, let alone sit up straight and talk on television. Those survivors all continued to be proud of their direct help.

Real suicide survivors are blamed for the death of their loved one, and the blame goes everywhere. Society has taught us to blame people for suicide, and this often creates hostile separations within families and without. It is assumed that survivors somehow "drove" their loved one to suicide. Suicide and guilt are equated. Even the nicest people will say things like, "Oh that poor family, they must feel terribly guilty." Why *must* they? Or we hear, "It must be awful for the family dealing with *all that guilt*." Society has taught us to assume suicide survivors are guilty and in collusion with the deaths. Suicide survivors are accused of complicity; "rational suicide" survivors actually are in complicity.

Horrible Prognostications

Suicide survivors go through the same grieving process others do, but because of the taboo and stigma they have many extra burdens. Horrible prognostications are made about them:
- That their guilt will be massive and overwhelming
- That they were in some way in complicity in the death
- That they will be unable to "admit" it was a suicide
- That their marriages will probably break up
- That they and their families are at high risk for suicide
- That they will suffer from it all their lives
- That they will never "get over" a suicide death

The only ray of hope cast to them is that through years of therapy they may "get over it." Even if this were true, there will never be enough therapists to reach all of the suicide survivors. Every year there are about 30,000 suicides, and they leave behind at least 300,000 survivors. This means there are millions of suicide survivors. If all the predictions were true, suicide survivors would be a readily observable, deeply disturbed group of people. Suicide survivors have a right to recover as other people, and they do.

In *real* suicide, there is a strong message that suicide survivors will *never* know *why* someone kills her or himself. However, it *is* known why people kill themselves; they were very sick, and they died. The way people die from biological brain diseases is by suicide. It is as if advocates of "rational suicide" have on blinders that block out the evidence from psychiatry and neuroscience since the 1960s. But there are thousands upon thousands of therapists who have their feet firmly planted in the psychodynamic past. There's a new disorder named "pathological grief" and many new "grief counseling" specialties. Suicide survivors need to "work through their grief" and "deal with it," they say. Suicide has been with us since the beginning of time, and up until this century survivors have "dealt with it" and moved on to re-build their lives.

For suicide survivors, there is the assumption that there was a lack of love and understanding of the suicidal person that was at fault in the relationship—that we did not love them well enough, or pay enough attention to them, and were so preoccupied with our own lives that we ignored their cries for help.

A sampling of philosophers show they do not know the *real* world of suicide. For example, [bioethicists] Karen Lebacqz and Tristan Engelhardt say: "Persons should be *permitted* to take their own lives when they have chosen to do so *freely and rationally* and when there are *no other duties* which would over-ride this freedom."

Manipulated Suicide

Who gives this kind of permission? A person determined to suicide doesn't ask permission; she or he does it. Her or his remaining loved ones certainly do not give permission for the devastation in their lives. What omnipotent person decides that such a person's decision is rational? How can any-one know this? Or do they suggest that the suicidal person fill out a form, or make an affidavit attesting to her or his rationality? As to "no other duties," one always has duties, es-pecially to one's family. [Philosophy professor] Margaret Pabst Battin made a chilling statement when she said that,

> Social acceptance of the notion of rational suicide . . . opens the way for both individual and societal manipulation of in-dividuals into choosing to end their lives when they would not otherwise have done so. . . . However, . . . if we accept

the notion of rational suicide, we cannot object to the manipulated suicides that do occur.

I find this unusual because she defines "manipulated suicides" very clearly, and the lines from manipulated suicide to assisted suicide to homicide can blur into one another. Suicide survivors are always subjected to a police investigation; it is the duty of the police to determine what happens in a sudden death. A survivor told me of returning home to discover his son dead with his face all bloodied. The police tore up the house looking for a gun. They gave up when they found the family dog with blood all over his face. The man had actually poisoned himself, and the dog had eaten off his face.

There is a great deal of hypocrisy in "rational suicide." A few years ago a woman, named Bertha X, wrote a letter to the *Hemlock Quarterly*. She told of the "rational suicide" pact she and her husband had. But he suffered a stroke and died in a nursing home. She was writing to warn people not to wait too long to take their store of pills. My question was, "Bertha! if suicide is so terrific, why are you still here?"

Abandonment of Suicidal Sufferers

Consider this definition closely: All suicidal people have severe psychological pain or mentally debilitating conditions. Every suicidal person by definition believes that his quality of life is unacceptable. In the name of nonjudgmentalism, rational suicide transforms self-destruction into just another choice. It is also a warrant for the abandonment of suicidal sufferers by psychologists, psychiatrists, and social workers, the very people who are often the last line of defense between a despairing person and a leap into eternity.

Wesley J. Smith, *Weekly Standard*, May 29, 2000.

In one "rational suicide," an elderly woman wanted the plastic bag removed from her head; her daughter and husband removed it, bathed her face with cool water, and put the bag on again. She died. Roswell Gilbert "helped" his wife in dying by shooting her in the back of the head—twice. Was it for her relief, or his?

Then there was the case of Morgan Sibbitt. He declared to Mike Wallace of *60 Minutes* that he and his wife had a suicide pact, the necessary prescription pills, and the will to kill themselves. He also stated he had "aided" seven people in their suicides. In a follow-up, Mike Wallace said,

> As for Morgan Sibbitt, he died seven months ago after a 20-month battle with lung cancer. He was 71. His wife wrote us: "He never took the pills for suicide, despite his pain and breathing discomfort—especially in the final weeks. He died a natural death; I guess his human instincts came through."

Like Bertha, she never took the pills either. Similarly, many years ago Elizabeth Bouvia made an international scene over her "right" to not be force-fed, but she is still alive and living quietly in a Los Angeles nursing home.

Talkers, Not Doers

These are examples of why I believe the advocates of "rational suicide" are talkers, not doers. I know of no evidence, other than anecdotal, that has shown that any members of the Hemlock Society died by suicide, or any philosophers and others who discuss "rational suicide" so earnestly actually killed themselves.

The advocates of "rational suicide" appear not to have concern about the "rights" of the survivors. The rights of those left behind after suicide are not considered. There are degrees of reactions in *real* suicide. It is not true that direct relatives of a suicide are always affected the most. A longtime friend of someone who died may be closer to the person than a sister who is 15 years older and lives across the country. The sister cares but may never have had the time it takes to maintain a close relationship because of distance and time. A wife may not always grieve a husband's death. He may have been an abusive alcoholic for years, and she, understandably, may feel only relief after his suicide.

Relief is one of the only things in grief that feels good. The advocates of "rational suicide" seem to confuse it with feelings that a death was a "blessing." This happens after a long drawn-out death in which survivors suffer from watching the misery of the dying person. This is similar to the reactions of some suicide survivors. Many of them lived under extreme tension before their loved one died. It is not true that all suicide survivors were ignorant of what was happening. Many lived with a chronically ill person who had the "mental cancers" of major depression, manic-depression, schizophrenia, or panic disorder. Some survivors suffered so long watching someone they loved who was so ill that there is hardly any emotion left for grief. Relief comes because their stress is gone, and a long ordeal is finished. This usually is not the case in suicide.

The Real World of Suicide

The real world of suicide is that of my friend whose 70-year-old father cut his wrists, and stabbed himself over his whole body. He bled to death in his bed, and his wife found him. The real world of suicide is finding your son hanged to death in the basement. The real world of suicide is the death of your husband who jumped from a high bridge. The real world of suicide is finding your loved one dead from a self-inflicted gunshot.

People shoot themselves, they hang themselves, they burn themselves to death, and kill themselves in many other ways. These deaths are all ugly and undignified, and terribly tragic. "Rational suicide" may be a vain attempt to understand suicide and to make it legitimate. The advocates of "rational suicide" are fastidious; they want people to have a lethal quantity of pills so they may gently sleep away. The Hemlock Society recommends a good dose of alcohol before taking the pills. It also recommends death by placing a plastic bag over one's head "to make sure". These combination methods seem hardly more dignified than shooting or hanging.

Reality for survivors is ugly, and people who advocate "rational suicide" have to realize that. "Rational suicide" advocates are silent in the aftermath of suicide; their focus seems to be on a "dignified" death that is an end in itself. The answer to terminal illness is the hospice movement, not suicide. The answer to suicide is not more death, but less. Just because we have not supported hospice or better care to the dying does not mean that we should advocate suicide. And beyond just the "right" to kill one's self, now the advocates want "assisted" suicide.

In "rational suicide" there is no room for grief. The survivors are too busy patting themselves on the back. In *real* suicide, grief is devastating. Because of the stigma and taboo, there is so little understanding of suicide that survivors are completely bewildered; they do not know what hit them. They are in denial—denial before death and after death. Very troubling things they saw or heard before death come tumbling back into their minds as things they should have seen or done. Denial after death helps them get through their initial and continuing journey through grief.

In an effort to make sense of the death, suicide survivors have to make some kind of reconstruction of events— whether it is based on facts or blaming. Recovery from grief entails pulling themselves from the past, which is the only place their loved one still lives, into the present in which they must rebuild their lives. People do recover from suicide grief.

A Coerced Choice

Suicide is not a rational or clearly thought-out action. If there is any kind of a "choice," it is a coerced choice, in which someone survivors loved was unable to see alternatives or consequences. Having said that, it is nonetheless true that it is the person who died who decided *when* all else had failed, *when* everything he or she tried had not worked, and *when* the pain was too much to bear any longer. Someone once said the life of a suicide was like being in a room of unbearable pain where the only door out was marked "suicide." The only decision the person made was that "the time to kill myself is *now*."

Love—as a human, religious, and philosophical issue—is missing from the arguments for "rational suicide." If love were included, the arguments would get all muddied up with grief, despair and anguish. [Psychologist] Edwin Shneidman has written:

> Most suicide is a dreary and dismal wintry storm within the mind, where staying afloat or going under is the vital decision being debated. It is a place where we can't reach them, and their memories cannot save them.

There is a story about the mother of a family talking to John; she is telling him he must go to school. "But I don't want to," he says. "You must," she replies. "I don't want to; all the kids pick on me." "Never mind, you have to go to school." He says, "I don't want to; all the teachers pick on me too." She says, "John, you're the principal and you *have* to go to school."

The reason suicide survivors go on is because they are the principal in their lives, and they *have* to go on. They plant a stake in the future when they feel least able to do it. They go on for their own sake, for their family's, for their friend's, and for the memory of their loved one.

Real suicide survivors are sturdy people who have lost faith in themselves after a suicide. Trying to make sense of so shocking and tragic a death as suicide, in the face of society's blame, is more than one person should have to bear. Survivors feel they cannot carry on, but they do. They feel it is more than they can bear, but it is not. They feel it is tragically unfair, and it is. They feel they will never get over it, but they do. Why? Because they have to. One way or another survivors do survive, and most do it very well.

I believe the advocates of "rational suicide" are playing at death, titillating themselves, and perhaps, whistling in the dark.

Periodical Bibliography

The following articles have been selected to supplement the diverse views presented in this chapter.

Johann Christoph Arnold	"Talking About Suicide," *Plough*, Autumn 1998.
Daniel Avila	"Suicide and the Alienated Life," *First Things*, June 2001.
David M. Clarke	"Autonomy, Rationality, and the Wish to Die," *Journal of Medical Ethics*, December 1999.
Bobbie Farsides and Robert J. Dunlop	"Is There Such a Thing as a Life Not Worth Living?" *British Medical Journal*, June 16, 2001.
R.G. Frey	"Hume on Suicide," *Journal of Medicine and Philosophy*, August 1999.
Sohail H. Hashmi	"Not What the Prophet Would Want; How Can Islamic Scholars Sanction Suicide Attacks?" *Washington Post*, June 9, 2002.
Philip Higgs	"Unplanned Legacy: My Friend Killed Himself, but to Me, It Wasn't a Suicide," *New York Times Magazine*, February 17, 2002.
Human Life Review	"The Body Bag," Spring 1998.
Bill Murchinson	"The Dark, Dark Wood of Suicide," *Chronicles*, August 1998.
Robert Parry	"The Biblical Teachings on Suicide," *Issues in Law and Medicine*, February 1, 1998.
Wesley J. Smith	"Don't Rationalize Suicide," *Wall Street Journal*, August 3, 1999.
Jean-Pierre Soubrier	"Souvenirs to Remember and Meditate," *Suicide and Life-Threatening Behavior*, Summer 1998.
Matthew Stevenson	"Suicide Soldiering: Through the Ages," *American Enterprise*, December 2001.
Thomas Szasz	"Suicide as a Moral Issue," *Freeman*, July 1999.

CHAPTER 2

What Are the Causes of Teen Suicide?

Chapter Preface

According to the U.S. Centers for Disease Control, suicide is the third leading cause of death for persons between fifteen and twenty-four years old, behind automobile accidents and homicide. It is estimated that one out of thirteen teens age nineteen and under attempts suicide each year, a rate that has increased threefold over the last two decades. With the rate of teen suicide increasing, many analysts have naturally turned their attention to the question of what causes adolescents to kill themselves. One possible cause that has garnered much attention is bullying.

In recent years, numerous teens who committed suicide blamed the teasing and torment they endured from bullies for their tragic actions. For example, in March 1999, fourteen-year-old Kerby Guerra shot herself in her home in Colorado Springs, Colorado. In a suicide note she had written a month earlier, Kerby wrote, "All my life I've been teased and harassed. I just couldn't stand it anymore." A year later, fourteen-year-old Hamed Nastoh of Surrey, Canada, leaped off a bridge to his death. He wrote a letter to his family lamenting the harassment that drove him to kill himself: "Mom, I was teased at school by my mates, my classmates, even my own friends laughed at me."

Some experts agree that the victims of bullying are at increased risk of suicide. Glenn Stutzy, a school violence specialist at Michigan State University, argues, "Suicide is bullying's quiet little secret. It's picking off our children one at a time." A 2001 study of middle and high school students reports that the victims and bystanders of bullying were prone to experience suicidal impulses and feelings of hopelessness and low self-esteem.

On the contrary, other commentators believe that focusing on bullying may not offer a satisfactory explanation of teen suicide, especially when other factors that may heighten the risk of suicide are present. For instance, Kerby Guerra was diagnosed with a mood disorder that needed medical treatment and lived in a home where a firearm was accessible—factors that some experts believe increase the risk of teen suicide. Furthermore, other analysts suggest that a one-sided campaign against bullies may be ineffective at preventing suicides because bullies themselves suffer from serious emotional problems. According to a 1999 Finnish study, bullies are just as—and even more prone to—depression and suicidal ideation as their victims.

As teen suicide rates climb, experts are increasingly concerned about identifying the factors that lead to adolescent suicides. In the following chapter, the authors offer different opinions on the causes of teen suicide. As the relationship between teen suicides and bullying becomes increasingly publicized, it is certain that many experts will study the effects of such behavior on both the victims of bullying and the bullies themselves. Determining whether bullying increases the odds of teen suicide could lead to possible solutions and the saving of many teen lives.

> "The existing evidence points to an
> inordinate risk of suicide facing
> homosexual and bisexual youth."

Homosexual Teens Are at High Risk for Suicide

Gary Remafedi

In the following viewpoint, Gary Remafedi contends that many studies show a high rate of suicide attempts among gay teenagers. However, he argues, this link between homosexuality and suicide has often been overlooked due to the lack of government support of these studies, the sensitive and controversial subject matter, and the difficulty determining if suicide victims were homosexual. It is important, Remafedi asserts, that future studies of teen suicide address the issue of homosexuality. Remafedi is the author of several articles on gay youth and suicide. He is also an associate professor of pediatrics and the director of Youth and AIDS Projects at the University of Minnesota.

As you read, consider the following questions:
1. According to Remafedi, by what percentage have teenage suicide rates increased since 1960?
2. Why was the *Report of the Secretary's Task Force on Youth Suicide* almost suppressed, in the author's opinion?
3. What characteristics of gay teens are linked to a high risk of attempted suicide, according to the author?

Gary Remafedi, *Death by Denial: Studies of Suicide in Gay and Lesbian Teenagers.* New York: Alyson Publications, Inc., 1994. Copyright © 1994 by Gary Remafedi. Reproduced by permission.

A connection between suicide and homosexuality has long been recognized in the popular culture, reflected in music (e.g., "The Ode to Billie Joe"), movies (e.g., *The Boys in the Band*), theater (e.g., Lillian Hellman's *The Children's Hour*), and other art forms. Yet, few researchers have ventured to explore the link between sexual orientation and self-injury. Early evidence of an association appeared as incidental findings in studies of adult sexuality. They revealed that gay men were much more likely to have attempted suicide than heterosexual men and that their attempts often occurred during adolescence. Newer studies have provided consistent evidence of unusually high rates of attempted suicide among gay youth, in the range of 20–30 percent, regardless of geographic and ethnic variability.

A Leading Killer

In the U.S., suicide is the third leading killer of youth, accounting for 14 percent of all deaths in the teen age-range. For uncertain reasons, teenage suicide rates have risen by more than 200 percent since 1960, as compared to a 17 percent increase in the general population. Surveys of youth have found that 6–13 percent of adolescents have attempted suicide at least once in their lives, but only a small percentage of attempters have received appropriate help.

These disturbing observations have led to considerable epidemiological, psychological, medical, and sociological research to understand the epidemic of self-injury and death among youth. However, the unifying characteristics of young victims are still incompletely understood, despite considerable progress and new information. It appears that adolescent suicide victims are a diverse group. While most have discernible psychiatric symptoms, a sizeable minority have not exhibited psychological or behavioral problems before death. Given the many unanswered questions regarding epidemiological trends and causative factors, no stone should be left unturned by scientists exploring the issues.

Unfortunately, the potentially important link between suicide and homosexuality has been overlooked until recent years for a variety of reasons:

1. Governmental agencies have not adequately supported

the study of suicide in homosexual populations. Given the events surrounding the [U.S. Department of Health and Human Services'] federally commissioned *Report of the Secretary's Task Force on Youth Suicide*, it appears that political forces were at work to suppress the collection or publication of information which has been perceived to benefit homosexual communities. The report's controversial chapter on gay and lesbian youth almost led to a rejection of the whole volume. After considerable debate, the report ultimately was accepted in its entirety, but published only in limited edition. . . .

The Technical Challenges

2. Another set of impediments to studies of suicide and sexual orientation are the technical challenges. Both are extremely sensitive and controversial subjects, difficult to broach with institutional review boards, professionals, and participants alike. Because adults and, especially, adolescents may keep their sexual orientation hidden, identifying representative samples of gays, lesbians, and bisexuals has been virtually impossible in the climate of American society. Only in the past decade have investigators succeeded in launching research with sizeable samples of gay, lesbian, and bisexual youth, albeit volunteers with unknown biases for participation. Despite the sampling limitations, the works by Stephen G. Schneider et al. and Gary Remafedi et al. are important illustrations of the general feasibility of suicide research with homosexual youth.

These studies also have helped clarify that the risk of attempted suicide is not uniformly distributed among homosexual youth, but linked to particular characteristics. Some characteristics resemble familiar risk factors in the general adolescent population, such as family dysfunction, substance abuse, and sexual abuse. Others are unique to studies of gay and bisexual youth: gender attypicality, young age at the time of gay identity formation, intrapersonal conflict regarding sexuality, and nondisclosure of orientation to others. Although derived from homosexual youth, these data regarding predictions of attempted suicide might help scientists understand other populations as well. For example, the observed relationship between gender nonconformity and attempted suicide may be relevant to any adolescent group, regardless of sexual orientation. . . .

A Paucity of Information

3. A final, noteworthy barrier to the recognition of the risk for suicide among homosexual youth has been the paucity of information about the sexual orientation of actual suicide victims. Only a small percentage of attempters ultimately will die at their own hands. Suicide attempts are 50–200 times more common than completed suicides. Suicide completers may be a unique subset of all attempters, and data derived from attempters may not be generalizable to those persons who will someday succeed.

Suicidality of Sexual Minority Students

Category/ Problem	Sexual Minority Students 5.5% (243 total)	Other Students 94.5% (4,172 total)	Greater Likelihood for Problem
Considered Suicide	49% (119)	20% (834)	2.4 Times
Planning a Suicide	39% (95)	15% (626)	2.6 Times
Attempting Suicide	29% (71)	7% (292)	4.1 Times
Suicide Attempt & Receiving Medical Attention	18% (44)	3% (125)	6.0 Times

Massachusetts Department of Education, *Youth Risk Behavior Survey, Massachusetts*, 1999.

In the *Report of the Secretary's Task Force*, Paul Gibson projected that gay and lesbian youth may account for 30 percent of all youth suicides, based on existing data about the prevalence of homosexuality and the relative risk of attempted suicide. Although this alarming and hotly contested figure may indeed be accurate, it will be important for future studies to gather empirical evidence from the psychological autopsies of adolescent suicide victims. In this type of study, health care records, personal documents, and interviews with friends and family members are used retrospectively to reconstruct the circumstances contributing to a suicide death.

In lieu of psychological autopsies, the existing information on attempted suicide for gay youth reflects grave potential for lethality. From Ronald F.C. Kourany, we learn that two-thirds of randomly sampled U.S. psychiatrists believed that the self-injurious acts of homosexual adolescents were more serious and lethal than those of heterosexual youth. Moreover, the attempts that my colleagues and I studied were characterized by moderate to high lethality and inaccessibility to rescue in 54 percent and 62 percent of cases, respectively.

To my knowledge, the only psychological autopsy study to examine the sexual orientation of victims systematically has been the work of Charles L. Rich et al. The investigators set out to determine the orientation of adult suicide victims in San Diego County during a specified time frame in the pre-AIDS era. That 10 percent of suicide victims were found to be gay men is impressive, since the proportion of openly gay men in the U.S. is now thought to be less than 10 percent of males. Moreover, since suicide attempts in homosexual persons have been found to be associated with nondisclosure of orientation, it is reasonable to expect that the 10 percent figure is the lowest possible estimate of the actual proportion of gay suicides in the San Diego cohort. Unfortunately, the authors minimized their own findings by overestimating the prevalence of homosexuality in the general population and underestimating the likelihood of missed cases of gay and lesbian suicide.

The Future of Research

What lies ahead in the future of research and suicide prevention programs for homosexual youth? From the perspective of research design, studies of suicide attempters should move beyond the use of volunteers. Future population-based surveys of adolescent health should routinely ascertain the sexual orientation of respondents, thereby enabling analyses of suicide risk (as well as any number of other health problems) in relation to sexual orientation within respective cohorts of youth. However, even with this improved sampling strategy, investigators will continue to wrestle with the validity of self-reported sexual orientation and the generalizability of findings to youth who cannot disclose their feelings honestly.

It is imperative that future psychological autopsies of adolescent victims address the issue of sexual orientation. Surely, this will require an unprecedented collaboration between suicidologists and sexologists to devise appropriate methods to uncover sensitive sexual information from all available sources at the postmortem. Since gay and lesbian youth who complete suicide may not be "out" to families, it will be important to question friends, teachers, and counselors and to examine other variables which indirectly reflect orientation such as manifest gender role, dating behaviors, pornographic materials, diaries and personal artifacts, telephone records, and other novel strategies.

In the future, investigations of attempted and completed suicide should address the issue of suicide risk for young lesbian women. A retrospective review of records from 500 homosexual youth at the Hetrick-Martin Institute in New York found that female victims of violence reported suicide attempts more often than males (41 percent vs. 34 percent). It remains to be determined whether lesbian status itself is a relative protection or a risk factor for suicide. Both Joseph Harry and I have found gender nonconformity to be a risk for young men. Is it also true of young lesbians, or can we expect the opposite effect? Answering this question may shed new light on the well-recognized, but poorly understood, gender differences in suicidal behavior in the general population. Females attempt suicide at least three times as often as males; but males are approximately four times as likely to die from an attempt (rate of 18.0 per 100,000 vs. 4.4).

Important Implications

Beyond academic interest, research pertaining to homosexuality and suicide has important implications for clinical practice and public policy. Completed suicides have been found to be associated with other health problems like substance abuse and HIV/AIDS, all of which are overrepresented in gay communities. Understanding and attacking the root causes of self-injurious behavior in the form of suicide may benefit other community health outcomes, too. From a clinical perspective, neglecting the interrelatedness of risky behavior can adversely affect individual young clients. For example, programs offering HIV-antibody counseling and testing to high-risk adolescents should be mindful of their multiple risks for suicide and proceed with caution. . . .

In my own mind, there is no doubt that the existing evidence points to an inordinate risk of suicide facing homosexual and bisexual youth. Also apparent is the need to expand understanding of the subject. Given what is already known, there is ample reason to earmark research funds for this purpose and to alert human services professionals and students to the current state of knowledge. To ignore the problem now is a missed opportunity to save thousands of young lives, tantamount to sanctioning death by denial.

"Americans concerned about teen suicide should seek out the true causes and not become muddled in the myth of homosexual teen suicide."

The Extent of Homosexual Teen Suicide Is Exaggerated

Concerned Women for America

Concerned Women for America (CWA) is a conservative organization of women that advocates Christian beliefs and traditional family values. In the following viewpoint, CWA argues that homosexual activists have exaggerated the rate of gay teen suicide. According to the organization, the study that gay activists use to support their claim that 30 percent of all completed suicides are committed by homosexual teens is seriously flawed. CWA asserts that young gay men and lesbians are not being driven to suicide by society's disapproval of homosexuality. On the contrary, homosexual activists are manipulating the teen suicide crisis to promote their unhealthy lifestyle.

As you read, consider the following questions:
1. According to Marshall Kirk and Hunter Madsen, why do homosexuals portray themselves as victims?
2. How does CWA support its argument that Paul Gibson's study on homosexual teens and suicide is flawed?
3. What benefits has the homosexual movement gained from manipulating the teen suicide crisis, as stated by CWA?

Since 1965, the rate of teen suicide in America has nearly tripled. Such statistics have our nation reeling to find the source of this tragedy. Unfortunately, homosexual activists have capitalized on America's concern. They have transformed this national tragedy into a vehicle to drive the homosexual agenda into the mainstream of our lives. Homosexual activists claim gay youths account for 30 percent of all teen suicides. They suggest that society's aversion to homosexuality victimizes gay teens, compelling them to commit suicide. Therefore, they say, the only way to stop this tragedy is to embrace and accept homosexuality as a normal and healthy lifestyle.

The strategy of preying on American sympathies is not new to the homosexual movement. Homosexual advocates Marshall Kirk and Hunter Madsen described the plan in their book *After the Ball*. Kirk and Madsen urged homosexuals to cast themselves as victims. By doing so, homosexuals are able to "invite straights to be their protectors."

The myth of gay teen suicide stems mainly from a study by Paul Gibson titled "Gay Male and Lesbian Youth Suicide." This study was included in a 1989 report published by the Department of Health and Human Services (HHS). Gibson is a homosexual social worker living in San Francisco. And he concluded that 30 percent of teen suicides are committed by gay youth.

Skewed Statistics

When the Gibson paper was included in the HHS report, then-HHS Secretary Dr. Louis Sullivan quickly took steps to distance himself from the controversial Gibson findings. He wrote, ". . . the views expressed in the paper entitled 'Gay Male and Lesbian Youth Suicide' do not in any way represent my personal beliefs or the policy of this Department."

But because the Gibson paper was included in the government report, the myth of gay teen suicide was granted new legitimacy in the public forum. Now homosexual activists could point to Gibson's skewed statistics and attribute them to government sources.

And his statistics were indeed skewed. Gibson harvested his statistics primarily from homosexual sources and then applied them to the masses using the discredited estimate by Dr. Alfred Kinsey that 10 percent of the population is homosexual. Furthermore, the Gibson report is riddled with statistical inconsistencies. For example, Gibson refers to an author who, in the *Washington Blade* (a Washington, D.C.-area homosexual newspaper), stated that as many as 3,000 gay youths commit suicide each year. However, that would be impossible since the total number of annual teen suicides amounts to about 2,000.

Fundamentally Flawed

Beyond the statistics, there are some fundamental flaws in the study's assumptions. Gibson assumes that sexual orientation is normal and natural. His study begins with the presupposition that homosexuality is unchangeable and fixed at birth. Although scientists have spent countless hours and research dollars trying to prove this theory, they have yet to produce any conclusive evidence.

The Gibson study also fails to acknowledge other psychological factors that could contribute to a homosexual youth committing suicide, such as family problems, abuse, etc.

A Precipitant, Not a Cause

[Researcher Susan] Blumenthal writes that although the humiliation related to homosexuality may be a precipitant of a suicide attempt, that does not make it the *cause:* ". . . [T]he most important risk factor is the presence of mental illness . . . those gay and heterosexual youths at highest risk may have certain predisposing factors, such as a family history of suicide and a biological vulnerability that interacts with risk factors developed later in life, including a psychiatric illness, substance abuse, and poor social supports."

Peter LaBarbera, *Insight,* February 1994.

Moreover, a 1991 Gallup poll of teens provides little support for Gibson's theory. Sixty percent of kids polled said they knew a teen who had attempted suicide. But none suggested that homosexuality factored into the teen's decision to try to take his own life.

Experts have blasted the Gibson study for its inaccuracies.

Dr. David Shaffer, a psychiatrist at Columbia University and a leading expert on teen suicide, explained that the Gibson paper "was never subjected to the rigorous peer review that is required for publication in a scientific journal and contained no new research findings."

A Powerful Weapon

Despite the Gibson study's innumerable flaws, it has spurred the creation of gay and lesbian youth programs. Massachusetts Governor William Weld's Commission on Gay and Lesbian Youth cites the study to justify a series of pro-homosexual recommendations including: school-based support groups that affirm homosexuality; gay and lesbian books and resources in the school library; and curriculum that affirms and promotes the gay lifestyle as normal and healthy.

In 1992, in Columbia Maryland, the school district conducted a one-day conference on homosexuality for teachers and counselors. The speakers instructed teachers to affirm a child's homosexuality. They suggested that schools put up posters in the hallway that portray various families, such as one made up of two lesbian mothers.

Speakers also encouraged teachers and counselors to keep parents out of the loop. When one teacher asked about whether she should contact the parents about the child's homosexual feelings, she was told "no." That might lead to the family's rejection of the child, which in turn might lead the child to commit suicide. In fact, any time a person suggested an approach to dealing with the child that did not "affirm" homosexuality, they were told, "but if you do that, he might commit suicide."

The pro-gay education effort reaches into even the earliest grades. The Sex Information and Education Council of the United States (SIECUS) creates general guidelines for sex education in America's schools. These guidelines blatantly promote homosexuality even in the youngest grades. The 1990 guidelines suggest that children ages five through eight should be taught that "some men and women are homosexual, which means they will be attracted to and fall in love with someone of the same gender."

The skyrocketing rate of teen suicide in America is a

tragedy. And homosexual activists are manipulating this tragedy to further their own agenda and lure youth into a disease-ridden lifestyle. Americans must not be taken in by these tactics. Americans concerned about teen suicide should seek out the true causes and not become muddled in the myth of homosexual teen suicide.

"*Whatever the eventual catalyst, every suicidal youth's life story has a uniquely tragic plot.*"

Many Factors Contribute to Teen Suicide

Jessica Portner

Depression and the accessibility of guns are routinely blamed for teen suicide. However, in the following viewpoint, Jessica Portner contends that other factors are frequently involved in teens killing themselves. She maintains that teens' tendency for risk-taking, the breakdown of the traditional family, media violence, drug abuse, and hostile school environments are contributing factors in many teen suicides. In addition, teen suicide seems to result only when more than one risk factor is present: A survey of teens who attempted suicide revealed that among the top three motivations for committing suicide— conflict with parents, troubled relationships, and difficulties in school—none were reported to be the sole reason. Portner is a writer and journalist for the *San Jose Mercury News*.

As you read, consider the following questions:
1. In the author's view, which teenagers are more likely to commit suicide?
2. According to the author, how has media violence affected suicidal teens' views of violence?
3. How does illicit drug use affect teenagers' moods, as stated by the author?

W hile suicide rates among adults have steadied or even declined over the past few decades, teenage suicide rates have tripled. In 1960, the suicide rate among 15- to 19-year-olds was 3.6 per 100,000. But by 1990, 11.1 out of every 100,000 teenagers 15 and older committed suicide, according to the U.S. Centers for Disease Control and Prevention (CDC).

In 1997, more than 30,000 suicides were recorded in the United States; about 9 percent of those were committed by people age 19 or younger. "Where it used to be your grand-father, now it's your son," said Tom Simon, a suicide re-searcher at the CDC. He added that more Americans under age 19 now die each year from suicide than from cancer, heart disease, AIDS, pneumonia, lung disease, and birth de-fects combined.

Likely Victims

Which teenagers are most likely to take their own lives? Federal statisticians say the surge in suicides among the na-tion's youths is fueled by unprecedented increases in such deaths in certain populations. For example, suicide rates among 10- to 14-year-olds have nearly doubled in the past few decades. And black teenagers are now more than twice as likely to kill themselves as they were just 20 years ago. But white teenagers, particularly boys, still tower over their peers in their rates of self-destructiveness.

For every teenager who commits suicide, 100 more will try. Every year, one in 13 high school students attempts sui-cide, a 1997 federally funded Youth Risk Behavior Survey found. Half of all high school students report they have "se-riously considered" suicide by the time they graduate, the survey says. That's an estimated 700,000 American high school students annually who attempt to kill themselves, and millions who say they have contemplated doing so. . . .

Impulsive Youths

Young people are more vulnerable than adults to thoughts of suicide, experts say, because they often don't comprehend in a rational sense that death is final. Suicide notes collected by researchers show children fantasizing about what they will do when they are dead. Young people often see suicide as the end of their problems, not their existence. "The developmental stage of adolescence is consistent with not thinking of the long- or short-term consequences of behavior," said Mr. Simon of the CDC.

Another tenet of child development is that adolescents are risk-takers by nature who change friends, clothing styles, and attitudes constantly and for no apparent reason. Such impulsivity still rules when teenagers want to chuck more than their wardrobes.

But those traits are most often coupled with environmental stresses before a young person decides to commit suicide.

The impetus for inner turmoil in the hearts of American adolescents in recent years cannot be gleaned from superficial clues such as whether a teenager plays violent video games, listens to Marilyn Manson CDs, or dons black trench coats, school psychologists say. Young people, they say, rarely wear their angst so conveniently on their sleeves.

In his 1991 book, *The Enigma of Suicide*, journalist George Howe Colt writes that searching for a single cause for suicide is as futile as "trying to pinpoint what causes us to fall in love or what causes war."

Finding an answer to the riddle of self-murder is not like tracing the origins of a disease to a single genetic marker. Suicide is more akin to a multicolored tapestry whose yarn must be unraveled strand by strand.

Looking for Reasons

Sociologists and mental-health experts point to a tangle of cultural, psychological, and medical factors that have in the past 30 years fueled teenagers' heightened self-destructiveness: a higher divorce rate, parental abuse, poor impulse control stemming from exposure to television, the availability of handguns, lack of access to mental-health services, and a general sense of isolation and alienation from caring adults both at home and at school.

Some experts argue that the leading reason why young people are more at risk for suicide now than they were a generation or two ago is the decline of the traditional family unit.

The teenage suicide rate began its climb just as the divorce rate started to surge upward in the 1970s. Half of U.S. marriages now end in divorce, compared with 28 percent in the 1960s; 70 percent of children who attempt suicide have parents who are divorced. In addition, the percentage of children living with two parents declined from 85 percent in 1970 to 68 percent in 1996, federal statistics show.

The dissolution of a two-parent family, whether from divorce, desertion, or the death of a parent, makes children more vulnerable, experts say. Ultimately, though, it's the quality of the parenting, not the constitution of the family unit, that matters most, children's advocates say.

Whether married, divorced, or single, most parents are now working more than in the past and, as a result, have far less free time to spend with their children.

"We are benefiting in this society from everyone working, women working, the gross-national-product productivity per dollar increasing," said Kevin Dwyer, the president of the National Association of School Psychologists (NASP). "But now kids are growing up without the supports they had in the past." The term "latchkey kid," for children left to fend for themselves at home after school, was coined in the 1980s.

Television and the Parenting Void

To fill the parenting void and the decreasing ratio of caring adults to children, television increasingly has become children's stalwart companion after school. Parents spend an average of just two minutes a day communicating with their child, while the TV set spends an average of 3 1/2 hours a day with that child, Mr. Colt writes in his book.

Studies are mixed on how exposure to media images of murders and assaults affects children's behavior, though many youth advocates are convinced that violent television shows, movies, and computer games inflame destructive tendencies. More than 86 percent of television shows and movies depict characters who solve interpersonal problems with violence, according to NASP.

By the end of elementary school, the average child will have witnessed more than 100,000 acts of violence on television, including 8,000 murders, according to the Center for Media Education in Washington.

Served the common fare of shootouts and knifings on TV, children come to believe that violence is an appropriate solution to problems, Mr. Dwyer said.

In today's media-saturated, high-velocity society, youths with poor impulse control are given the message that it's only natural that they should want everything yesterday.

Teen Suicide Risk Factors

Teens who are at increased risk for suicide include those who:

- face problems that are out of their control, such as divorce, alcoholism of a family member, or exposure to domestic violence
- have suffered physical or sexual abuse
- have poor relationships with their parents, lack a support network, are socially isolated, devalued, or rejected
- have a family history of depression or suicide . . .
- experience the feelings of helplessness and worthlessness that often accompany depression . . .
- are dealing with homosexual feelings in an unsupportive family or community or hostile school environment . . .
- use alcohol or drugs in an attempt to numb their pain . . .
- express their feelings violently
- have had a previous suicide attempt

Kidshealth.org, "Understanding and Preventing Teen Suicide," December 2001.

While the video-game industry rejects the idea that some of its games are virtual training classes for potential gunmen, some recent, controversial studies contend that playing violent video games helps youths' dexterity with real firearms and desensitizes them to the visceral realities of violence. In one recent study, high school students interviewed after suicide attempts expressed surprise that their actions were so painful because it didn't look that way on TV.

The Media Factor

Some research suggests that the news media may foster children's self-destructive and violent behavior simply by reporting horrific events.

A 1986 study by Madelyn Gould, a professor of psychiatry at Columbia University who examined media coverage of suicides, found that the suicide of a person reported either on television or in newspapers makes at-risk individuals who are exposed to the coverage feel that suicide is a "reasonable, and even appealing, decision."

After 1999's shootings at Columbine High School, which touched off weeks of intensive coverage by the national news media, there was a spike in teenage suicides across the nation, according to several experts. In Los Angeles County alone, six students killed themselves within six weeks of the shootings. In the four of those cases in which notes were left, three mentioned Columbine as an inspiration. "If you plaster their face up on the news for 20 minutes, that's going to make the difference," said Dr. Pollack of Harvard. Media coverage of suicides isn't *the* reason for a child's decision to kill himself, Dr. Pollack said, but it's a contributing factor.

"These things open the floodgate," he said of news accounts. "But to flood, the waters have to already be at a high level."

Keeping Afloat Emotionally

Keeping afloat emotionally is challenging for many young people because the violence they're exposed to is not just on their television screens. Not surprisingly, children who suffer chronic physical or emotional abuse at home or who witness domestic violence, are much more likely to kill themselves than their peers who do not witness such violence.

"A child doesn't just wake up suicidal," said Richard Lieberman, a school psychologist with the suicide-prevention unit of the Los Angeles public schools who handles distress calls from school officials 24 hours a day. "Kids are dealing with more loss. Families are under more stress."

In all areas of the country—poor, rich, urban, suburban, and rural—reports of child abuse have accelerated dramatically in the past few decades. Though a small portion of the increase is attributable to better reporting, the bulk represents a real and disturbing trend, according to federal health officials. In 1997, 42 out of every 1,000 children in the United States were reported as victims of child abuse, a 320 percent leap from 10 per 1,000 children in 1976, figures from the U.S. Department of Health and Human Services (HHS) show. Newspapers regularly report stories that were once rare: children locked in basements without food; battered and bruised toddlers entering shelters; teenage girls sexually assaulted by their fathers.

Changing School Climate

While home environments in general seem to have become more hazardous, so in large part have schools, say researchers who monitor school climate. Apart from the increasing rates of assaults and shootings since the 1970s, garden-variety bullying behavior is rampant, says Dorothy Espelage, a professor of educational psychology at the University of Illinois at Urbana-Champaign. In a study published [in fall 1999], Ms. Espelage found that 80 percent of the 558 Illinois middle school students surveyed reported they had been "threatened, ridiculed, or been physically aggressive" with at least one classmate in the past 30 days.

Other experts suggest that the increased emphasis on raising academic standards and student-achievement levels adds pressure to the mix.

"We have become so focused on raising standards and testing students, and we are paying very little attention that this is working against creating a motivating environment for kids to come to school," said Howard Adelman, a professor of psychology at the University of California, Los Angeles, who runs a project to promote mental health in schools.

Of course, not every student who feels pressured at school, is harassed, or even has a chaotic home life becomes suicidal.

A suicidal teenager is often fundamentally unstable, mental-health experts say.

Currently in the United States, they note, an estimated 11 percent of children ages 9 to 17—or 4 million children—have a diagnosable mental disorder, ranging from obsessive-compulsive disorders to major depression. The rate of depression has been rising among the young, researchers say, in part because the average age of puberty has declined, and depressive illness tends to emerge after puberty.

Paralyzed Vital Forces

Clinically depressed adolescents are five times more likely to attempt suicide than their nondepressed peers, according to a 15-year study that tracked 73 depressed adolescents and compared them with peers who were not clinically depressed. . . .

In a new book, *Night Falls Fast: Understanding Suicide*, Dr. Kay Redfield Jamison, a professor of psychiatry at Johns Hopkins University, says clinical depression is quite distinguishable from common adolescent angst. "In its severe forms, depression paralyzes all of the otherwise vital forces that make us human, leaving instead a bleak, fatiguing, deadened state," she writes.

In *Darkness Visible*, the author William Styron describes his own severe depression as "a hurricane of the mind." And five years before killing herself, poet Sylvia Plath said of her depressive moods: "I felt as if I were smothering. As if a great muscular owl were sitting on my chest, its talons clenching and constricting my heart."

A growing number of children are now being treated for mood disorders. In 1996, 600,000 children under age 18 with clinical depression were prescribed the antidepressants Prozac, Paxil, and Zoloft, according to IMS America, a research group in New York City. Because no long-term studies on the use of anti-depressants by children have been conducted, it is difficult to determine whether such medicinal remedies can lift the suffocating darkness that Dr. Jamison describes.

Whatever the effect, the upsurge in prescribing psychiatric medications has occurred mainly in middle- and upper-class populations, in which children have more access to health care. For millions of teenagers, the last trip to any kind of doctor was for childhood inoculations.

A study released last fall by the University of North Carolina at Chapel Hill found that one-fifth of teenagers said they had had no health care in the past six months, even though they had a condition that warranted a medical visit. That situation represents a lost opportunity, suicide experts say, because family doctors can detect sudden changes in mood, sleeping patterns, and eating habits—indicators of depression.

Illegal Drugs

Some depressed teenagers, who are either embarrassed to seek help or can't afford it, eschew traditional medical care in favor of illicit drugs to elevate their moods. There is a strong link between the use of illegal drugs and suicide; alcohol and certain drugs are depressants and can often have the effect of deepening one's mood. And, because they knock down inhibitions, teenagers feel freer to act on their suicidal fantasies.

Autopsies of adolescent suicide victims show that one-third to one-half of the teenagers were under the influence of drugs or alcohol shortly before they killed themselves, according to HHS statistics. The rate of overall teenage drug use has fluctuated over the past three decades, peaking in the 1970s and then receding somewhat in the 1980s. Use of marijuana and alcohol—both depressants—surged in the 1990s.

Teenagers haven't been gravitating much toward church for comfort. Religious affiliation as a buffer against the harsh realities of the world has a solid grounding in research. For example, studies have shown that elderly people who participate in church-based activities—such as social events and bingo games—have a decreased risk of mortality. That finding, researchers say, could be due as much to the balm of faith as to the fact that attending places of worship decreases isolation.

But while teenage attendance at religious services rose in the late 1990s, far fewer adolescents attend than did 20 years ago.

Means and Reasons

The burgeoning numbers of isolated, despondent teenagers now more than ever have lethal means at their fingertips.

The federal Bureau of Alcohol, Tobacco, and Firearms reports that in 1960, 90 million guns were in circulation; today, there are an estimated 200 million firearms in private hands. That's enough weaponry, if distributed among the U.S. population, for three out of four Americans to be armed. Despite state and federal laws banning possession of handguns by anyone under 18, for many young people, finding a firearm is no more complicated than pilfering from a parent's closet. Other teenagers know where to buy guns illegally on the streets.

Guns are the method of choice for suicidal youths: More than 67 percent of boys and nearly 52 percent of girls ages 10 to 19 who kill themselves use a firearm. Hanging or suffocation follows far behind—the choice of roughly 23 percent of both male and female suicide victims. Smaller percentages die by overdosing on drugs, drowning, in falls, or by slitting their wrists.

Before a youth pulls the trigger, experts say, some event usually has to set him or her off.

A recent survey of 15- to 19-year-old students in Oregon who had attempted suicide found that the top three things that spurred them to act—while none was the sole reason—were conflict with parents, relationship problems, or difficulties at school.

Whatever the eventual catalyst, every suicidal youth's life story has a uniquely tragic plot. More often than not, it's a circuitous route that leads him or her toward suicide.

| *"Over 90 percent of . . . adolescents who commit suicide have a mental disorder."*

Mood Disorders Contribute to Teen Suicide

David Satcher

David Satcher, who served as the U.S. Surgeon General between 1998 and 2002, is director of the National Center for Primary Care at the Morehouse School of Medicine. In the following viewpoint, Satcher contends that the presence of mood disorders such as depression significantly increases teens' risk for suicide. He maintains that depression is the most significant risk factor leading to suicide for girls and the second most significant risk factor for boys. The author also acknowledges other possible risk factors for teen suicide, such as stressful life events and intensive media coverage of suicide.

As you read, consider the following questions:
1. According to Satcher, what behaviors characterize teens suffering from bipolar disorder?
2. What emotions and perceptions persist after adolescents have experienced depression, according to Satcher?
3. What is the relationship between schizophrenia and teen suicide, as stated by the author?

David Satcher, "Depression and Suicide in Children and Adolescents," *Mental Health: A Report of the Surgeon General*, December 1999.

In children and adolescents, the most frequently diagnosed mood disorders are major depressive disorder, dysthymic disorder, and bipolar disorder. Because mood disorders such as depression substantially increase the risk of suicide, suicidal behavior is a matter of serious concern for clinicians who deal with the mental health problems of children and adolescents. The incidence of suicide attempts reaches a peak during the midadolescent years, and mortality from suicide, which increases steadily through the teens, is the third leading cause of death at that age. Although suicide cannot be defined as a mental disorder, the various risk factors—especially the presence of mood disorders—that predispose young people to such behavior are given special emphasis in this viewpoint, as is a discussion of the effectiveness of various forms of treatment. The evidence is strong that over 90 percent of children and adolescents who commit suicide have a mental disorder as explained later in this viewpoint.

Major Depressive Disorder

Major depressive disorder is a serious condition characterized by one or more major depressive episodes. In children and adolescents, an episode lasts on average from 7 to 9 months and has many clinical features similar to those in adults. Depressed children are sad, they lose interest in activities that used to please them, and they criticize themselves and feel that others criticize them. They feel unloved, pessimistic, or even hopeless about the future; they think that life is not worth living, and thoughts of suicide may be present. Depressed children and adolescents are often irritable, and their irritability may lead to aggressive behavior. They are indecisive, have problems concentrating, and may lack energy or motivation; they may neglect their appearance and hygiene; and their normal sleep patterns are disturbed.

Despite some similarities, childhood depression differs in important ways from adult depression. Psychotic features do not occur as often in depressed children and adolescents, and when they occur, auditory hallucinations are more common than delusions. Associated anxiety symptoms, such as fears of separation or reluctance to meet people, and somatic symptoms, such as general aches and pains, stomachaches, and headaches, are more common in depressed children and adolescents than in adults with depression.

Dysthymic Disorder

Dysthymic disorder is a mood disorder like major depressive disorder, but it has fewer symptoms and is more chronic. Because of its persistent nature, the disorder is especially likely to interfere with normal adjustment. The onset of dysthymic disorder (also called dysthymia) is usually in childhood or adolescence. The child or adolescent is depressed for most of the day, on most days, and symptoms continue for several years. The average duration of a dysthymic period in children and adolescents is about 4 years. Sometimes children are depressed for so long that they do not recognize their mood as out of the ordinary and thus may not complain of feeling depressed. Seventy percent of children and adolescents with dysthymia eventually experience an episode of major depression. When a combination of major depression and dysthymia occurs, the condition is referred to as *double depression*.

Bipolar Disorder

Bipolar disorder is a mood disorder in which episodes of mania alternate with episodes of depression. Frequently, the condition begins in adolescence. The first manifestation of bipolar illness is usually a depressive episode. The first manic features may not occur for months or even years thereafter, or may occur either during the first depressive illness or later, after a symptom-free period.

The clinical problems of mania are very different from those of depression. Adolescents with mania or hypomania feel energetic, confident, and special; they usually have difficulty sleeping but do not tire; and they talk a great deal, often speaking very rapidly or loudly. They may complain that their thoughts are racing. They may do schoolwork quickly and creatively but in a disorganized, chaotic fashion. When manic, adolescents may have exaggerated or even delusional ideas about their capabilities and importance, may become overconfident, and may be "fresh" and uninhibited with others; they start numerous projects that they do not finish and may engage in reckless or risky behavior, such as fast driving or unsafe sex. . . .

Prevalence of Depressive Disorders and Suicide

Major Depression Population studies show that at any one time between 10 and 15 percent of the child and adolescent population has *some* symptoms of depression. The prevalence of the full-fledged diagnosis of major depression among all children ages 9 to 17 has been estimated at 5 percent. Estimates of 1-year prevalence in children range from 0.4 and 2.5 percent and in adolescents, considerably higher (in some studies, as high as 8.3 percent). For purposes of comparison, 1-year prevalence in adults is about 5.3 percent.

Dysthymic Disorder The prevalence of dysthymic disorder in adolescents has been estimated at around 3 percent. Before puberty, major depressive disorder and dysthymic disorder are equally common in boys and girls. But after age 15, depression is twice as common in girls and women as in boys and men.

Suicide In 1996, the age-specific mortality rate from suicide was 1.6 per 100,000 for 10- to 14-year-olds, 9.5 per 100,000 for 15- to 19-year-olds (i.e., about six times higher than in the younger age group; in this age group, boys are about four times as likely to commit suicide than are girls, while girls are twice as likely to attempt suicide), compared with 13.6 per 100,000 for 20- to 24-year-olds. Hispanic high school students are more likely than other students to attempt suicide. There have been some notable changes in these rates over the past few decades: since the early 1960s, the reported suicide rate among 15- to 19-year-old males increased threefold but remained stable among females in that age group and among 10- to 14-year-olds; the rate among white adolescent males reached a peak in the late 1980s (18.0 per 100,000 in 1986) and has since declined somewhat (16.0 per 100,000 in 1997), whereas among African American male adolescents, the rate increased substantially in the same period (from 7.1 per 100,000 in 1986 to 11.4 per 100,000 in 1997). From 1979 to 1992, the Native American male adolescent and young adult suicide rate in Indian Health Service Areas was the highest in the Nation, with a suicide rate of 62.0 per 100,000.

It has been proposed that the rise in suicidal behavior

among teenage boys results from increased availability of firearms and increased substance abuse in the youth population. However, although the rate of suicide by firearms increased more than suicide by other methods, suicide rates also increased markedly in many other countries in Europe, in Australia, and in New Zealand, where suicide by firearms is rare. . . .

The precise causes of depression are not known. Extensive research on adults with depression generally points to both biological and psychosocial factors. However, there has been substantially less research on the causes of depression in children and adolescents. . . .

Serotonin and Suicide

Recent studies indicate that those who have attempted suicide may . . . have low levels of the brain chemical serotonin. Serotonin helps control impulsivity, and low levels of the brain chemical are thought to cause more impulsive behavior. Suicides are often committed out of impulse. Antidepressant drugs affecting serotonin are used to treat depression, impulsivity and suicidal thoughts. However, much more research is needed to confirm these hypotheses and, hopefully, eventually lead to more definite indicators of and treatment for those prone to suicide.

The Nation's Voice on Mental Illness (NAMI), "Teenage Suicide," n.d.

Cognitive Factors For over two decades there has been considerable interest in the relationship between a particular "mindset" or approach to perceiving external events and a predisposition to depression. The mindset in question is known as a pessimistic "attribution bias". A person with this mindset is one who readily assumes personal blame for negative events ("All the problems in the family are my fault"), who expects that one negative experience is part of a pattern of many other negative events ("Everything I do is wrong"), and who believes that a currently negative situation will endure permanently ("Nothing I do is going to make anything better"). Such pessimistic individuals take a characteristically negative view of positive events (i.e., that they are a result of someone else's effort, that they are isolated events, and that they are unlikely to recur). Individuals with this mindset react more passively, helplessly, and ineffectively to negative events than those without a pessimistic mindset. . . .

There is evidence that children and adolescents who previously have been depressed may learn, during their depression, to interpret events in this fashion. This may make them prone to react similarly to negative events experienced after recovery, which could be one of the reasons why previously depressed children and adolescents are at continuing risk for depression.

Perceptions of hopelessness, negative views about one's own competence, poor self-esteem, a sense of responsibility for negative events, and the immutability of these distorted attributions may contribute to the hopelessness that has been repeatedly found to be associated with suicidality.

Risk Factors for Suicide and Suicidal Behavior

There is good evidence that over 90 percent of children and adolescents who commit suicide have a mental disorder before their death. The most common disorders that predispose to suicide are some form of mood disorder, with or without alcoholism or other substance abuse problem, and/or certain forms of anxiety disorder. Psychological postmortem studies also show that a significant proportion of suicide victims suffered from an anxiety disorder at the time of their death, but the number of victims has been too small to yield precise odds ratios for the calculation of an effect. Although the rate of suicide is greatly increased in schizophrenia, because of its rarity, it accounts for very few suicides in the child and adolescent age group. . . .

Among girls, the most significant risk factor is the presence of major depression, which, in some studies, increases the risk of suicide 12-fold. The next most important risk factor is a previous suicide attempt, which increases the risk approximately threefold. Among boys, a previous suicide attempt is the most potent predictor, increasing the rate over 30-fold. It is followed by depression (increasing the rate by about 12-fold), disruptive behavior (increasing the rate by twofold), and substance abuse (increasing the rate by just under twofold).

Stressful Life Events

Stressful life events often precede a suicide and/or suicide attempt. As indicated earlier, these stressful life events include getting into trouble at school or with a law enforcement agency; a ruptured relationship with a boyfriend or a girlfriend; or a fight among friends. They are rarely a sufficient cause of suicide, but they can be precipitating factors in young people.

Controlled studies indicate that low levels of communication between parents and children may act as a significant risk factor. While family discord, lack of family warmth, and disturbed parent-child relationship are commonly associated with child and adolescent psychopathology (violent behavior, mood disorder, alcohol and substance abuse disorders), these factors do not play a specific role in suicide.

Exposure to Suicide

Evidence has accumulated that supports the observation that suicide can be facilitated in vulnerable teens by exposure to real or fictional accounts of suicide, including media coverage of suicide, such as intensive reporting of the suicide of a celebrity, or the fictional representation of a suicide in a popular movie or TV show. The risk is especially high in the young, and it lasts for several weeks. The suicide of a prominent person reported on television or in the newspaper or exposure to some sympathetic fictional representation of suicide may also tip the balance and make the at-risk individual feel that suicide is a reasonable, acceptable, and in some instances even heroic, decision.

The phenomenon of suicide clusters is presumed to be related to imitation. Suicide clusters nearly always involve previously disturbed young people who knew about each other's death but rarely knew the other victims personally.

Consequences

Both major depressive disorder and dysthymic disorder are inevitably associated with personal distress, and if they last a long time or occur repeatedly, they can lead to a circumscribed life with fewer friends and sources of support, more stress, and missed educational and job opportunities. The psychological scars of depression include an enduring pessimistic style of interpreting events, which may increase the risk of further depressive episodes. Impairment is greater for those with dysthymic disorder than for those with major depression, presumably because of the longer duration of depression in dysthymic disorder, which is also a prime risk factor for suicide. In a 10- to 15-year followup study of 73 adolescents diagnosed with major depression, 7 percent of the adolescents had committed suicide sometime later. The depressed adolescents were five times more likely to have attempted suicide as well, compared with a control group of age peers without depression.

> "*Competitive, self-critical, high-achieving*
> *students make up an estimated one-third*
> *of all teenage suicides.*"

High-Achieving Teens Are at Risk for Suicide

Julian Guthrie

In the following viewpoint, Julian Guthrie reports that high-achieving teens are at higher risk for suicide than commonly perceived. He suggests that the pressure to succeed and feelings of inadequacy can overwhelm even the most successful and popular students. Moreover, he claims that high-achieving teens who are contemplating suicide are hard to identify because they often appear to be untroubled. Guthrie is a reporter for the *San Francisco Chronicle*.

As you read, consider the following questions:
1. How does Guthrie describe student Thomas Ray Hoo?
2. What evidence does the author use to support his claim that completed suicides represent only a small percentage of total attempted suicides?
3. According to Guthrie, what factors at school made Hoo feel inadequate?

Julian Guthrie, "When Success Turns to Suicide; Lowell High Student's Death Shows How High-Achieving Teens Are Also at Risk," *San Francisco Chronicle*, June 2, 2002, p. A17. Copyright © 2002 by *San Francisco Chronicle*. Reproduced by permission.

On the surface, Thomas Ray Hoo, a Lowell High School junior [in San Francisco] was a model student and athlete. He was captain of the football team, placed second in all-city wrestling, had good grades and lots of friends.

To all at his school, he was not a likely candidate for suicide.

But, below the surface, behind the shy, goofy smile and confident mien, was a nagging sense of inadequacy. He never felt big enough, fast enough, smart enough.

In late May 2002, the 16-year-old killed himself.

Popularity and Success Mask the Pain

Hoo is not an isolated case. Competitive, self-critical, high-achieving students make up an estimated one-third of all teenage suicides. Experts who work to understand the phenomenon say that it is these students who present the greatest challenge because they appear to be untroubled. Popularity and success often mask pain and depression.

"Those are the ones who present a paradox," said Dr. David Shaffer, a Columbia University psychiatrist who runs the American Foundation for Suicide Prevention. "On the surface, it's a puzzle. But if you dig deeper, it's not a puzzle.

"You see these kids have done well because of certain levels of anxiety. That anxiety can also get the best of them."

While the number of teens who commit suicide is startling, it represents a fraction of those who try to end their lives. For every death, there are 200 failed attempts, according to the American Association of Suicidology.

A recent study of 150 San Francisco high school students found that 30 percent are at risk of suicide, a figure that is in line with national statistics.

Lowell, known for its intense academic rigor, was chosen [in fall 2001] as one of six San Francisco schools to be included in a national pilot program aimed at helping depressed and alienated kids, those most at risk for attempting suicide.

Shaffer said that nearly everyone who commits suicide has a "somewhat treatable mental illness." It is the high-achieving kids who generally go undiagnosed, he said.

"They're seen as good, rather serious kids who always do well. Rather than parents pushing them, (their parents) tell them not to worry so much."

Family and Friends Are Shocked

Shaffer's description is reflected in the words of Hoo's grandfather, Linkee Hoo. Standing outside the Lowell auditorium where a memorial service was held May 30th, he described a seemingly untroubled teen.

"Every night, after studying one or two hours, after he brushed his teeth and washed his face, he came to kiss me good night," Hoo said, trembling as he talked. "He was just a baby. He was a very good boy."

According to friends and faculty at Lowell, Hoo never accepted that he was a success. The unyielding pressure to do better appeared to come from within.

"People are trying to analyze this, to find a reason," said Lowell Principal Paul Cheng. "I think there was something about his sense of striving. He was a perfectionist. He was meticulous. But those are elements that many of us have, at Lowell and elsewhere. If they're not recognized and modified so that a person has a more balanced perspective and goals, it can get to the extreme."

Kevin Hines, now 20, was also a striver when he attempted suicide at age 18. Like Hoo, he was a star wrestler and football player and was popular. He now cautions against assuming successful kids can't also be suffering from depression.

"The thing about mental illness is that it's in the brain and with many people, it's subtle or you can't see it at all," said Hines.

Feelings of Inadequacy

No one ever considered that Hoo's personal sense of inadequacy reflected anything more than a drive to do better. In retrospect, friends and teachers say they wish they had been able to convince him he was good enough.

Instead of being exultant over placing second in all-city wrestling competition held in March 2002, Hoo was depressed he hadn't come in first. Instead of being honored to have been selected captain of next year's football team, he worried he would falter as a leader. He questioned the merits of being captain when he wasn't going to be in the starting lineup.

He felt inadequate because of his size, telling football teammates how lucky they were to be bigger and beefier. He was 5-foot-4 and weighed 150 pounds during football season and 130 during wrestling. Although he maintained a solid B or B-plus average, his grades had dropped in recent months because of the demands of sports. He was surrounded by students with straight A's.

Suicide and Perfectionism

Why do people commit suicide? Does the problem lie with the suicidal person, the society, or a combination of the individual and the environment? So far as the individual is concerned, the problem often is his or her striving to reach a high goal and the failure to achieve that goal. [According to behavioral science writer Howard Rosenthal,] "At the core of every suicidal individual's personality is a demanding perfectionistic streak consumed with criticizing, cutting down, nitpicking, and downright tyrannizing every major, minor, and even minuscule behavior. The perfectionist leaves no stone unturned in order to yield an unfavorable report card of one's self."

Judy Cushman, "What You Should Know, How You Should Relate," www.adventist.org, September 1, 1997.

One of the only things he was satisfied with was his ability to bench-press 205 pounds.

Two days before Hoo committed suicide, Lowell's head football coach Jason Krolikowski called the student into his office because he had heard rumors that Hoo wanted to quit the team.

Hoo asked his coach why he kept coaching when he didn't always win.

"I said that one of these days, we're going to, and I won't stop until we do. I thought he embodied the same mentality. He had this amazing work ethic and a special energy reserve."

Krolikowski said he thought Hoo was going through a rough time, nothing more.

"He was so strong in everything. He would always come back and try harder," the coach said. It was "inconceivable" Hoo would commit suicide.

Many at Lowell questioned how such a high achiever could reach such an unseen low.

When Hoo took his life at home around 2 a.m., it was reportedly with a gun that had been stashed away and forgotten in the family garage a decade earlier. He left behind his grandparents, his mother and father and two older sisters, one a senior at Lowell.

Identifying Those at Risk

The pilot program to identify at-risk students at Lowell and other San Francisco schools is being conducted by researchers from the University of North Carolina at Chapel Hill. The program began at Mission, Lincoln and Balboa high schools, and includes Lowell and a school to be named in the fall of 2002.

Denise Hallfors, director of the Reconnecting Youth Program funded by the National Institutes of Health, was troubled but not surprised to find that 30 percent of students surveyed in random samples in San Francisco were at risk of suicide.

"We know that a high percentage of students think of suicide," Hallfors said. "What is more difficult, what we'd like to understand, is who the young people are who would go that extra step."

That was Hines in 2000. Like Hoo, his suicide attempt was unthinkable, largely because he excelled in school and at sports. The successes couldn't stop him, though, from jumping off the Golden Gate Bridge.

Of the estimated 10,000 people who have jumped off the Golden Gate Bridge, Hines is one of 15 known survivors. Of those, he is one of only four who can walk.

Now, Hines visits schools to talk about mental illness and suicide prevention. He tells students that he suffered from bipolar disorder and, at the time of his suicide attempt, was overcome by paranoia and depression. "I just wanted to end the pain," he said.

"I changed my mind the second I jumped off the bridge," he said. "I knew I wanted to live. In my case, I was given a second chance."

He tells students and adults that they're not alone in feeling depressed and that help is available. He is now on medication that effectively controls his disorder.

"I thought no one else was going through what I was," said Hines, who is 20. "But I've learned that people are going through that and worse. You can never look at a student and say, 'Oh, she or he would never do that.' You don't know what's going on in the brain."

Periodical Bibliography

The following articles have been selected to supplement the diverse views presented in this chapter.

Francesca Delbanco   "The Heart of Darkness," *Seventeen*, November 1998.

Economist (US)   "Such a Waste; Teenage Suicide," December 8, 2001.

Marilyn Elias   "Gay Teens Less Suicidal than Thought, Report Says," *USA Today*, November 26, 2001.

Chris Heredia   "More Suicide Attempts Found Among Gay Teens; Study Finds Rate Twice That of Straight Kids," *San Francisco Chronicle*, August 7, 2001.

Richard Jerome   "The Lost Boy: Grieving Mom Julie Bishop Blames Acne Drug for Her Son's Bizarre, Tragic Suicide," *People Weekly*, April 29, 2002.

Pediatrics   "Suicide and Suicide Attempts in Adolescents," April 2000.

Patrick Perry   "Teens at Risk," *Saturday Evening Post*, January/February 1999.

Gabriel Rotello   "Calling All Parents," *Advocate*, January 16, 2001.

Michael D. Simpson   "Student Suicide: Who's Liable?" *NEA Today*, February 1999.

Ron Stodghill II   "Lost Boys (African American Males Committing Suicide)," *Essence*, November 1, 1998.

Gloria Troyer   "Does God Love Gabe?" *Presbyterian Record*, October 2001.

Robert Wright   "'I'd Sell You Suicide': Pop Music and Moral Panic in the Age of Marilyn Manson," *Popular Music*, October 2000.

Alan J. Zametkin, Marisa R. Alter, and Tamar Yemini   "Suicide in Teenagers: Assessment, Management, and Prevention," *The Journal of the American Medical Association*, December 26, 2001.

CHAPTER 3

Should Physician-Assisted Suicide Be Legalized?

Chapter Preface

In the debate over legalizing assisted suicide, the terms *assisted suicide* and *euthanasia* are often used synonymously. However, the terms actually describe the different levels of autonomy, responsibility, and choice the patient may or may not exercise in hastening his or her own death. In an assisted suicide, a physician, family member, or friend provides the lethal dose of medication or other means of dying to the patient, but the patient is responsible for carrying out the suicide. In contrast, euthanasia involves someone other than the patient directly causing death. There are two kinds of euthanasia: passive and active. Passive euthanasia is when life-sustaining medical treatment—such as a respirator, a feeding tube, or medication—is withdrawn and the patient is allowed to die naturally from the underlying illness, injury, or condition. Active euthanasia is when someone else directly causes the patient's death—by lethal injection, for example. Both passive and active euthanasia can be voluntary or involuntary, depending on whether the procedure is performed with the patient's awareness and permission (voluntary) or without such awareness or permission (involuntary).

Opponents of physician-assisted suicide assert that legalizing the practice will lead to the acceptance and legalization of voluntary euthanasia, which would inevitably open the door to the practice of involuntary euthanasia. They allege that the Netherlands, where assisted suicide is tolerated, now condones euthanasia for those who cannot volunteer for the procedure, such as comatose patients. On the other hand, proponents of physician-assisted suicide argue that enforcing strict safeguards would give physicians the authority to help their patients commit suicide without putting other patients at risk for involuntary euthanasia. In the following chapter, the authors debate the benefits, risks, and ethical implications of legalizing assisted suicide.

"No matter how good [end-of-life] care gets, there still will be a need to have assisted death as one choice."

Physician-Assisted Suicide Should Be Legalized

Faye Girsh

Faye Girsh is executive director of the Hemlock Society, a nonprofit organization that works to legalize voluntary physician-assisted suicide for terminally ill consenting adults. In the following viewpoint, Girsh asserts that physician-assisted suicide must be a legal choice for the terminally ill when suffering becomes unbearable. Because there is a legal right to commit suicide and refuse unwanted medical treatment, she claims that in order to be ethically consistent, assisted death should be legalized. Furthermore, legalizing physician-assisted suicide would not lead to the deaths of patients against their will as detractors argue because the practice would be strictly monitored.

As you read, consider the following questions:

1. According to Girsh, why do most terminally ill patients ask for a hastened death?
2. In Girsh's opinion, how has the right-to-die movement affected end-of-life care?
3. What objectives would legalizing physician-assisted suicide accomplish, as stated by the author?

Faye Girsh, "Q: Should Assisted Suicide Be Legalized by the States? Yes: Don't Make Doctors Criminals for Helping People Escape Painful Terminal Illnesses," *Insight*, vol. 15, March 8, 1999, p. 24. Copyright © 1999 by Insight on the News. Reproduced by permission.

Many people agree that there are horrifying situations at the end of life which cry out for the help of a doctor to end the suffering by providing a peaceful, wished-for death. But, opponents argue, that does not mean that the practice should be legalized. They contend that these are the exceptional cases from which bad law would result.

A Peaceful End

I disagree. It is precisely these kinds of hard deaths that people fear and that happen to 7 to 10 percent of those who are dying that convince them to support the right to choose a hastened death with medical assistance. The reason that polls in this country—and in Canada, Australia, Great Britain and other parts of Europe—show 60 to 80 percent support for legalization of assisted suicide is that people want to know they will have a way out if their suffering becomes too great. They dread losing control not only of their bodies but of what will happen to them in the medical system. As a multiple-sclerosis patient wrote to the Hemlock Society: "I feel like I am just rotting away. . . . If there is something that gives life meaning and purpose it is this: a peaceful end to a good life before the last part of it becomes even more hellish."

Even with the best of hospice care people want to know that there can be some way to shorten a tortured dying process. A man whose wife was dying from cancer wrote, "For us, hospice care was our choice. We, however, still had 'our way,' also our choice, as 'our alternative.' We were prepared. And the 'choice' should be that of the patient and family."

It is not pain that causes people to ask for a hastened death but the indignities and suffering accompanying some terminal disorders such as cancer, stroke and AIDS. A survey in the Netherlands found that the primary reason to choose help in dying was to avoid "senseless suffering."

Hospice can make people more comfortable, can bring spiritual solace and can work with the family, but—as long as hospice is sworn neither to prolong nor hasten death—it will not be the whole answer for everyone. People should not have to make a choice between seeking hospice care and choosing to hasten the dying process. The best hospice care should be available to everyone, as should the option of a quick, gentle, certain death with loved ones around when the suffering has become unbearable. Both should be part of the continuum of care at the end of life.

A Difference Without Distinction

We have the right to commit suicide and the right to refuse unwanted medical treatment, including food and water. But what we don't have—unless we live in Oregon—is the right to get help from a doctor to achieve a peaceful death. As the trial judge in the Florida case of *Kirscher vs McIver*, an AIDS patient who wanted his doctor's help in dying, said in his decision: "Physicians are permitted to assist their terminal patients by disconnecting life support or by prescribing medication to ease their starvation. Yet medications to produce a quick death, free of pain and protracted agony, are prohibited. This is a difference without distinction."

The Oregon example has shown us that, although a large number of people want to know the choice is there, only a small number will take advantage of it. During the first eight months of the Oregon "Death with Dignity" law, only 10 people took the opportunity to obtain the medications and eight used them to end their lives. In the Netherlands it consistently has been less than 5 percent of the total number of people who die every year who choose to get help in doing so from their doctor.

In Switzerland, where physician-assisted death also is legal, about 120 people die annually with the help of medical assistance. There is no deluge of people wanting to put themselves out of their misery nor of greedy doctors and hospitals encouraging that alternative. People want to live as long as possible. There are repeated testimonials to the fact that people can live longer and with less anguish once they know that help will be available if they want to end it. Even Jack Kevorkian, who says he helped 130 people die since 1990, has averaged only 14 deaths a year.

To the credit of the right-to-die movement, end-of-life care has improved because of the push for assisted dying. In Oregon, end-of-life care is the best in the country: Oregon is No. 1 in morphine use, twice as many people there use hospice as the national average and more people die at home than in the hospital. In Maine there will be an initiative on the ballot in 2000 to legalize physician aid in dying, and in Arizona a physician-assisted-dying bill has been introduced. In both states the Robert Woods Johnson Foundation has awarded sizable grants to expand hospice care and to improve end-of-life care. [The Maine initiative and the Arizona bill did not pass.]

Medical Reality

The good news is that many adults are now capable, with the help of pharmacological and technological advances in medicine, of having long lives with a remarkable health status that would have been unachievable earlier in this century and unimaginable before that. The bad news is that some adults are caught in an existential situation dominated by intractable pain, severe disability, progressive dementia, a deteriorating neurological condition, a terminal condition, or some combination of these that makes life seem not to be worth living. An unknown number of these persons decide that death is a preferable option to the suffering that life holds for them and, for their own personal reasons, ask their physicians to help them end the suffering.

It is this part of medical reality—the realistic limits of physicians to heal all their patients and effectively relieve suffering—that represents the ethical core of the debate over physician-assisted suicide (PAS). Rather than quoting a passage from the Hippocratic Oath ["First, do no harm."] about what physicians cannot do for their patients, contemporary physicians should address medical reality as it currently exists in their patients—some with terminal conditions, and an increasing number with chronic and degenerative diseases—and consider again what they might do for that small minority of patients who find their lives to be intolerable and who, perhaps as a last resort, turn to their physicians for help in bringing about death.

Robert F. Weir, *Law, Medicine and Health Care* 20, 1992.

It is gratifying that the specter of assisted dying has spurred such concern for care at the end of life. Clearly, if we take the pressure off, the issue will disappear back into the closet. No matter how good the care gets, there still will be a need to have an assisted death as one choice. The better the care gets, the less that need will exist.

The Culture of Death

The pope and his minions in the Catholic Church, as well as the religious right, announce that assisted dying is part of the "culture of death." Murder, lawlessness, suicide, the cheapening of life with killing in the media, the accessibility of guns, war—those create a culture of death, not providing help to a dying person who repeatedly requests an end to his or her suffering by a day or a week. Not all religious people believe that. The Rev. Bishop Spong of the Episcopal Diocese of Newark, New Jersey, said: "My personal creed asserts that every person is sacred. I see the holiness of life enhanced, not diminished, by letting people have a say in how they choose to die. Many of us want the moral and legal right to choose to die with our faculties intact, surrounded by those we love before we are reduced to breathing cadavers with no human dignity attached to our final days. Life must not be identified with the extension of biological existence. [Assisted suicide] is a life-affirming moral choice."

The Catholic belief that suicide is a sin which will cause a person to burn in hell is at the root of the well-financed, virulent opposition to physician aid in dying. This has resulted in expenditures of more than $10 million in losing efforts to defeat the two Oregon initiatives and a successful campaign to defeat the recent Michigan measure. And $6 million was spent in Michigan, most of which came from Catholic donors, to show four TV ads six weeks before voters saw the issue on the 1998 ballot. The ads never attacked the concept of physician aid in dying, but hammered on the well-crafted Proposal B. Surely that money could have been spent to protect life in better ways than to frustrate people who have come to terms with their deaths and want to move on. The arguments that life is sacred and that it is a gift from God rarely are heard now from the opposition. Most Americans do not want to be governed by religious beliefs they don't share, so the argument has shifted to "protection of the vulnerable and the slippery slope." Note, however, that the proposed death-with-dignity laws carefully are written to protect the vulnerable. The request for physician-assisted death must be voluntary, must be from a competent adult and must be documented and repeated during a waiting period. Two doctors must examine the patient and, if there is any question of depression or incompetence or coercion, a mental-health professional can be consulted. After that it must be up to the requester to mix and swallow the lethal medication. No one forces anyone to do anything!

The same arguments were raised in 1976 when the first "living-will" law was passed in California. It again was raised in 1990 when the Supreme Court ruled that every American has the right to refuse medical treatment, including food and hydration, and to designate a proxy to make those decisions if they cannot. This has not been a downhill slope since 1976 but an expansion of rights and choices. It has not led to abuse but rather to more freedom. Those who raise the specter of the Nazis must remember that we are in greater danger of having our freedoms limited by religious dogma than of having them expanded so that more choices are available. When the state dictates how the most intimate and personal choices will be made, based on how some religious groups think it should be, then we as individuals and as a country are in serious trouble.

Enhancing Freedom

One observer said about the Oregon Death With Dignity law: "This is a permissive law. It allows something. It requires nothing. It forbids nothing and taxes no one. It enhances freedom. It lets people do a little more of what they want without hurting anyone else. It removes a slight bit of the weight of government regulation and threat of punishment that hangs over all of us all the time if we step out of line."

Making physician aid in dying legal as a matter of public policy will accomplish several objectives. Right now we have a model of prohibition. There is an underground cadre of doctors—of whom Kevorkian is the tip of the iceberg—who are helping people die. The number varies, according to survey, from 6 to 16 percent to 20 to 53 percent. The 53 percent is for doctors in San Francisco who work with people with AIDS where networks for assisted dying have existed for many years. This practice is not regulated or reported; the criteria and methods used are unknown. There is some information that the majority of these deaths are done by lethal injection. Millions of viewers witnessed on *60 Minutes* the videotape of Kevorkian using this method to assist in the death of Thomas Youk. If the practice is regulated, there will be more uniformity, doctors will be able to and will have to obtain a second opinion and will have the option of having a mental-health professional consult on the case. Most importantly for patients, they will be able to talk about all their options openly with their health-care providers and their loved ones.

Another consequence is that desperately ill people will not have to resort to dying in a Michigan motel with Kevorkian's assistance, with a plastic bag on their heads, with a gun in their mouth or, worse, botching the job and winding up in worse shape and traumatizing their families. They won't have to die the way someone else wants them to die, rather than the way they choose. As philosophy professor Ronald Dworkin said in *Life's Dominion*: "Making someone die in a way others approve, but he believes a horrifying contradiction of his life, is a devastating, odious form of tyranny."

"On closer inspection, there are many reasons that legalizing assisted suicide is a terrible idea."

Physician-Assisted Suicide Should Not Be Legalized

Marilyn Golden

Marilyn Golden is a member of the Executive Committee for the California Disability Alliance. In the following viewpoint, Golden argues that making physician-assisted suicide legal would have many negative, unintended consequences. For instance, she contends that legalizing physician-assisted suicide would likely result in for-profit health care organizations pressuring doctors to deny terminally ill patients medical treatment. Moreover, Golden claims that proposals for assisted suicide would inevitably expand to include a variety of conditions, putting patients who are not suffering from terminal or painful illnesses at risk for involuntary euthanasia.

As you read, consider the following questions:
1. In the author's opinion, which groups of people are discriminated against in the health care system?
2. What is Golden's view of life expectancy prognoses for terminally ill patients?
3. How might physician-assisted suicide become a coerced choice rather than a personal decision for some people, as stated by Golden?

Marilyn Golden, "Why Assisted Suicide Must Not Be Legalized," www. euthanasiaprevention.on.ca, 1999. Copyright © 1999 by California Disability Alliance. Reproduced by permission.

A ssisted suicide seems, at first blush, like a good thing to have available. But on closer inspection, there are many reasons that legalizing assisted suicide is a terrible idea.

While an extremely small number of people may benefit, they will tend to be at the upper end of the income scale, white, and have good health insurance coverage. At the same time, large numbers of people, particularly among those less privileged in society, would be at significant risk of substantial harm. We must separate our private wishes for what we each may hope to have available for ourselves some day and, rather, focus on the significant dangers of legalizing assisted suicide as public policy in this society as it is today. Assisted suicide would have many unintended consequences.

Managed Care and Assisted Suicide Are a Deadly Mix

Perhaps the most significant problem is the deadly mix between assisted suicide and profit-driven managed health care. Health maintenance organizations (HMO's) and managed care bureaucrats are already overruling doctors' treatment decisions, sometimes hastening patients' deaths. The cost of the lethal medication generally used for assisted suicide is about $35–$50, far cheaper than the cost of treatment for most long-term medical conditions. The incentive to save money by denying treatment is already a significant danger; it would be far greater if assisted suicide is legal. It's not coincidental that the author of Oregon's assisted suicide law, Barbara Coombs Lee, was an HMO executive when she drafted it. Assisted suicide will accelerate the decline in quality of our health care system.

A 1998 study from Georgetown University's Center for Clinical Bioethics underscored the link between profit-driven managed health care and assisted suicide. The research found a strong link between cost-cutting pressure on doctors and their willingness to prescribe lethal drugs to patients, were it legal to do so. The study warns there must be "a sobering degree of caution in legalizing [physician-assisted suicide] in a medical care environment that is characterized by increasing pressure on physicians to control the cost of care."

The deadly impact would come down the hardest on socially and economically disadvantaged groups who have less access to medical resources and who already find themselves discriminated against by the health care system: poor people, people of color, elderly people, people with chronic or progressive conditions or disabilities, and anyone who is, in fact, terminally ill will be put at serious risk.

Dr. Rex Greene, a cancer specialist in Los Angeles for over twenty years and a leader in his field, underscored the heightened danger to the poor. He said, "The most powerful predictor of ill health is [people's] income. [Legalization of assisted suicide] plays right into the hands of managed care."

Supporters of assisted suicide frequently say that HMO's will not use assisted suicide as a way to deal with costly patients. They cite a 1998 study in the *New England Journal of Medicine* that found the savings of allowing people to die before their last month of life would be $627 million, which is only .07% of the nation's total health care costs per year. But this study has several significant problems that make it an unsuitable basis for claims about assisted suicide's potential impact. The researchers based their findings on the average cost to Medicare of patients with only four weeks or less to live. But assisted suicide proposals (as well as the law in Oregon, the only state where assisted suicide is legal) define terminal illness as having six months to live. The researchers also assumed that about 2.7% of the total number of people who die in the U.S. would opt for physician-assisted suicide, based on reported physician-assisted suicide and euthanasia deaths in the Netherlands. But Dutch doctors are not required to report such deaths, which casts considerable doubt on this figure. And how can you compare the U.S. to a country that has universal health care? All these considerations would skew the costs much higher.

Fear, Bias, and Prejudice Against Disability

Another major problem with assisted suicide is who ends up using it, both in Oregon and in the only other place on earth where it is legally tolerated, the Netherlands. The point of assisted suicide is purported to be relief from untreatable pain at the end of life. However, all but one of the people in

Oregon who were reported to have used that state's assisted suicide law during its first year wanted suicide not because of pain, but for fear of losing functional ability, autonomy, or control of bodily functions. Oregon's second year report has similar results. Further, in the Netherlands, more than half the doctors surveyed say the main reason given by patients for seeking death is "loss of dignity."

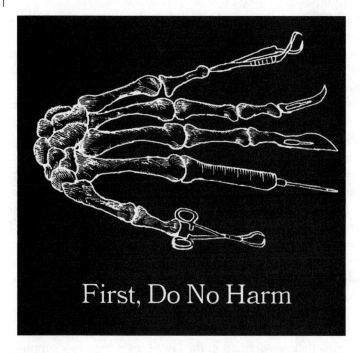

First, Do No Harm

Podwal. © 1994 by *New York Times*. Reprinted with permission.

This fear of disability typically underlies assisted suicide. Said one assisted suicide advocate, "Pain is not the main reason we want to die. It's the indignity. It's the inability to get out of bed or get onto the toilet . . . [People] . . . say, 'I can't stand my mother—my husband—wiping my behind.' It's about dignity." But needing help is not undignified, and death is not better than dependency. Have we gotten to the point that we will abet suicides because people need help using the toilet?

Assisted suicide proposals are based on the faulty assumption that you can make a clear distinction between who is terminally ill with 6 months to live, and everyone else. Everyone else is supposedly protected and not eligible for assisted suicide. But it is extremely common for medical predictions of a short life expectancy to be wrong. Studies show that only cancer patients show a predictable decline, and even then, it's only in the last few weeks of life. And with every disease other than cancer, there is no predictability. Prognoses are based on statistical averages, which are nearly useless in predicting what will happen to an individual patient. Moreover, doctors and the courts frequently classify people with long-term disabilities as "terminally ill." Thus, the potential effect of assisted suicide is extremely broad, far beyond the supposedly narrow group the proponents claim.

This poses considerable danger to people with new or increasing disabilities or diseases. Research overwhelmingly shows that people with new disabilities frequently go through initial despondency and suicidal feelings, but later adapt well and find great satisfaction in their lives. However, the adaptation usually takes considerably longer than the mere two week waiting period required by assisted suicide proposals and Oregon's law. People with new diagnoses of terminal illness appear to go through similar stages. In that early period before one learns the truth about how good one's quality of life can be, it would be all too easy to make the final choice one that is irrevocable, if assisted suicide is legal.

In Oregon's law and similar proposals, doctors are not supposed to write a lethal prescription under inappropriate conditions that are defined in the law. This is seen as a supposed safeguard. But what's happened in several cases in Oregon is "doctor shopping"—if one physician refuses assisted suicide because the patient doesn't meet the conditions in the law, another physician is sought who will approve it, often one who's an assisted suicide advocate. Such was the case of Kate Cheney, age 85, whose case was described in the *Oregonian* in October 1999. Her doctor refused to prescribe the lethal medication, because he thought the request was actually the result of pressure by an assertive daughter who was stuck with caregiving, rather than the free choice of the mother. So the family found another doctor, and Ms. Cheney is now dead.

There is one safeguard in most assisted suicide proposals—for HMO's and doctors: the "good faith" standard. This "safeguard" provides that no person will be subject to any form of legal liability if they claim that they acted in "good faith." A claimed "good faith" belief that the requirements of the law are satisfied is virtually impossible to disprove, rendering all other proposed "safeguards" effectively unenforceable.

"Narrow" Proposals Will Inevitably Expand

As the New York State Task Force on Life and the Law wrote, "Once society authorizes assisted suicide for . . . terminally ill patients experiencing unrelievable suffering, it will be difficult if not impossible to contain the option to such a limited group. Individuals who are not (able to make the choice for themselves), who are not terminally ill, or who cannot self-administer lethal drugs will also seek the option of assisted suicide, and no principled basis will exist to deny (it)."

The longest experience we have with assisted suicide is in the Netherlands, where not only assisted suicide but also active euthanasia is practiced. The Netherlands is a very frightening laboratory experiment where, because of assisted suicide and euthanasia, "pressure for improved palliative care appears to have evaporated," according to Dr. Herbert Hendin in Congressional testimony in 1996. Assisted suicide and euthanasia have become not just the exception, but the rule for people with terminal illness.

"Over the past two decades," Hendin continued, "the Netherlands has moved from assisted suicide to euthanasia, from euthanasia for the terminally ill to euthanasia for the chronically ill, from euthanasia for physical illness to euthanasia for psychological distress and from voluntary euthanasia to nonvoluntary and involuntary euthanasia. Once the Dutch accepted assisted suicide it was not possible legally or morally to deny more active medical (assistance to die), i.e. euthanasia, to those who could not effect their own deaths. Nor could they deny assisted suicide or euthanasia to the chronically ill who have longer to suffer than the terminally ill or to those who have psychological pain not associated with physical disease. To do so would be a form of discrimination. Involuntary euthanasia has been justified as necessitated by the need to make decisions for patients not competent to choose for themselves." In other words, for a substantial number of people in the Netherlands, doctors have decided patients should die without consultation with the patients.

Furthermore, assisted suicide proponents and medical personnel alike have documented how taking lethal drugs by mouth is often ineffective in fulfilling its intended purpose. The body expels the drugs through vomiting, or the person falls into a lengthy state of unconsciousness rather than dying promptly, as so-called "death with dignity" advocates wish. Such ineffective suicide attempts happen in a substantial percentage of cases—estimates range from 15% to 25%. The way to prevent these "problems," in the view of euthanasia advocates, is by legalizing lethal injections by doctors, which is active euthanasia. This is an inevitable next step if society first accepts assisted suicide as a legitimate legal option.

We are told by assisted suicide proponents that these things will not happen. But why not? How can the proponents, or anyone, stop it? The courts have already completely blurred these categories. If the next step is wrong, then taking this step is tantamount to taking the next step.

Not Truly Free Choice

Assisted suicide purports to be about free choice. But there are significant dangers that many people would take this "out" due to pressure, such as elderly individuals who don't want to be a financial or caretaking burden on their families. There's a significant amount of well-documented elder abuse in this country, and it's very often by family members, which could easily lead to such pressures. Also, leaders and researchers in the black and Latino communities have stated their fears that pressures to choose death would be applied disproportionately to their communities. Other people would undergo assisted suicide because they lack good health care, or in-home support, and are terrified about going to a nursing home. Assisted suicide would actually result in deaths due to a lack of choices for many people. Given the absence of any real choice, death by assisted suicide becomes not an act of personal autonomy, but an act of desperation. It is fictional freedom; it is phony autonomy.

"Euthanasia, physician-assisted suicide, and aid-in-dying are primarily about increased liberty, not about killing and letting die."

Physician-Assisted Suicide Is Moral

Tom L. Beauchamp

Honoring a patient's request to die by ending medical treatment is widely accepted. However, hastening a patient's death through physician-assisted suicide is still controversial. In the following viewpoint, Tom L. Beauchamp claims that physician-assisted suicide is morally acceptable. According to Beauchamp, there is no difference between allowing terminally ill patients to die through the cessation of medical treatment and actively helping them die by administering a lethal dose of medication. Beauchamp argues that both acts are moral provided that the patient has clearly and voluntarily requested them. Beauchamp is a philosophy professor at the Kennedy Institute of Ethics at Georgetown University in Washington, D.C.

As you read, consider the following questions:

1. According to Beauchamp, how has patient autonomy influenced the physician-assisted suicide debate?
2. In the author's opinion, what are some generally accepted justifications for killing?
3. What is a physician's moral responsibility to a patient who has refused medical treatment?

Tom L. Beauchamp, "The Medical Ethics of Physician-Assisted Suicide," *Journal of Medical Ethics*, vol. 25, December 1999, pp. 437–39. Copyright © 1999 by *Journal of Medical Ethics*. Reproduced by permission.

A bsolute prohibitions of physician assistance in suicide have long been canonical in medical ethics, but a powerful reformation of views on euthanasia and physician-assisted suicide is now underway in several countries. The law on physician-assisted suicide in the state of Oregon, social approval of euthanasia in the Netherlands, and the (in principle) legality of active euthanasia in Japan are clear signs of the future. The key moral issue that will drive discussion is the liberty to choose the means to one's death and the justification, if any, for limiting that liberty.

Until very recently the consensus view in most countries was that a passive euthanasia of letting die is acceptable, but an active euthanasia of killing is not. An extraordinary transformation in our conception of the role of patient autonomy had occurred to bring about this consensus. We migrated from a fear of any form of intentional hastening of death to a confidence that it is permissible under a variety of conditions intentionally to forgo life-sustaining technologies of all types, knowing that death will ensue.

This history is now shifting from *refusal* of treatment—where the consensus was originally formed—to *request* for aid that involves physicians (or other second parties). The issues of first-party refusals of life-sustaining technologies are behind us. The issues are now about how patients will be able to request aid. My concern here is not with issues of legalisation or appropriate public policy. I want to suggest why certain acts that have traditionally been considered mercy killings are better framed as forms of requested aid-in-dying. The term "killing" has done more to confuse than to clarify thinking about these matters. None the less, killing remains the centrepiece of the current discussion.

Killing and Letting Die

The influential distinction between killing and letting die is essential to the traditional view that killing (even at another's request) is prohibited and letting die permitted under specified conditions. However, the multi-purpose term "killing" does not entail a wrongful act or a crime, and there are several generally accepted justifications of killing, such as killing in self-defence and killing to rescue a person endangered by the immoral acts of other persons. Correctly to apply the label "killing" or the label "letting die" to a set of events will therefore not determine whether the set of events is morally acceptable or unacceptable. This is as true in medicine as elsewhere. Killing may typically be wrong and letting die rarely wrong, but this conclusion is contingent on the features of particular circumstances, not merely on whether the act is a killing or a letting die.

This result is not surprising inasmuch as killings are rarely authorised by appropriate parties (excepting capital punishment), whereas cases of letting die generally are authorised appropriately. Be that as it may, the *frequency* with which one kind of act is justified, by contrast to the other kind of act, is not relevant to the moral (or legal) justification of either kind of act. Forgoings that let a patient die can be both as intentional and as immoral as actions that involve direct interventions to bring about death (and both can be forms of killing).

Largely Irrelevant

Furthermore, the killing/letting-die distinction is largely irrelevant to today's mainstream issues about physician-assisted suicide, because the cases are not ones in which physicians are involved in either killing or of letting die. For example, a physician who prescribes a lethal medication at a patient's request does not thereby cause the patient's death and neither kills the patient nor lets the patient die, whether or not the patient voluntarily ingests the medication and dies.

A common thesis is that "letting die" occurs in medicine by "ceasing useless medical technologies", but "letting die" actually occurs in medicine under two circumstances: one is the cessation of medical technology because it is *useless* and the other is the cessation of medical technology because it has been *refused*. Honouring a refusal of a useful treatment knowing of a fatal outcome is letting someone die, not killing the person. The type of action—a killing or a letting die—can thus depend entirely on whether a valid refusal justifies the forgoing of medical technology. If there is no valid refusal, the act is an unjustified killing; if the act is of an identical type but is underwritten by a valid refusal, it is a justified letting die.

The received account of letting die in both law and medicine relies on a doctrine about the causation of death. The thesis is that intentionally forgoing a medical technology qualifies as letting die, rather than killing, if and only if an underlying disease or injury causes death. Despite its venerability, this received view is unsatisfactory. To obtain a satisfactory position, it must be added that the forgoing of the medical technology is validly authorised and for this reason is justified. Otherwise, allowing a "natural" death would be a killing. Again we see the absolutely central conceptual and moral role of valid authorisation.

In many cases of justified withdrawing or withholding of a medical treatment, death is not caused by an underlying condition of disease or injury. For example, an act of removing a nasogastric tube to abate hydration or nutrition leads to death from malnutrition, not death from an underlying condition of disease or injury. The disease or injury motivates and justifies the decision to forgo treatment, but does not cause death.

Life Is a Choice

Life is a choice, not a duty. The joys of life are not an entitlement for anyone with a heartbeat, they are to be chosen and actively grasped. Forced life is meaningless. So while I have difficulty imagining pain great enough to motivate a person to choose death, I recognize that to make the choice to live meaningfully there must be a viable alternative choice. The lives of those who persevere mean that much more because they could have chosen another way out.

Those who argue that the sanctity of life is so great that we cannot allow it to be taken under any circumstances miss the reason we consider life sacred. We consider life sacred as a reminder that it is something none of us may take from another person. However, assisted suicide is not murder. A person's life is his or her own.

Stentor Danielson, *Colgate Maroon-News*, November 9, 2001.

From both a legal and a moral point of view, one reason why physicians do not injure or maltreat patients when they withhold or withdraw medical technology (often with the intention of bringing about death) is that physicians are morally and legally obligated to recognise and act upon a valid refusal, irrespective of the causal outcome of doing so. Since a valid refusal of treatment obligates the physician to forgo treatment, it would be absurd to hold that these legal and moral duties require physicians to cause the deaths of their patients—in the legal and moral sense of "cause"—and thereby to kill them.

The particular form or mode of causation of death is not therefore the material matter in the justification of assistance in dying by forgoing treatment. As long as a refusal of medical technology is valid, there exists no problem about responsibility for the death that ensues or about the justification of the action.

Valid Refusals and Valid Requests

The issue of valid requests for active assistance in dying is more difficult than these issues about valid refusals of treatment, but consider the logic of the law on physician-assisted suicide in Oregon: a valid request for assistance removes legal culpability for the death that is arranged, but in the absence of a valid request, the same act is one of killing, indeed murder. This logic is why opponents of that law so deeply abhor it. It underwrites the principle that valid requests for assistance legitimate responses by physicians to such requests.

Of course, refusal and request are not so alike that the physician must act on whatever the patient or family wishes. Whereas a health professional is obligated to honour a refusal, he or she is not obligated to honour a request. Valid refusals obligate a physician to do something (or forbear from doing something) that leads to death, whereas valid requests only make it permissible for a physician (or some other person) to lend aid in dying. A physician who in principle accepts the permissibility of assistance in bringing about death may still refuse to honour a particular request if there is good moral reason for doing so.

Causing a person's death is morally wrong, when it is wrong, not merely because the death is caused by someone, but because an unauthorised and unjustified harm or loss to the person occurs. The death is bad for the person only if there is an unauthorised and unjustified deprivation of opportunities and goods that life would otherwise have afforded. If a person freely elects and authorises death and sees that event as a personal benefit, rather than a setback, then meeting the person's request involves no clear harm or moral wrong.

If letting die based on valid refusals does not harm or wrong persons or violate their rights, how can assisted suicide or voluntary active euthanasia harm or wrong a person who dies? In each case, persons seek what for them in their bleak circumstances is the best means to the end of quitting life. Their judgment is that lingering in life is worse than death. The person in search of assisted suicide, the person who seeks active euthanasia, and the person who forgoes life-sustaining technology to end life may be identically situated. They simply select different means to the end of their lives.

Looking to the Future

In the twenty-first century we can expect the following to happen: the laws or precedents permitting physician-assistance in death will prove manageable and even be improved in the Netherlands, Oregon, Japan, and other locations. In the meanwhile, law, ethics, and medicine will struggle to find more conservative alternatives.

One option will be the cultivation of a wider array of circumstances under which competent patients are allowed to refuse nutrition and hydration in order to end their lives. The refusal of nutrition and hydration appears to encounter no legal or moral problems in many countries, despite the fact that there is no clear distinction between starving oneself to death and suicide or between a physician's starving a patient to death at the patient's request and physician-assisted suicide. The other option that is certain to come into increased favour is a dramatically improved style of palliative care. There is already a consensus that better end-of-life care, including palliative care, is needed, and we can expect to see more resources and training in support of this commendable goal.

No one of these three different options: (1) provision of fatal means to death, (2) planned forgoing of nutrition and hydration, and (3) improved palliative care will necessarily be best for each patient. The presentation of these options is also consistent with the larger argument I have presented, which is that these issues of euthanasia, physician-assisted suicide, and aid-in-dying are primarily about increased liberty, not about killing and letting die.

"[Physician-assisted suicide], like murder, involves premeditated intent and therefore should be condemned as immoral and even criminal."

Physician-Assisted Suicide Is Immoral

Kerby Anderson

In the following viewpoint, Kerby Anderson contends that physician-assisted suicide is immoral because it violates the sanctity of life. He argues that suicide undermines God's authority over life and death. In addition, Anderson repudiates the argument that hastening a patient's death through assisted suicide and the withdrawal of medical treatment are the same because there is a moral difference between killing and letting death run its course. Anderson is president of Probe Ministries, a nonprofit organization that promotes Christian values, and author of *Genetic Engineering, Origin Science*, and *Moral Dilemmas*.

As you read, consider the following questions:
1. What has been the Dutch experience with euthanasia and assisted suicide, as described by the author?
2. According to Anderson, how do physician-assisted suicide and euthanasia undermine the value of human life?
3. What is Anderson's view of extraordinary measures to save life?

It is helpful to distinguish between mercy-killing and what could be called mercy-dying. Taking a human life is not the same as allowing nature to take its course by allowing a terminal patient to die. The former is immoral (and perhaps even criminal), while the latter is not.

However, drawing a sharp line between these two categories is not as easy as it used to be. Modern medical technology has significantly blurred the line between hastening death and allowing nature to take its course.

Certain analgesics, for example, ease pain, but they can also shorten a patient's life by affecting respiration. An artificial heart will continue to beat even after the patient has died and therefore must be turned off by the doctor. So the distinction between actively promoting death and passively allowing nature to take its course is sometimes difficult to determine in practice. But this fundamental distinction between life-taking and death-permitting is still an important philosophical distinction. . . .

The Dutch Experience

A survey of Dutch physicians was done in 1990 by the Remmelink Committee. They found that 1,030 patients were killed without their consent. Of these, 140 were fully mentally competent and 110 were only slightly mentally impaired. The report also found that another 14,175 patients (1,701 of whom were mentally competent) were denied medical treatment without their consent and died.

A more recent survey of the Dutch experience is even less encouraging. Doctors in the United States and the Netherlands have found that though euthanasia was originally intended for exceptional cases, it has become an accepted way of dealing with serious or terminal illness. The original guidelines (that patients with a terminal illness make a voluntary, persistent request that their lives be ended) have been expanded to include chronic ailments and psychological distress. They also found that 60 percent of Dutch physicians do not report their cases of assisted suicide (even though reporting is required by law) and about 25 percent of the physicians admit to ending patients' lives without their consent. . . .

In recent years media and political attention has been

given to the idea of physician-assisted suicide. Some states have even attempted to pass legislation that would allow physicians in this country the legal right to put terminally ill patients to death. While the Dutch experience should be enough to demonstrate the danger of granting such rights, there are other good reasons to reject this idea.

First, physician-assisted suicide would change the nature of the medical profession itself. Physicians would be cast in the role of killers rather than healers. The Hippocratic Oath was written to place the medical profession on the foundation of healing, not killing. For 2,400 years patients have had the assurance that doctors follow an oath to heal them, not kill them. This would change with legalized euthanasia.

Second, medical care would be affected. Physicians would begin to ration health care so that elderly and severely disabled patients would not be receiving the same quality of care as everyone else. Legalizing euthanasia would result in less care, rather than better care, for the dying.

Third, legalizing euthanasia through physician-assisted suicide would effectively establish a right to die. The Constitution affirms that fundamental rights cannot be limited to one group (e.g., the terminally ill). They must apply to all. Legalizing physician-assisted suicide would open the door to anyone wanting the "right" to kill themselves. Soon this would apply not only to voluntary euthanasia but also to involuntary euthanasia as various court precedents begin to broaden the application of the right to die to other groups in society like the disabled or the clinically depressed.

Biblical Analysis

Foundational to a biblical perspective on euthanasia is a proper understanding of the sanctity of human life. For centuries Western culture in general and Christians in particular have believed in the sanctity of human life. Unfortunately, this view is beginning to erode into a "quality of life" standard. The disabled, retarded, and infirm were seen as having a special place in God's world, but today medical personnel judge a person's fitness for life on the basis of a perceived quality of life or lack of such quality.

No longer is life seen as sacred and worthy of being saved.

Now patients are evaluated and life-saving treatment is frequently denied, based on a subjective and arbitrary standard for the supposed quality of life. If a life is judged not worthy to be lived any longer, people feel obliged to end that life.

The Darkness of Physician-Assisted Suicide

The darkness that is shrouded by this euphemism physician-assisted suicide is murder. We would be much better off as a society if we would stop playing semantic games and call things what they are. To help someone kill himself or herself is as wrong as murder. Even the president of the Nebraska Hemlock Society [Carl Schmitthausler] has said: When you strip away all the euphemisms, we're talking about doctors killing patients.

That the healing art of the physician should be perverted in such a way as to make the physician an agent of death is nothing short of monstrous. The physician's vocation is to heal, to comfort not to kill! However compelling the reasons advanced for this action may appear, the knowing and willing participation in the death of another human being is nothing short of murder. Any society which condones such killing is writing its own death warrant.

Cardinal Bernard Law, Cardinal Law's Statement on Physician-Assisted Suicide Before the State House of Massachusetts, May 9, 1997.

The Bible teaches that human beings are created in the image of God (Gen. 1:26) and therefore have dignity and value. Human life is sacred and should not be terminated merely because life is difficult or inconvenient. Psalm 139 teaches that humans are fearfully and wonderfully made. Society must not place an arbitrary standard of quality above God's absolute standard of human value and worth. This does not mean that people will no longer need to make difficult decisions about treatment and care, but it does mean that these decisions will be guided by an objective, absolute standard of human worth.

The Bible also teaches that God is sovereign over life and death. Christians can agree with Job when he said, "The Lord gave and the Lord has taken away. Blessed be the name of the Lord" (Job 1:21). The Lord said, "See now that I myself am He! There is no god besides me. I put to death and I bring to life, I have wounded and I will heal, and no one can deliver out of my hand" (Deut. 32:39). God has ordained our days (Ps. 139:16) and is in control of our lives.

A Biblical View of Life-Taking

Another foundational principle involves a biblical view of life-taking. The Bible specifically condemns murder (Exod. 20:13), and this would include active forms of euthanasia in which another person (doctor, nurse, or friend) hastens death in a patient. While there are situations described in Scripture in which life-taking may be permitted (e.g., self-defense or a just war), euthanasia should not be included with any of these established biblical categories. Active euthanasia, like murder, involves premeditated intent and therefore should be condemned as immoral and even criminal.

Although the Bible does not specifically speak to the issue of euthanasia, the story of the death of King Saul (2 Sam. 1:9–16) is instructive. Saul asked that a soldier put him to death as he lay dying on the battlefield. When David heard of this act, he ordered the soldier put to death for "destroying the Lord's anointed." Though the context is not euthanasia per se, it does show the respect we must show for a human life even in such tragic circumstances.

A So-Called "Right to Die"

Christians should also reject the attempt by the modern euthanasia movement to promote a so-called "right to die." Secular society's attempt to establish this "right" is wrong for two reasons. First, giving a person a right to die is tantamount to promoting suicide, and suicide is condemned in the Bible. Man is forbidden to murder and that includes murder of oneself. Moreover, Christians are commanded to love others as they love themselves (Matt. 22:39; Eph. 5:29). Implicit in the command is an assumption of self-love as well as love for others.

Suicide, however, is hardly an example of self-love. It is perhaps the clearest example of self-hate. Suicide is also usually a selfish act. People kill themselves to get away from pain and problems, often leaving those problems to friends and family members who must pick up the pieces when the one who committed suicide is gone.

Second, this so-called "right to die" denies God the opportunity to work sovereignly within a shattered life and bring glory to Himself. When Joni Eareckson Tada realized that she would be spending the rest of her life as a quadraplegic, she asked in despair, "Why can't they just let me die?" When her friend Diana, trying to provide comfort, said to her, "The past is dead, Joni; you're alive," Joni responded, "Am I? This isn't living." But through God's grace Joni's despair gave way to her firm conviction that even her accident was within God's plan for her life. Now she shares with the world her firm conviction that "suffering gets us ready for heaven."

The Bible teaches that God's purposes are beyond our understanding. Job's reply to the Lord shows his acknowledgment of God's purposes: "I know that you can do all things; no plan of yours can be thwarted. You asked, 'Who is this that obscures my counsel without knowledge?' Surely I spoke of things I did not understand, things too wonderful for me to know" (Job 42:2–3). Isaiah 55:8–9 teaches, "For my thoughts are not your thoughts, neither are your ways my ways, declares the Lord. As the heavens are higher than the earth, so are my ways higher than your ways and my thoughts than your thoughts."

A Biblical View of Death

Another foundational principle is a biblical view of death. Death is both unnatural and inevitable. It is an unnatural intrusion into our lives as a consequence of the fall (Gen. 2:17). It is the last enemy to be destroyed (1 Cor. 15:26, 56). Therefore Christians can reject humanistic ideas that assume death as nothing more than a natural transition. But the Bible also teaches that death (under the present conditions) is inevitable. There is "a time to be born and a time to die" (Eccles. 3:2). Death is a part of life and the doorway to another, better life.

When does death occur? Modern medicine defines death primarily as a biological event; yet Scripture defines death as a spiritual event that has biological consequences. Death, according to the Bible, occurs when the spirit leaves the body (Eccles. 12:7; James 2:26).

Unfortunately this does not offer much by way of clinical diagnosis for medical personnel. But it does suggest that a rigorous medical definition for death be used. A comatose patient may not be conscious, but from both a medical and biblical perspective he is very much alive, and treatment should be continued unless crucial vital signs and brain activity have ceased.

On the other hand, Christians must also reject the notion that everything must be done to save life at all costs. Believers, knowing that to be at home in the body is to be away from the Lord (2 Cor. 5:6), long for the time when they will be absent from the body and at home with the Lord (5:8). Death is gain for Christians (Phil. 1:21). Therefore they need not be so tied to this earth that they perform futile operations just to extend life a few more hours or days.

In a patient's last days, everything possible should be done to alleviate physical and emotional pain. Giving drugs to a patient to relieve pain is morally justifiable. Proverbs 31:6 says, "Give strong drink to him who is perishing, and wine to him whose life is bitter." As previously mentioned, some analgesics have the secondary effect of shortening life. But these should be permitted since the primary purpose is to relieve pain, even though they may secondarily shorten life.

Moreover, believers should provide counsel and spiritual care to dying patients (Gal. 6:2). Frequently emotional needs can be met both in the patient and in the family. Such times of grief also provide opportunities for witnessing. Those suffering loss are often more open to the gospel than at any other time.

Difficult philosophical and biblical questions are certain to continue swirling around the issue of euthanasia. But in the midst of these confusing issues should be the objective, absolute standards of Scripture, which provide guidance for the hard choices of providing care to terminally ill patients.

*"The humanitarian benefits of legalizing
physician-assisted suicide outweigh [the
risks.]"*

The Arguments of Those Opposed to Assisted Suicide Are Flawed

Peter Rogatz

Peter Rogatz is a founding board member of Compassion in Dying of New York and a member of the Committee on Bioethical Issues of the Medical Society of the State of New York. In the following viewpoint, Rogatz claims that objections to assisted suicide are outweighed by arguments that promote patient autonomy and the physician's responsibility to relieve suffering. For instance, he argues that the desire for hastened death does not necessarily mean that the patient is receiving inadequate palliative care. Rather, Rogatz asserts that patients often request assisted suicide because of the misery and loss of dignity that accompanies the most debilitating conditions. In addition, he contends that physician-assisted suicide does not violate the Hippocratic oath, which states: Do no harm. According to Rogatz, bringing a patient's unbearable suffering to a painless end is an act of mercy.

As you read, consider the following questions:
1. How does legalizing physician-assisted suicide enhance patients' trust in their doctors, as stated by the author?
2. Give three criteria that Rogatz suggests to protect patients from coercion and involuntary euthanasia?

Peter Rogatz, "The Positive Virtues of Physician-Assisted Suicide: Physician-Assisted Suicide Is Among the Most Hotly Debated Bioethical Issues of Our Time," *Humanist*, vol. 61, November/December 2001, p. 31. Copyright © 2001 by Peter Rogatz. Reproduced by permission.

E very reasonable person prefers that no patient ever con-template suicide—with or without assistance—and recent improvements in pain management have begun to reduce the number of patients seeking such assistance. However, there are some patients who experience terrible suffering that can't be relieved by any of the therapeutic or palliative techniques medicine and nursing have to offer, and some of those patients desperately seek deliverance.

Physician-assisted suicide isn't about physicians becoming killers. It's about patients whose suffering we can't relieve and about not turning away from them when they ask for help. Will there be physicians who feel they can't do this? Of course, and they shouldn't be obliged to. But if other physicians consider it merciful to help such patients by merely writing a prescription, it is unreasonable to place them in jeopardy of criminal prosecution, loss of license, or other penalty for doing so.

Many arguments are put forward for maintaining the prohibition against physician-assisted suicide, but I believe they are outweighed by two fundamental principles that support ending the prohibition: patient autonomy—the right to control one's own body—and the physician's duty to relieve suffering.

Society recognizes the competent patient's right to autonomy—to decide what will or won't be done to his or her body. There is almost universal agreement that a competent adult has the right to self-determination, including the right to have life-sustaining treatment withheld or withdrawn. Suicide, once illegal throughout the United States, is no longer illegal in any part of the country. Yet assisting a person to take her or his own life is prohibited in every state but Oregon. If patients seek such help, it is cruel to leave them to fend for themselves, weighing options that are both traumatic and uncertain, when humane assistance could be made available.

The physician's obligations are many but, when cure is impossible and palliation has failed to achieve its objectives, there is always a residual obligation to relieve suffering. Ultimately, if the physician has exhausted all reasonable palliative measures, it is the patient—and only the patient—who can judge whether death is harmful or a good to be sought. Marcia Angell, former executive editor of the *New England*

Journal of Medicine, has put it this way:

> The highest ethical imperative of doctors should be to provide care in whatever way best serves patients' interests, in accord with each patient's wishes, not with a theoretical commitment to preserve life no matter what the cost in suffering.
> . . . The greatest harm we can do is to consign a desperate patient to unbearable suffering—or force the patient to seek out a stranger like Dr. Kevorkian.

The Key Arguments Against Assisted Suicide

Let's examine the key arguments made against physician-assisted suicide. First, much weight is placed on the Hippocratic injunction to do no harm. It has been asserted that sanctioning physician-assisted suicide "would give doctors a license to kill," and physicians who accede to such requests have been branded by some as murderers. This is both illogical and inflammatory. Withdrawal of life-sustaining treatment—for example, disconnecting a ventilator at a patient's request—is accepted by society, yet this requires a more definitive act by a physician than prescribing a medication that a patient has requested and is free to take or not, as he or she sees fit. Why should the latter be perceived as doing harm when the former is not? Rather than characterizing this as "killing," we should see it as bringing the dying process to a merciful end. The physician who complies with a plea for final release from a patient facing death under unbearable conditions is doing good, not harm, and her or his actions are entirely consonant with the Hippocratic tradition.

Second, it is argued that requests for assisted suicide come largely from patients who haven't received adequate pain control or who are clinically depressed and haven't been properly diagnosed or treated. There is no question that proper management of such conditions would significantly reduce the number of patients who consider suicide; any sanctioning of assistance should be contingent upon prior management of pain and depression.

However, treatable pain is not the only reason, or even the most common reason, why patients seek to end their lives. Severe body wasting, intractable vomiting, urinary and bowel incontinence, immobility, and total dependence are recognized as more important than pain in the desire for hastened death. There is a growing awareness that loss of dignity and of those attributes that we associate particularly with being human are the factors that most commonly reduce patients to a state of unrelieved misery and desperation.

A Medical Procedure

Nowhere is the concept of assisted suicide and the cruelty of making it illegal more pronounced than when individuals are unable to take their own lives. People in advanced stages of life-threatening illness, for example, sometimes either don't have the use of their limbs or are unable to gather the proper drugs or paraphernalia by which they might deliver themselves. Here, suicide is only available through assistance. By filling out the proper legal documents ahead of time, people can clearly indicate the point of deterioration after which they choose to no longer live. When this point is reached, death then becomes a medical procedure.

Peter McWilliams, *Ain't Nobody's Business If You Do*, 1996.

Third, it is argued that permitting physician-assisted suicide would undermine the sense of trust that patients have in their doctors. This is curious reasoning; patients are not lying in bed wondering if their physicians are going to kill them—and permitting assisted suicide shouldn't create such fears, since the act of administering a fatal dose would be solely within the control of the patient. Rather than undermining a patient's trust, I would expect the legalization of physician-assisted suicide to enhance that trust. I have spoken with a great many people who feel that they would like to be able to trust their physicians to provide such help in the event of unrelieved suffering—and making that possible would give such patients a greater sense of security. Furthermore, some patients have taken their own lives at a relatively early stage of terminal illness precisely because they feared that progressively increasing disability, without anyone to assist them, would rob them of this option at a later time when they were truly desperate. A patient contemplating suicide would be much less likely to take such a step if he or she were confident of receiving assistance in the future if so desired.

Fourth, it is argued that patients don't need assistance to commit suicide; they can manage it all by themselves. This seems both callous and unrealistic. Are patients to shoot themselves, jump from a window, starve themselves to death, or rig a pipe to the car exhaust? All of these methods have been used by patients in the final stages of desperation, but it is a hideous experience for both patient and survivors. Even patients who can't contemplate such traumatic acts and instead manage to hoard a supply of lethal drugs may be too weak to complete the process without help and therefore face a high risk of failure, with dreadful consequences for themselves and their families.

Rare Occurrences?

Fifth, it is argued that requests for assisted suicide are not frequent enough to warrant changing the law. Interestingly, some physicians say they have rarely, if ever, received such requests, while others say they have often received requests. This is a curious discrepancy, but I think it can be explained: the patient who seeks help with suicide will cautiously test a physician's receptivity to the idea and simply won't approach a physician who is unreceptive. Thus, there are two subsets of physicians in this situation: those who are open to the idea of assisted suicide and those who aren't. Patients are likely to seek help from the former but not from the latter.

A study carried out a few years ago by the University of Washington School of Medicine queried 828 physicians (a 25 percent sample of primary care physicians and all physicians in selected medical subspecialties) with a response rate of 57 percent. Of these respondents, 12 percent reported receiving one or more explicit requests for assisted suicide, and one-fourth of the patients requesting such assistance received prescriptions.

A survey of physicians in San Francisco treating AIDS patients brought responses from half, and 53 percent of those respondents reported helping patients take their own lives by prescribing lethal doses of narcotics. Clearly, requests for assisted suicide can't be dismissed as rare occurrences.

Sixth, it is argued that sanctioning assisted suicide would fail to address the needs of patients who are incompetent. This is obviously true, since proposals for legalization specify that assistance be given only to a patient who is competent and who requests it. However, in essence, this argument says that, because we can't establish a procedure that will deal with every patient, we won't make assisted suicide available to any patient. What logic! Imagine the outcry if that logic were applied to a procedure such as organ transplantation, which has benefited so many people in this country.

The Slippery Slope Argument

Seventh, it is argued that once we open the door to physician-assisted suicide we will find ourselves on a slippery slope leading to coercion and involuntary euthanasia of vulnerable patients. Why so? We have learned to grapple with many slippery slopes in medicine—such as Do Not Resuscitate (DNR) orders and the withdrawal of life support. We don't deal with those slippery slopes by prohibition but, rather, by adopting reasonable ground rules and setting appropriate limits.

The slippery slope argument discounts the real harm of failing to respond to the pleas of real people and considers only the potential harm that might be done to others at some future time and place. As in the case of other slippery slopes, theoretical future harm can be mitigated by establishing appropriate criteria that would have to be met before a patient could receive assistance. Such criteria have been outlined frequently. Stated briefly, they include:

1. The patient must have an incurable condition causing severe, unrelenting suffering.
2. The patient must understand his or her condition and prognosis, which must be verified by an independent second opinion.
3. All reasonable palliative measures must have been presented to and considered by the patient.
4. The patient must clearly and repeatedly request assistance in dying.
5. A psychiatric consultation must be held to establish if the patient is suffering from a treatable depression.
6. The prescribing physician, absent a close preexisting relationship (which would be ideal) must get to know the patient well enough to understand the reasons for her or his request.

7. No physician should be expected to violate his or her own basic values. A physician who is unwilling to assist the patient should facilitate transfer to another physician who would be prepared to do so.

8. All of the foregoing must be clearly documented.

Application of the above criteria would substantially reduce the risk of abuse but couldn't guarantee that abuse would never occur. We must recognize, however, that abuses occur today—in part because we tolerate covert action that is subject to no safeguards at all. "A more open process would," in the words of philosopher and ethicist Margaret Battin, "prod us to develop much stronger protections for the kinds of choices about death we already make in what are often quite casual, cavalier ways."

It seems improbable that assisted suicide would pose a special danger to the elderly, infirm, and disabled. To paraphrase John Maynard Keynes, in the long run we are all elderly, infirm, or disabled and, since society well knows this, serious attention would surely be given to adequate protections against abuse. It isn't my intention to dispose glibly of the fear that society would view vulnerable patients as a liability and would manipulate them to end their lives prematurely. Of course, this concern must be respected, but the risk can be minimized by applying the criteria listed above. Furthermore, this argument assumes that termination of life is invariably an evil against which we must protect vulnerable patients who are poor or otherwise lacking in societal support. But, by definition, we are speaking of patients who desperately wish final release from unrelieved suffering, and poor and vulnerable patients are least able to secure aid in dying if they want it. The well-to-do patient may, with some effort and some good luck, find a physician who is willing to provide covert help; the poor and disenfranchised rarely have access to such assistance in today's world.

Eighth, it is argued that the Netherlands experience proves that societal tolerance of physician-assisted suicide leads to serious abuse. Aside from the fact that the data are subject to varying interpretation depending upon which analysis one believes, the situation in the Netherlands holds few lessons for us, because for many years that country followed the ambiguous practice of technically prohibiting but tacitly permitting assisted suicide and euthanasia.

The climate in the United States is different; our regulatory mechanisms would be different—much stricter, of course—and we should expect different outcomes. The experience of Oregon—the only one of our fifty states to permit physician-assisted suicide—is instructive. During the first three years that Oregon's law [Death with Dignity Act] has been in effect, seventy terminally ill patients took advantage of the opportunity to self-administer medication to end protracted dying. Despite dire warnings, there was no precipitous rush by Oregonians to embrace assisted suicide. The poor and the uninsured weren't victimized; almost all of these seventy patients had health insurance, most were on hospice care, and most were people with at least some college education. There were no untoward complications. The Oregon experience is far more relevant for the United States than the Dutch experience, and it vindicates those who, despite extremely vocal opposition, advocated for the legislation.

Ninth, it has been argued that a society that doesn't assure all its citizens the right to basic health care and protect them against catastrophic health costs has no business considering physician-assisted suicide. I find this an astonishing argument. It says to every patient who seeks ultimate relief from severe suffering that his or her case won't be considered until all of us are assured basic health care and financial protection. These are certainly proper goals for any decent society, but they won't be attained in the United States until it becomes a more generous and responsible nation—and that day seems to be far off. Patients seeking deliverance from unrelieved suffering shouldn't be held hostage pending hoped-for future developments that are not even visible on the distant horizon.

Finally, it is argued that the status quo is acceptable—that a patient who is determined to end his or her life can find a sympathetic physician who will provide the necessary prescription and that physicians are virtually never prosecuted for such acts. There are at least four reasons to reject the status quo. First, it forces patients and physicians to undertake a clandestine conspiracy to violate the law, thus compromising the integrity of patient, physician, and family. Second, such secret compacts, by their very nature, are subject to faulty implementation with a high risk of failure and consequent tragedy for both patient and family. Third, the assumption that a determined patient can find a sympathetic physician applies, at best, to middle- and upper-income persons who have ongoing relationships with their physicians; the poor, as I've already noted, rarely have such an opportunity. Fourth, covert action places a physician in danger of criminal prosecution or loss of license and, although such penalties are assumed to be unlikely, that risk certainly inhibits some physicians from doing what they believe is proper to help their patients.

I believe that removing the prohibition against physician assistance, rather than opening the flood gates to ill-advised suicides, is likely to reduce the incentive for suicide: patients who fear great suffering in the final stages of illness would have the assurance that help would be available if needed and they would be more inclined to test their own abilities to withstand the trials that lie ahead.

Life is the most precious gift of all, and no sane person wants to part with it, but there are some circumstances where life has lost its value. A competent person who has thoughtfully considered his or her own situation and finds that unrelieved suffering outweighs the value of continued life shouldn't have to starve to death or find other drastic and violent solutions when more merciful means exist. Those physicians who wish to fulfill what they perceive to be their humane responsibilities to their patients shouldn't be forced by legislative prohibition into covert actions.

There is no risk-free solution to these very sensitive problems. However, I believe that reasonable protections can be put in place that will minimize the risk of abuse and that the humanitarian benefits of legalizing physician-assisted suicide outweigh that risk. All physicians are bound by the injunction to do no harm, but we must recognize that harm may result not only from the commission of a wrongful act but also from the omission of an act of mercy. While not every physician will feel comfortable offering help in these tragic situations, many believe it is right to do so and our society should not criminalize such humanitarian acts.

"The so-called 'right to die' mantra has become the 'duty to die.'"

The Arguments of Those in Favor of Assisted Suicide Are Flawed

Trudy Chun and Marian Wallace

In the following viewpoint, Trudy Chun and Marian Wallace assert that arguments for the legalization of physician-assisted suicide, which fundamentally advocate the right to die, are flawed because they trivialize the right to life, which supersedes all other rights. The authors allege that historically the right to die argument has been used to justify the systematic termination of the "unfit." For example, according to Chun and Wallace, in the Netherlands, where physician-assisted death was originally only permitted at the request of a terminally ill patient, comatose or severely deformed patients can now be put to death without their explicit consent. Chun is a former editor for Concerned Women for America, an organization of women that promotes Christian values, where Wallace is director of research and publications.

As you read, consider the following questions:
1. According to the authors, how has the right-to-die movement manipulated language?
2. How do Chun and Wallace support their claim that the wish to die among terminally ill patients can change?
3. What does the request for assisted suicide reveal about a patient's needs, as stated by Chun and Wallace?

Over the past several decades, America has witnessed a strange and subtle shift in how society views life. In the 1960s, the shift began as some states began to remove the criminal penalties for abortion. In the 1970s, the U.S. Supreme Court *Roe v. Wade* decision put the federal government's stamp of approval on abortion nationwide. Today, the value of life is being obscured at the other end of the spectrum as courts grant the elderly and sick the so-called "right to die."

Initiating the Desire for Death

This "right to die" movement has entered society in two forms: assisted suicide and euthanasia, with the former beginning to give way to the latter. Assisted suicide occurs when the doctor provides the patient the means to kill himself—the doctor acts as an accomplice in the self-murder, so to speak. Euthanasia is the active killing of the patient by the doctor—the physician is the murderer in this case. More often today, physicians are initiating the desire for death.

The very laws once designed to protect a person's inalienable right to life now permit the elimination of those deemed unworthy to live. And in the name of compassion, doctors trained to heal and to prolong life are shortening and even snuffing it out altogether. Killing the patient as the cure is becoming an acceptable medical procedure in some circles. Nonetheless, changing public opinion and advances in modern pain relief and end-of-life care are shifting the debate in favor of pro-life advocates.

Many Americans view physician-assisted suicide as an acceptable practice. According to a March 1999 Gallup poll, 61 percent of all Americans believe physician-assisted suicide should be legal—down from 75 percent in a May 1996 *USA Today* poll. When the issue becomes personal, fewer Americans support it. Fifty-one percent of Americans said they would not consider physician-assisted suicide to end pain from a terminal illness, while 40 percent said they would. As may be expected, support for the idea of physician-assisted suicide diminished with age in the Gallup poll. While 62 percent of those between the ages of 18 and 29 supported physician-assisted suicide, 51 percent of those aged 65 said they do.

While acceptance of euthanasia and assisted suicide has diminished somewhat, euthanasia advocates continue their campaign. The manipulation of terms in the debate reveals their strategy of courting acceptance.

Verbicide

Christian writer C.S. Lewis coined the term "verbicide" to denote the murder of a word. That is what euthanasia advocates have done with the language of "compassion" and "mercy." In order to advance their agenda with the public, euthanasia advocates are cloaking doctors' deliberate homicide of patients in rosy phrases such as: quality of life, death with dignity, voluntary euthanasia, and the right to die. Even "euthanasia"—which the dictionary defines as "killing an individual for reasons considered to be merciful"—comes from two Greek words meaning "good death." But no matter what they call it, euthanasia is still murder.

Dr. Jack Kevorkian cast physician-assisted suicide and euthanasia into the national spotlight in the early 1990s. Kevorkian, a retired Michigan pathologist, claims to have helped approximately 130 people kill themselves. He calls his practice "medicide" and himself an "obitiarist." The man they call "Dr. Death" also proposes professionally staffed, well-equipped "obitoriums"—where the sick, elderly, or depressed could go to their demise voluntarily. In 1996, he opened his first suicide center north of Detroit. Fortunately, the building owner terminated Dr. Kevorkian's lease and his suicide center closed. Then, in 1999, after a nationally televised videotape showed Dr. Kevorkian ending the life of a terminally ill man, a Michigan jury convicted him and sentenced him to prison for murder.

Death as a Civil Right

Although Dr. Kevorkian is no longer in the national spotlight, death as the option of choice—abortion, infanticide, euthanasia and suicide—now has high-profile, big-money organizational support. Some of the most visible pro-death groups are Planned Parenthood, the National Abortion and Reproductive Rights Action League, the Hemlock Society, Choice in Dying, Americans Against Human Suffering and

EXIT. Derek Humphry, cofounder of Hemlock, voices a common viewpoint: "Individual freedom requires that all persons be allowed to control their own destiny. . . . This is the ultimate civil liberty. . . . If we cannot die by our choice, then we are not free people." The decision to die is increasingly viewed as a civil "right."

In January 1997, lawyers representing some physicians and terminally ill patients urged the U.S. Supreme Court to rule that the Constitution allows individuals the right to terminate their lives with the assistance of a physician. This action came in response to appellate court rulings in Washington and New York, where state laws banned assisted suicide. Both rulings concluded that terminally ill patients had a right to a physician-assisted suicide. In its ruling, the U.S. Court of Appeals for the Ninth Circuit in Seattle said the constitutional "liberty" reasoning in *Planned Parenthood v. Casey*, which reaffirmed a woman's "right" to choose abortion, influenced their decision. That so-called "right," the judges concluded, also applied to the end of life.

In the New York state ruling, the Federal Court of Appeals for the Second Circuit based its similar finding on the 14th Amendment's "equal protection" clause. The judges argued that terminally ill patients had the right to hasten their own death by refusing treatment. Physicians therefore could lawfully order the removal of life-support systems. In addition, doctors should not be prosecuted for actively administering lethal drugs to patients when they request help in accelerating their deaths.

The *New York Times* editorialized that the two courts "have issued humane and sound rulings." In both cases, it noted the defendants "claimed a sovereign right over their own bodies." Ernest Van Den Haag, an advocate of suicide, observed in the June 12, 1995, issue of *National Review*, "Only in our time has it come to be believed that individuals . . . own themselves. . . . Owners can dispose of what they own as they see fit."

The U.S. Supreme Court reversed both decisions, however, stating that neither state law violated the 14th Amendment of the U.S. Constitution. The Court noted, "They neither infringe fundamental rights nor involve suspect classifications." Furthermore, the Court argued the Equal Protection Clause of the Fourteenth Amendment "creates no substantive rights," including a so-called right to die.

Redefining Personhood

Francis Schaeffer, renowned Christian philosopher and theologian, credited the influx of humanistic thought in society for the increasing disrespect for human life. "If man is not made in the image of God, nothing then stands in the way of inhumanity. There is no good reason why mankind should be perceived as special," he wrote in *Whatever Happened to the Human Race?*. "Human life is cheapened. We can see this in many of the major issues being debated in our society today: abortion, infanticide, euthanasia. . . ."

Euthanasia advocates are also redefining what it means to be a person. In their book, *In Defense of Life*, Keith Fournier and William Watkins dissect "ethicist" Joseph Fletcher's 15 "indicators of personhood." These include: an IQ greater than 40; self-awareness; self-control; a sense of time; capability of relating to and concern for others; communication; control of existence and [degree of brain] function.

Alarmed, Fournier and Watkins wrote: "When judged by these criteria, the preborn, newborn, and seriously developmentally disabled would be disqualified as human persons." Sufferers of dementia or anyone brain-damaged would also be non-persons. "Ethicist" Peter Singer agrees that personhood should be defined according to what we can do, rather than who we are. He has even advocated allowing parents of severely disabled infants to put their children to death in some painless way. This kind of thinking about "defective humans" is disturbingly reminiscent of the euthanasia program that accompanied the rise of Nazism.

A Nazi Legacy

In *A Sign For Cain*, the eminent Dr. Fredric Wertham documented exhaustively the physician-sponsored mass murder of civilians in pre–World War II Germany. Well before they were dismantled and moved to the concentration camps, gas chambers were installed in six leading psychiatric hospitals. Under the guise of "help for the dying," "mercy killings," and "destruction of life devoid of value," university professors of psychiatry, hospital directors and their staff members systematically exterminated hundreds of thousands of "superfluous people"—mental patients, the elderly, and sick and handicapped children. Criteria for such "undesirables" included "useless eaters," the unfit, unproductive and misfit.

Wertham stressed the concept of "life not worth living" was not a Nazi invention. As early as the 1920s, respected physicians wrote about "absolutely worthless human beings" and the urgently necessary "killing of those who cannot be rescued." In fact, even in 1895, a widely used German medical textbook advocated the "right to death."

However, in 1939, a note from Adolf Hitler to his own private doctor and chancellery officials extended "the authority of physicians" so that "a mercy death may be granted to patients who according to human judgment are incurably ill." Nearly the same language has been used in the various "right to die" decisions of America's high courts.

Holland's Contribution

In the Netherlands, the lower house of the Dutch parliament has passed a bill to permit euthanasia, paving the way for the open practice of giving doctors or relatives a "license to kill" unconscious patients. Dutch Dr. Karel Gunning, president of the World Federation of Pro-Life Doctors, revealed that official figures estimate approximately 3,200 cases of euthanasia occur each year. This practice has caused a number of sick and poor Dutch to start carrying a printed card in their pockets that states they do not want doctors to put them to death. According to Dr. Gunning, the euthanasia law simply legalizes what has been done secretly for years.

"In the beginning, the explicit request of the patient was necessary," he said. "Now, one can do away with the comatose and children with severe malformations. Initially, euthanasia was allowed only for terminal patients, but later it was extended to people with psychic depression." As happened in the United States, he also believes that this "path to death" began in 1971 when the Dutch Medical Association approved abortion. This act removed "the unconditional defense of human life."

America has been sliding down the same slippery slope as

Holland, spurred by the same pro-euthanasia arguments and utilizing the same tactics.

Just as Dutch doctors had secretly performed euthanasia before a law was passed allowing it, American doctors have done the same. In a Washington state survey, 26 percent of responding doctors anonymously admitted they had been asked to help a patient die. Those same doctors actually gave 24 percent of their ailing patients prescriptions that induced death. Although chronic pain was a factor, researchers found that patients were most often motivated toward suicide by nonphysical concerns, such as "losing control, being a burden, being dependent, and losing dignity."

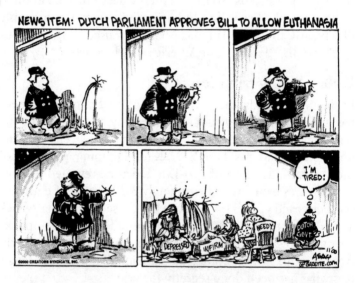

Asay. © 2000 by Gazette.com. Reprinted with permission of Creators Syndicate.

In February 1999, columnist Nat Hentoff wrote of Oregon's legalization of physician-assisted suicide and its decision to provide the service without cost to low-income residents. Noting the cruel hypocrisy of the decision, Hentoff quoted Ric Burger, spokesman for disabled citizens in Oregon, "The fact that the state of Oregon will not properly fund our personal-attendant services, yet will pay for us to die, amounts to nothing less than cultural genocide.". . .

Care vs. Killing

At its heart, the Hippocratic Oath taken by physicians enjoins "Do no harm" and states: "I will give no deadly medicine, even if asked." Thomas Reardon, past president of the American Medical Association (AMA) said, "Physicians are healers. . . . The inability of physicians to prevent death does not imply that they are free to help cause death."

Under-treatment has been a problem for many terminally ill patients, noted Dr. Richard Payne, chief of pain-control services at New York's Memorial Sloan-Kettering Cancer Center. The AMA has consistently opposed any attempts to legalize or promote physician-assisted suicide. In a policy paper on the issue, revised in 1999, the AMA even states, "Requests for physician-assisted suicide should be a signal to the physician that the patient's needs are unmet and further evaluation to identify the elements contributing to the patient's suffering is necessary." Physician-assisted suicide is "fundamentally incompatible with the physician's role as healer," states the AMA.

Even more encouraging are results of a 1998 survey of the 3,299 members of the American Society of Clinical Oncology (ASCO), published in the October 3, 2000, issue of the *Annals of Internal Medicine*, concerning euthanasia and physician-assisted suicide of terminally ill cancer patients. In 1994, 23 percent of ASCO members supported euthanasia for "dying cancer patients in excruciating pain." By 1998, that number dropped to *below 7 percent*. Likewise, 22 percent of the oncologists supported physician-assisted suicide in 1998, down from 45 percent in 1994. Lead researcher Ezekiel J. Emanuel, M.D., Ph.D., stated the survey's results "emphasize the need to educate physicians about ways to provide high-quality pain management and palliative care to dying patients."

"Modern medicine was so brilliant at saving lives that we . . . forgot our traditional role of providing comfort at the end of life," said Christine K. Cassel, M.D., chair of the Henry L. Schwartz Department of Geriatrics at Mount Sinai School of Medicine. "Now we need to take the advances in modern medicine and apply them to relieving suffering." The palliative care movement is growing.

The Joint Commission on Accreditation of Healthcare

Organizations (JCAHO) pushed physicians in this direction in 1999 by implementing required palliative care (pain relief) standards. It gave hospitals, nursing homes and outpatient clinics accredited by JCAHO until January 2001 to comply. The new standards require that every patient's pain be measured and relief be provided from the moment he checks into the facility. Otherwise, the health organization risks losing accreditation. Calling this a "watershed event," Dr. Russell Portenoy, pain medicine chairman of New York's Beth Israel Medical Center, commented, "No one has ever promised patients no pain." Yet euthanasia advocates have fought tooth and nail to make it easier to kill those same patients.

It is crucial the distinction be made between prolonging life artificially—with unwanted "heroic measures"—and terminating life prematurely through deliberate intervention. The first may be unacceptable to many. But the second is clearly murder. Rather, we must provide comforting care for the critically ill—food and water, pain medication, oxygen and a loving touch. Hospice programs nationwide offer medical, spiritual, legal and financial services for dying persons and their families. . . .

The Duty to Die

By definition, a terminally ill person's life will end—as will all our lives. The ethical challenge is how, when and at whose hand? Without question, watching a loved one waste away and suffer incurable pain is horrific. Along with them, we suffer intensely. But are we seeking to put others out of *our* misery? To end the life of another—or our own—because of wrenching debilitation or "lack of quality" is to deny the reality of death.

Fundamentally, assisted suicide and euthanasia are issues concerning morals and ethics. Indeed, the so-called "right to die" mantra has become the "duty to die." Professor David Currow, vice president of Palliative Care Australia, commented, "To make every person who's facing death think about euthanasia is an enormous impost on people who are already feeling isolated and frightened." The issue reaches to the very core of how a society views life. And it sets America sliding down a slippery slope toward destruction.

Periodical Bibliography

The following articles have been selected to supplement the diverse views presented in this chapter.

Carrie Carmichael "Last Right: When a Friend Asked for Help, I Couldn't Refuse. Her Choice Haunts Me Still," *New York Times Magazine*, May 20, 2001.

Adam Cohen "Showdown for Doctor Death: With His Latest Arrest, Kevorkian Pushes the Euthanasia Debate a Grisly Step Farther," *Time*, December 7, 1998.

Ezekiel J. Emanuel "What Is the Great Benefit of Legalizing Euthanasia or Physician-Assisted Suicide?" *Ethics*, April 1999.

August Gribbin "We Shall Not Fear . . ." *Insight on the News*, February 26, 2001.

Bill Hewitt "Last Wish: Defending Oregon's Assisted-Suicide Law, Four Terminally Ill Patients Try to Stop the Federal Government from Taking Away Their Right to Die with Dignity," *People Weekly*, November 26, 2001.

Nelson Lund "Why Ashcroft Is Wrong on Assisted Suicide," *Commentary Magazine*, February 2002.

Rita L. Marker "Ashcroft to Oregon: Stop Breaking the Law," *Human Life Review*, Fall 2001.

Richard A. McCormick "Bioethics: A Moral Vacuum?" *America*, May 1, 1999.

Jennifer A. Parks "Why Gender Matters in the Euthanasia Debate," *Hastings Center Report*, January 2000.

Richard D. Parry "Death, Dignity, and Morality," *America*, November 14, 1998.

Christina M. Puchalski "We Don't Give the Dying What We Need," *Los Angeles Times*, May 26, 1999.

Wesley J. Smith "Suicide Pays," *First Things*, June 1999.

Wall Street Journal "Going Dutch," October 6, 1999.

Washington Post "Leave Oregon Alone," April 20, 2002.

CHAPTER 4

How Should Society Address Suicide?

Chapter Preface

According to psychiatry professor Yeates Conwell, "In general, our society tends to regard suicide among older adults as more acceptable than suicide among younger people." Conwell contends that while persons seventy years old and over are at a highest risk for suicide than any other group in the United States, suicide prevention measures often place more urgency upon preventing youth suicide.

Experts maintain that confronting society's attitudes toward the elderly is key to preventing suicide among older people. Gerontology professor Nancy J. Osgood and sociology professor Susan A. Eisenhandler claim that "the rapid rate of cultural change . . . has spawned moral and ethical dilemmas about suicide and assisted suicide among older persons." These cultural changes, states psychology professor John L. McIntosh, "exist in subtle and more obvious ways in our society. The old tend to be viewed as expendable, as having lived long enough and, perhaps, as having outlived their usefulness. Daily, the high value of youth and the devaluing of old age are apparent in advertisements, television, and other media." Adversely affected by these attitudes, the elderly are at higher risk of depression, low self-esteem, and suicide. To counter the effects of these cultural attitudes upon the elderly and help prevent suicide, experts recommend that they be treated with compassion, respect, and as the valuable members of society that they are. Improved attitudes toward older people are especially important to the elderly residing in assisted-living facilities and nursing homes, where they are likely to feel that their autonomy and sense of dignity are compromised.

In addition to changing attitudes about the elderly, many experts are working to identify other causes of elderly suicide. For example, affective disorders such as depression contribute to suicide by older people. Another factor in elderly suicide is bereavement. Conwell claims that "risk of [elderly] suicide is increased . . . for up to four years following the death of a spouse." In addition, he asserts that illnesses and conditions that lead to physical impairment may also increase the risk for suicide. Conwell asserts that treatment and counseling for the elderly to address these and other factors may prevent suicide. He reports that more than twelve thousand at-risk senior citizens who were enrolled in a telephone outreach program, in which they were provided with call-in services and support for several years, experienced a low number of suicides for their age group.

Creating special programs and addressing cultural attitudes to prevent suicide among the elderly demonstrate how suicide prevention measures attempt to address the unique needs and circumstances of individuals contemplating suicide. In the following chapter, the authors present various views on how society should respond to suicide.

> *"Increasingly, suicide is being viewed as a serious and preventable public health problem."*

Suicide Must Be Prevented

Evangelical Lutheran Church in America (ELCA)

The Evangelical Lutheran Church in America (ELCA) is an organization of Lutheran churches in the United States. Its members include Lutheran congregations, educational and social institutions, and individuals nationwide. In the following viewpoint, the ELCA contends that suicide must be prevented because life is a precious gift from God. Moreover, the organization claims that every individual has a responsibility to help those in need. The ELCA states that increased awareness and discussion of suicide as a preventable public health problem will help suicidal or depressed individuals get help.

As you read, consider the following questions:
1. According to the ELCA, what ethnic groups are experiencing increases in suicide rates?
2. In the author's view, how does the failure to understand depression as an illness obstruct suicide prevention?
3. How does the ELCA counter the myth that suicide can be a careful, rational decision?

Each year more than 30,000 persons in the United States take their own life. Suicide is the eighth leading cause of death and the third leading cause among persons who are 15 to 24. More persons die by suicide than by homicide. Each year nearly 500,000 persons make a suicide attempt serious enough to receive emergency room treatment. Millions have suicidal thoughts.

These numbers, we know, speak of individuals whose stories and relationships are unique. They speak of persons with whom we live in our families, congregations, neighborhoods, and work places. Some of us have attempted suicide, and others of us have made sure a relative or friend who is threatening suicide gets help. Many of us have mourned and anguished over the suicidal death of a loved one, and others of us will some day experience such unspeakable grief and suffering.

Suicide testifies to life's tragic brokenness. We believe that life is God's good and precious gift to us, and yet life for us ourselves and others sometimes appears to be hell, a torment without hope. When we would prefer to ignore, reject, or shy away from those who despair of life, we need to recall what we have heard: God's boundless love in Jesus Christ will leave no one alone and abandoned. We who lean on God's love to live are called to "bear one another's burdens and so fulfill the law of Christ" (Galatians 6:2). Our efforts to prevent suicide grow out of our obligation to protect and promote life, our hope in God amid suffering and adversity, and our love for our troubled neighbor.

Increasingly, suicide is being viewed as a serious and preventable public health problem. Suicide and its prevention are complex and multi-dimensional and need to be approached openly and comprehensively. Suicide prevention requires concerted and collaborative efforts from all sectors of society. . . .

Becoming Aware

Suicide occurs in all social groups. It occurs among young, middle-aged, and older people; men and women; rich, middle class, and poor people; all ethnic and religious groups; married and single people; the employed and unemployed, and the healthy and the sick.

Yet statistics indicate that suicide is more prevalent among some groups than others:

- White males account for nearly three-fourths of all completed suicides.
- While there are four male suicides for every female one, women attempt suicide twice as often as do men.
- The highest suicide rates are found among white men over 50, who represent 10 percent of the population and who are responsible for 33 percent of the suicides. Suicide rates for men over 65 are on the increase after a steady decrease from 1950–1980.
- Since 1950 the suicide rate for young men aged 15–24 has tripled, and for young women, it has more than doubled.
- Although suicide among children is a rare event, there has been a dramatic increase in the reported suicide rate among persons aged 10–14.
- Suicide rates for American Indians and Alaska Natives are well above the national average, with a disproportionate number of suicides among young men.
- Suicide among young African American males, once uncommon, has increased sharply in recent years.
- Suicide rates among some professions, such as police, farmers, dentists, and doctors, have been found to be higher than the national average.
- Attempted suicide rates among youth struggling with questions about their sexual orientation are higher than among others of the same age.
- Nearly 60 percent of all suicides are carried out with a firearm. People living in a household with a firearm are almost five times more likely to die by suicide than people who live in gun-free homes.

Risk Factors

While there is no one cause of suicide, researchers tell us that suicidal behavior is associated with a number of risk factors that frequently occur in combination. These include:

- Clinical depression and other mental illnesses. More than 60 percent of all people who complete suicide suffer from major depression. If one includes people who abuse alcohol and are depressed, the figure rises to 75 percent. Almost all people who take their own life have a diagnosable mental or substance abuse disorder or both.

- Alcohol and substance abuse. Alcoholism is a factor in 30 percent of all completed suicides.
- Adverse life events. Such events may be confusion about one's personal identity or a feeling of being cut off from others among young people; a family crisis like death or divorce; the loss of one's livelihood, perhaps caused by rural economic crisis, business downsizing, a cutting off of government programs, or addictive behavior; chronic, acute, or terminal illness; or the effects of a natural or social disaster. For most people, adverse life events do not lead to suicidal behavior. They may contribute to suicidal behavior in the context of mental illness and substance abuse.
- Familial factors, such as a family history of suicide, of mental illness and substance abuse, of violence and sexual abuse.
- Cultural or religious factors, such as beliefs that suicide is a noble resolution of a personal dilemma, or the destruction of a people's traditional culture that may lead to feelings of disconnectedness from the past, isolation, and hopelessness.
- Prior suicide attempt, firearm in the home, incarceration, impulsive or aggressive tendencies, and exposure to the suicidal behavior of others (by family members or peers, or through inappropriate media coverage or fiction stories). Suicides among young people sometimes occur in clusters and may even become an epidemic. Young people are particularly susceptible to imitating behavior leading to unintended suicide. . . .

Looking at Attitudes

Certain social attitudes form obstacles to suicide prevention. One such set of beliefs says that nothing can be done. "If it's going to happen, it will." "It's not worth trying to help, because these people have such huge problems that nothing can be done." "Suicide has been around forever; we're not going to change that fact." "Let them alone. If they want to kill themselves, that's their business."

Punitive attitudes form another obstacle to suicide prevention. These attitudes are eager to punish suicidal behavior and often blame the living for suicidal deaths. They create an environment in which suicidal behavior is concealed and persons with suicidal thoughts are reluctant to talk. Punitive attitudes are a carry over from the time when suicide was considered a crime and an unpardonable sin, and when those who completed suicide were denied Christian burial.

Failure to understand major depression as an illness also obstructs suicide prevention. Some misguided attitudes view serious depression as a character deficit, a human weakness, or a rare, untreatable, and permanent condition. These convey to depressed people that they should "tough it out" or be embarrassed or ashamed by how they feel. In truth, clinical depression is a disease involving changes in brain chemistry. It is one of the most common diseases, and can happen to people who have no apparent reason "to be depressed." Although clinical depression often goes untreated because it is not recognized, it is a very treatable mental illness. Depressed people cannot treat themselves, but they can be helped by professionals through medication or therapy, or a combination of the two. Suicide is not an inevitable or acceptable outcome of depression.

Experts speak of common misunderstandings that stand in the way of suicide prevention:

- *Myth:* Persons who talk about suicide rarely actually complete suicide; they are just wanting attention and should be challenged in order to "call their bluff." The truth is that persons who talk about suicide are serious and may be giving a clue or warning of their intentions. They should not be challenged but given assistance in obtaining professional help.
- *Myth:* A person who has made a serious suicide attempt is unlikely to make another. The truth is that persons who have made prior attempts are often at greater risk of completing suicide. A suicide attempt is a cry for help and a warning that something is terribly wrong and should be taken with utmost seriousness.
- *Myth:* The suicidal person wants to die and feels there is

no turning back. The truth is that suicidal persons often feel ambivalent about dying. They often go through a long process in which they try various ways to reduce their profound emotional pain. The balance between their contradictory desires to live and to die shifts back and forth, even up to the time of taking their life.

- *Myth:* Most people who take their life have made a careful, well-considered, rational decision. The truth is that persons considering suicide often have "tunnel vision": in their unbearable pain they are blind to available alternatives. Frequently, the suicide act is impulsive. When their suffering and pain are reduced, most will choose to live.

- *Myth:* Asking about suicidal feelings will cause one to attempt suicide. The truth is that asking a person about suicidal feelings provides an opportunity to get help that may save a life. The listener should ask if the person has formulated a plan and has access to the means to carry it out. If the intent, a plan, and the means are there, the suicidal person should not be left alone but be helped to get treatment immediately, by calling 911 if necessary. . . .

Receiving and Giving Help

"The church," [religious reformer] Martin Luther once wrote, "is the inn and the infirmary for those who are sick and in need of being made well." Luther's image of the Church as a hospital reminds us who we are: a community of vulnerable people in need of help; living by the hope of the Gospel, we also are a community of healing. At the same time vulnerable and healed, we are freed for a life of receiving and giving help. In the mutual bearing of burdens, we learn to be persons who are willing to ask for healing and to provide it.

Whoever among us experiences suicidal thoughts should know that the rest of us expect, pray, and plead for them to reach out for help. "Talk to someone. Don't bear your hidden pain by yourself." The notion is all-too-common that one should "go it alone": Persons are not supposed to be vulnerable, and when they are, they should conceal it and handle things on their own. In the Church, however, we admit that we all share the "need of being made well." There is no shame in having suicidal thoughts or asking for help. Indeed, when life's difficulties and disappointments threaten to overwhelm our desire to live, we are urged and invited to talk with trusted others and draw upon their strength.

Suicide Completions in 1999

- Average of 1 person every 18 minutes killed themselves.
- Average of 1 old person every 1 hour 35.8 minutes killed themselves.
- Average of 1 young person every 2 hours 14.7 minutes killed themselves. (If the 244 suicides below age 15 are included, 1 young person every 2 hours 6.8 minutes.)
- 11th ranking cause of death in U.S.—3rd for young.
- 4.1 male completions for each female completion.
- Suicide ranks 11th as a cause of death; Homicide ranks 14th.

John L. McIntosh for the American Association of Suicidology, "U.S.A. Suicide: 1999 Official Final Data," November 16, 2001.

When, on the other hand, a loved one talks to us of suicide or we sense that something is seriously amiss, we are called to be our brother's or sister's keeper. The experience may be frightening, and we may want to deny or minimize the suicidal communication. We may want to shy away because we feel unprepared to help someone with suicidal thoughts or think that we may make matters worse. Yet our responsibility is to listen, to encourage the person to talk, and to get him or her appropriate help. Beyond the crisis situation, we will want that person to hear the healing comfort of the Gospel and receive the care of the congregation. That care might, for example, involve creating an ongoing support network for a person and his or her family. . . .

Suicide prevention is broader than responding to a crisis situation. Prevention efforts also aim to reduce or reverse risk factors and to enhance protective factors before vulnerable persons reach the point of danger. They go together with efforts to prevent drug and alcohol abuse as well as violence. Protective factors include:

- Effective and appropriate clinical care for mental, physical, and substance abuse disorders

- Easy access to a variety of clinical interventions and support for help seeking
- Restricted access to highly lethal methods of suicide
- Family and community support
- Support from ongoing medical and mental health care relationships
- Learned skills in problem solving, conflict resolution, and nonviolent handling of disputes
- Cultural and religious beliefs that discourage suicide and support self-preservation instincts.

Stimulating Discussion, Reflection, and Action

What can we do in our congregations and communities to prevent suicide? The following is intended to stimulate discussion, reflection, and action.

Let us first recognize that the day-to-day preaching, teaching, and living of the Christian faith in congregations contribute to suicide prevention in indirect yet significant ways. In the community of the baptized, we come to know that we belong to God and to one another. There we give thanks to God for life and for our new life in Christ, and we are empowered to persevere during adversities and to hope in God when all else fails. We learn that human life is a sacred trust from God and that "deliberately destroying life created in the image of God is contrary to our Christian conscience." We are equipped to empathize with others in their suffering and joy and are prepared to act for their well-being. We are given a reason to live, forgiveness to start anew, and confidence that neither life nor death can separate us from "the love of God in Christ Jesus our Lord" (Romans 8:38). How, we might ask, do we do such things better?

When discussing love for others . . . could we talk about what to do if a friend hints at suicide? How does our congregation ensure that all members are known and none are invisible? How do we become more attentive to changes in a person's participation that may indicate personal distress or depression? How do we strengthen the bonds of community with persons going through stressful periods in their lives and with older persons living alone so they do not feel isolated and abandoned? . . .

How do we honor the vocation of members who are social workers, psychologists, doctors, nurses, counselors, and other caregivers who often work with suicidal persons? How do we find ways to assure them that when a person they are helping takes his or her life, they are not responsible for not "saving a life?" We also can draw upon these caregivers as well as upon survivors and advocates for suicide prevention to help educate other members about suicide.

What in our community, we should ask, are the cultural and social dynamics that lead to isolation and hopelessness? How do we address them? What are the resources in our community to respond to suicidal behavior? Do members know how to access them? We can join with other churches and community groups to help ensure that adequate treatment resources are available. What about our schools? Is suicide prevention a part of their programs that focus on mental health, substance abuse, aggressive behavior, and coping skills? Are there peer counseling or ministry programs in our schools and congregations?

What about the firearms in our homes? Most gun owners reportedly keep a firearm in their home for "protection" or "self-defense," yet 83 percent of gun-related deaths in these homes are suicide, often by someone other than the gun owner. Are our homes really safer with guns in them?, we might ask.

How do we counter the stigma often associated with mental illness? Should not the crucial role of untreated depression in suicidal behavior be an important consideration in debates on insurance coverage for mental illnesses? What might we do as citizens to promote accessible and affordable mental health services to enable all persons at risk for suicide to obtain needed substance abuse and treatment services?

We can encourage, use, and learn from suicide prevention programs in our social ministry organizations and at our colleges and universities. What, we should ask, could our church-related day schools do to prevent suicide? How are our seminaries preparing pastors to minister with suicidal persons? Should suicide prevention be a part of continuing education for rostered persons? Could we create opportunities at events for youth, women, and men and in our camping and retreat programs to learn about suicide and its prevention?

> "When a psychiatrist uses the power of the State to prevent a person who wants to kill himself from killing himself . . . we should regard it as a punishment, not as a treatment."

Suicide Should Not Be Prevented

Thomas Szasz

In the following viewpoint, Thomas Szasz argues that individuals should not be prevented from committing suicide if they do not voluntarily seek protection from their suicidal urges. He contends that suicide is an individual choice and should not be medicalized and treated as a disease. Preventing suicide through medical or state coercion infringes upon the individual freedom to kill oneself, according to Szasz. Szasz is the author of numerous books exploring psychology, medicine, human behavior, and individual rights, including *The Myth of Mental Illness* and *Fatal Freedom: The Ethics and Politics of Suicide*, from which the following excerpt is taken.

As you read, consider the following questions:
1. What analogy does Szasz use to explain his view that suicide prevention is an act of totalitarianism?
2. How does linking the terms "suicide" and "prevention" manipulate language, as stated by the author?
3. According to the author, how often do physicians and psychiatrists commit suicide?

D isapproved behaviors of all sorts are defined as diseases, and approved behaviors of all sorts are defined as treatments. The concepts of *disease* and *treatment* are now thoroughly politicized. Doctors, judges, journalists, civil libertarians, everyone accepts, or pretends to accept, that killing oneself without physician approval is a disease justifying State coercion, and that killing oneself with physician approval is a treatment justifying State exemption from the strictures of drug prohibition. Not surprisingly, these novel concepts of disease and treatment conflict with the traditional meaning of "helping" as aiding a person to attain his self-chosen goal or persuading him to change it. Helping a person against his will—that is, forcing him to pursue a goal he does not want to pursue—is a contradiction of terms. Joining suicide prevention and coercion as if they were indissolubly united makes us neglect the possibilities of noncoercive suicide prevention, an option we cannot consider so long as we view suicide as the consequence of untreated (mental-brain) disease.

Benevolent Coercion

Suicide prevention (SP) is a modern idea, the product of the concept of suicide as a sickness and its prevention as a species of disease prevention. It is a counterproductive policy that rests on a fallacious analogy: Suicide may be said to be *like* a disease, but it is not a disease. Some years ago I proposed comparing the would-be suicide with the would-be emigrant: One wants to leave life, the other wants to leave his homeland. Killing oneself is a decision, not a disease. The political analogy fits it more closely than does the medical analogy.

One of the most important differences between free and totalitarian countries is that people can leave the former without permission by authorities of the State, but they can leave the latter only with their explicit authorization. The coercive psychiatric prevention of suicide resembles the coercive political prevention of emigration: Psychiatric bureaucrats insist that the would-be suicide should not leave his life, much as totalitarian bureaucrats insist that the would-be emigrant must not leave his country. The sincerity or cynicism of the agents does not matter; what matters is the coerced person's loss of liberty, justified by patriotic or psychiatric rationalization and rhetoric. To one who believes in benevolent coercion, the beneficiary who rejects his benefactor and wants to vote with his feet perforce appears to be bad or mad or both, and must therefore be forcibly prevented from doing what he wants to do. "What's a government for," asks National Public Radio correspondent Susan Stamberg, "if it doesn't step in and say, 'You can't commit suicide'?"

Punishment Masquerading as Treatment

If a person fears that he might kill himself and seeks help because he considers *that* a problem, we do not say that he is receiving a "suicide prevention service." We call such a service "psychotherapy." Trying to persuade another person to refrain from an action which we believe is injurious to his best medical, moral, or financial interests is always permissible and may or may not be meritorious; however, that does not justify replacing suasion with coercion. We reserve the term "suicide prevention" for interventions such as the following:

- A young man fails to return home. His relatives call the police and say they fear he may be suicidal. The police find the man in the woods and *arrest him "on a charge of violation of the Mental Health Law."*
- A man calls the Los Angeles Suicide Prevention Center and says he wants to shoot himself. When the worker asks for his address, he refuses to give it. "Silently but urgently, [the worker] signaled a co-worker to begin *tracing the call. . . .* An agonizing 40 minutes passed. Then she heard the voice of a policeman come on the phone to say the man was safe."
- A man threatens to jump from an overpass to the highway below. Police officers arrive: "'We told him we wouldn't hurt him and just wanted to help.' . . . When he climbed back over, the officers ran to him and *handcuffed him.*" The man was taken to a mental hospital.

If a person is determined to kill himself and is physically able to do so, it is virtually impossible to prevent his suicide. This truism is regularly documented by newspaper stories. In March 1997, Pittsburgh police discovered the dismembered body of a woman in the basement of a condemned row house. The tenement's owner was arrested by the police and placed in the back of the police van. The man was "shackled and his hands were cuffed behind his back in the van, yet he still managed to remove his belt, loop it around the grating, and hang himself during the 12-minute ride to the police station."

The Semantics of Suicide Prevention

The practice of SP rests on civil commitment, that is, the involuntary detention of the subject in a building called "hospital." Is such a place of detention a hospital or a prison? *Webster's Dictionary* defines prison as: "A place or condition of confinement or restraint." *Black's Law Dictionary* offers the following definitions: "[Prevent, v.] To hinder, frustrate, prohibit, impede, or preclude; to obstruct; to intercept. . . . [Prison] A public building or other place for the confinement or safe custody of persons, whether as a punishment imposed by the law or otherwise in the course of the administration of justice."

Linking the terms "suicide" and "prevention" is an abuse of language, similar to linking the terms "mental" and "hospital." "Prevention" and "hospital" imply consent and cooperation. Only when a woman wants to avert her own pregnancy do we speak of "preventing pregnancy." When the State uses force to prevent a woman who wants to become pregnant from becoming pregnant, we call the intervention "forcible sterilization." By the same token, when a psychiatrist uses the power of the State to prevent a person who wants to kill himself from killing himself, we should call the intervention "coercive psychiatric suicide prevention" and we should regard it as a punishment, not as a treatment. Regardless of the coercer's intention, the person whose freedom is abridged experiences the abridgment as punishment. When a mother tells her son to go to his room and stay there for an hour, he perceives it as punishment. To say that her intention is to correct the child's behavior does not invalidate his experiencing her action as punishment, nor does it negate the likelihood that her intention may be punitive as well. As long as we pretend that procedures called "treatments" *ipso facto* help the recipients, and procedures called "punishments" *ipso facto* harm them, we foreclose the possibility of an open-minded examination of these interventions.

The Transient Desire for Suicide

Even if the desire for suicide is transient in most cases, that in itself will not justify the claim that all suicide should be prevented. One can easily imagine cases in which individuals think long and hard on the suicidal option before embracing it.

Further, why should the simple fact that a desire is transient justify others in preventing its realization? The desire to do something very good for others might be fleeting, but that in itself does not show that others are justified in preventing its realization. Clearly, the lifespan of a desire does not *in itself* determine whether or not one should prevent its realization, otherwise one would have to say that a transitory desire to do good for others must be frustrated.

Victor Cosculluela, *The Ethics of Suicide*, 1995.

Individuals, groups, and the State regularly use actual or threatened punishment to prevent, or try to prevent, people from engaging in certain behaviors, for example, selling and buying certain books or drugs. In every such situation the persons prevented from realizing their intentions regard the restraint as a form of *unjust and unmerited punishment.* It is disingenuous to expect that the person forcibly restrained in the name of suicide prevention should regard his situation differently. Indeed, the cruelty of his punishment is compounded by the fact that his physician and his family insist that they are helping him, thus invalidating his perception that they are harming him. . . .

Does "Suicide Prevention" Prevent Suicide?

The answer to that question is a flat-out no. Not only is there absolutely no evidence that coerced psychiatric suicide prevention (CPSP) reduces the frequency of suicide; what evidence there is suggests that the practice is likely to increase it. The late [law and behavioral sciences professor] Jonas Robitscher cogently observed: "Free mental health services, particularly when other meaningful forms of help are absent, are seductive. . . . Cities where suicide prevention services are offered, for example, show a rise and not a fall in suicides . . .

there is the possibility—not sufficiently studied—that the services do actually engender pathology."

A group of investigators reviewed published studies and "concluded that the suicide prevention center does not reach the highest risk population and it may possibly shape the low-risk person toward the act." A report published in a January 1998 issue of *Psychiatric News*, the American Psychiatric Association's official newspaper, informed the reader that "despite decades of progress in developing psychiatric medications, there has been little change in the rate of suicide in the last quarter century." Even [psychiatrist] Erwin Stengel, one of the most respected advocates of SP, acknowledged that instead of reducing the incidence of suicide, "the triumphs of scientific medicine [have], on the contrary, tended to increase it."

However, SP programs are counterproductive not because of the "triumphs of scientific medicine," but because of the *threats and terrors of psychiatric incarceration*, on which they depend. Ernest Hemingway, Sylvia Plath, and Virginia Woolf are only a few of the famous persons whose suicides may, in part at least, have been provoked by the fear of psychiatric incarceration and involuntary psychiatric treatment. The necessity to make this point is evidence of the biased character of the professional literature on suicide and of the media's uncritical acceptance of the benevolence of psychiatric coercion. [Philosopher and playwright] Antonin Artaud knew better. He wrote: "I myself spent nine years in an insane asylum and I never had the obsession of suicide, but I know that each conversation with a psychiatrist, every morning at the time of his visit, made me want to hang myself, realizing that I would not be able to slit his throat." . . .

Nevertheless, most (American) psychiatrists resolutely defend CPSP. It is psychiatric doctrine that the psychiatrist has a professional duty to "protect the patient from his own [suicidal] wishes," [states expert P. Solomon]. This creed follows inexorably from the psychiatrist's perception of the suicidal person as a kind of existential Siamese twin, one wanting to die, the other to live. The psychiatrist diagnoses the suicidal twin as irrational and ill, and the nonsuicidal twin as rational and healthy; he concludes that both need his help, the former to protect him from his illness, the latter, to protect him from his (self)murderous twin. He proceeds to incarcerate the patient in a mental hospital. Intoxicated with the cause of suicide prevention, the psychiatrist inverts [American revolutionist] Patrick Henry's "Give *me* liberty, or give me death!" declaring: "Give *him (the patient)* commitment, give him drugs, give him electric shock treatment, give him lobotomy, but do not let him choose death!" By so radically illegitimizing another person's wish to die, the suicide-preventer redefines the aspiration of the Other as not an aspiration at all. The result is the utter infantilization and dehumanization of the suicidal person. . . .

Suicide as a Public Health Problem

Webster's Dictionary defines the term "public health" as "The art and science dealing with the protection and improvement of community health by organized community effort." Traditionally, the term denoted activities undertaken by a governmental agency, using the economic and coercive powers of the State, to protect groups (the inhabitants of a city, military personnel) from disease-causing agents or conditions in the environment. Typical public health measures are sanitation (sewage disposal, the provision of clean water and pure food) and the control of infectious diseases (protection from microbial diseases, such as cholera and typhoid). By contrast, measures that individuals can take to protect themselves from disease or injury have traditionally been viewed as matters of *private health* (a term I use here to underscore the distinction between it and public health).

Today's State controls of personal behavior, justified by appeals to physical and mental health, closely resemble yesterday's State controls of personal behavior, justified by appeals to spiritual health. Thomas Jefferson recognized this problem at a very early stage. In the birth year of the United States, he issued this warning: "The care of every man's soul belongs to himself. But what if he neglects the care of it? Well what if he neglects the care of his health or estate, which more nearly relates to the state. Will the magistrate make a law that he shall not be poor or sick? Laws provide against injury from others; but not from ourselves. God himself will not save men against their wills."

Interventions justified in the name of health—defined as therapeutic not punitive—fall outside the scope of the criminal law and are therefore exempt from constitutional restraints on state coercion. Promoted as protecting the best interests of both the patients *and* the public, such measures are viewed as valuable public services. Therein, precisely, lies the danger.

Freedom means the opportunity to act wisely or unwisely, to help or harm ourselves. Free access to a particular drug, like free access to any object, increases our opportunities for both using and abusing it. Because it is true that no man is an island, and because every private act may be deemed to harm not only the actor's best interests, but also the economic, existential, medical, or religious well-being of others, no private behavior is safe from being classified as a public health problem and from being controlled by means of medical sanctions.

What is private and what is not—where we draw the line between the private sphere and the public sphere or whether we draw such a line at all—is a matter of convention. Ever since the beginning of this century, especially in recent decades, we have been moving toward redefining certain personal choices as public health problems. The 1997 Washington State "Drug Medicalization and Prevention Act" is an example. The act asserts that "we need to . . . recognize that drug abuse and addiction are public health problems that should be treated as diseases." This interpretation flies in the face of the common-sense secular view that what we put into our bodies is a matter of *private health, not public health*. If the State lets us poison ourselves slowly with cigarettes, by what logic or right can it prevent us from poisoning ourselves quickly with barbiturates? In the privacy of their minds, many people might still acknowledge that killing oneself is, or ought to be, recognized as a private (family) affair. . . .

Self-Serving Propaganda

The modern psychiatrist insists that mental illnesses are "treatable" and that, if the patient rejects treatment, psychiatric intervention ought to be imposed on him by force. This is a pathognomonic sign of *furor therapeuticus*,[1] an ailment most likely to affect physicians when they are most helpless. In the past, this *furor* led to bloodletting as a panacea, with George Washington as one of its most distinguished victims. Today, it leads to the use of so-called psychiatric drugs as a panacea for mental diseases, especially for "patients" who refuse to assume the patient role: The most conspicuous victims of contemporary *furor therapeuticus* are children and old persons. There is bitter irony in this situation. When the physician has an effective treatment for a real disease, he and the courts insist that the patient be granted the right to refuse it; but when he has an ineffective (non)treatment for a nondisease, he and the courts are eager to deprive the patient of his right to refuse treatment. The upshot is that psychiatrists oppose suicide that is unassisted by a physician *and* support suicide that is assisted by a physician. Physicians in general and psychiatrists in particular are ill suited, existentially as well as professionally, for the role of preventing suicide or providing assistance with it. Statistics about suicide among physicians support this view.

Preaching water but drinking wine disqualifies the speaker as a credible person and moral authority. Ophthalmologists do not go blind from untreated glaucoma more often than do lay persons. Pulmonary disease specialists do not develop emphysema more often than do lay persons. This rule holds true for all diseases except suicide. Then, physicians fail miserably: They preach suicide prevention but kill themselves more often than do lay persons: "Psychiatrists [commit] suicide, regularly, year by year, at rates about twice those expected." "The suicide rate of male physicians is about three times that of the general U.S. population . . . [and] of female physicians at least three times that of women in the general population." "Each year among the physician population, the equivalent of an average-sized medical school graduating class commits suicide." Undaunted, physicians redouble their effort to hold on to the mantle of experts in suicide prevention: The House

---

1. An attitude marked by overly ambitious—almost frenzied—therapeutic work (www.syntheory.com).

of Delegates of the American Medical Association (AMA) "has voted to explore the possibility of developing a suicide-prevention program to be run by the AMA."

Actions speak louder than words. The fact that physicians commit suicide more frequently than do lay persons ought to unmask their claims about suicide prevention as self-serving propaganda.

> "*Gun control measures that reduced gun availability among suicide-prone persons might save at least a few lives.*"

Restricting Access to Guns May Prevent Some Suicides

Gary Kleck

Although gun restrictions do not prevent individuals from attempting or committing suicide by means other than fire-arms, Gary Kleck asserts in the following viewpoint that such measures may prevent suicide deaths because of the high lethality of guns. He suggests that if a suicidal person is denied a gun and is forced to use a slower-acting method to commit suicide, he or she has a greater chance of changing his or her mind about dying or being saved by others. Kleck also contends that if a person is denied a gun during the first suicide attempt, he or she is more likely to survive that at-tempt and less likely to attempt suicide again. Kleck is a criminology and criminal justice professor at Florida State University and author of *Targeting Guns: Firearms and Their Control*, from which the following viewpoint was taken.

As you read, consider the following questions:
1. In the author's view, what role may alcohol and drugs play in suicide attempts?
2. What percentage of survivors of initial gun attempts did not subsequently commit suicide, according to Kleck?
3. According to Kleck, what are "transitory" suicidal impulses?

Gary Kleck, *Targeting Guns: Firearms and Their Control*. New York: Aldine de Gruyter, 1997. Copyright © 1997 by Walter de Gruyter, Inc. Reproduced by permission.

G un control opponents argue that the majority of suicide attempters who use guns are determined, at least at that moment, to kill themselves. Because almost all suicide attempters have other highly lethal means available to them, the absence of guns would make very little difference as to how many of them would succeed in killing themselves. Virtually all would substitute essentially equally lethal methods, hanging or drowning themselves, breathing exhaust fumes, or using some other method if a gun were not available.

Substitution-of-Other-Means

Note that the substitution-of-other-means issue is different with suicide than with homicide. Unlike murderers, suicide attempters are largely in control of the violent event, usually able to determine whether the "victim" dies, without interference from others. Further, being both offender and victim, so to speak, they rarely face anyone able to prevent the acquisition and use of available tools for producing death. In contrast, homicides usually involve a victim who does not want to die and who will use any means available to avoid death. This sharply restricts the killer's choice of methods for killing, especially in those homicides that are the impulsive, unpremeditated act of an enraged attacker. Such an assaulter would have a hard time shoving poisons down an adult victim's throat, putting a rope around his neck and hanging him, or even throwing him from a high place or drowning him. Consequently, guns would seem to be essential or very helpful in a much larger share of homicides than of suicides, and substitution of other means should be correspondingly higher with suicides.

Nevertheless, there still may be potential suicidal situations in which the availability of guns could make a difference as to whether the attempter lived or died. Therefore, hypothetical gun suicide scenarios where a death could potentially be prevented by eliminating the immediate availability of guns will be described. It should be kept in mind that, in real life, suicide situations are often combinations of the scenarios; they are described separately to clarify the elements that might make a suicide preventable through the elimination of gun availability.

Guns and Lethality

1. *A nonserious attempter uses a gun because he does not fully understand its lethality. He would not have died had he used a method better suited to his nonlethal intentions.* It might be impossible to prevent people seriously and persistently intent on killing themselves from doing so. However, it is possible that some persons who are not truly determined to die nevertheless use guns in their attempts and end up killing themselves due to unexpected or misunderstood lethality of firearms. In such suicides there is a mismatch of intention and method, with the lethality of the latter exceeding that of the former. It is unlikely that any sober, mentally healthy person would not be aware of the great lethality of firearms. If anything, their reputation for lethality is probably exaggerated by movies and television. However, at least at the time of the act, some suicide attempters are cognitively disordered or impaired in some way. Estimates of the fraction of suicides who are mentally ill have been as high as 60%, depending on how mental illness is defined, though figures around a third are more common.

Similarly, use of alcohol and other drugs could impair thought processes in such a way as to encourage nonserious suicide attempters to use guns in a lethal fashion. [Researchers] Norman Shneidman and E.S. Farberow found that 24% of the males and 11% of the females who committed suicide had at least some alcohol in their bodies at the time of autopsy. Of course, the suicide decision may have preceded the alcohol consumption. It is, moreover, impossible to estimate from these data how often thought processes were distorted to the point at which gun lethality could not have been sufficiently appreciated. Questioning of survivors of gun suicide attempts could shed light on this matter, but no such evidence has yet been produced. If a nonserious attempter of this sort could be denied access to firearms, one would not necessarily expect substitution of other equally lethal methods, unless there were similar misperceptions of the lethality of these other methods. Thus reduction of gun availability might prevent some suicides like this scenario.

2. *A suicide attempter is set on using only firearms and will not make an attempt of any kind if a gun is not available.* [Clinical

psychologist] Henry M. Seiden argued that at least some suicide attempters are set on using only one particular method and are unable to quickly switch to any other method. If this were true for any prospective gun suicide attempters, eliminating the availability of guns could prevent suicides. Seiden presented no evidence that this is true for any gun users, relying for support on another study's evidence concerning persons who jumped off the Golden Gate Bridge. [Psychology professor] David Rosen interviewed six persons who survived such a jump, and four of them said that they would not have used any other method had that bridge not been available. However these survivors also stated that the Golden Gate Bridge had special romance and notorious fame as a suicide locale, suggesting that their views on substitution of other methods may be peculiar to this unique "suicide shrine," as Rosen phrased it. Consequently, it is questionable whether these results can be generalized to other suicide methods.

Ambivalence and Impulse

3. *A gun user's intentions are ambivalent and he leaves his death up to chance; gun use tips the odds in favor of death.* Seiden and others have noted that many suicide attempters are ambivalent about whether they really want to die. Such persons may leave it up to the vagaries and uncertainties of the methods they use or to the unknown chances of someone effectively intervening in their attempt. This scenario is certainly plausible with regard to attempters who use less lethal methods such as drug self-poisonings, where the lethal dosage is so often unknown, or with self-inflicted cuttings, where it is uncertain how many cuts are needed, how deep they must be, or where they have to be located in order to produce death. However, it seems less plausible with shooting than with almost any other method. Because guns are ordinarily perceived to be so lethal, few prospective suicides are likely to view them as chancy or uncertain tools of self-destruction. And shooting attempts can easily produce death so quickly that intervention is categorically ruled out. However, if scenario 1 applied, i.e., the attempter's thinking was distorted, scenario 3 might occur.

4. *An impulsive suicide is precipitated by the knowledge that a uniquely quick, easy method of suicide is immediately available; no attempt would have been made without a gun being available.* [Researchers] George D. Newton and Franklin Zimring suggested that for a depressed person, "the knowledge of having a quick and effective way of ending his life might precipitate a suicide attempt on impulse". Although an interesting speculation, this ignores the almost universal availability of other quick and effective means for killing one's self, such as hanging. If a suicide attempt by a depressed person could be precipitated by the mere knowledge of the availability of such means, eliminating gun availability would make little or no difference (assuming scenario 2 does not apply) and such attempts would ordinarily be impossible to prevent.

Suicide, Homicide, and Guns

In 1998, 17,424 people committed suicide with a firearm, while 12,102 homicides involved a gun injury.

Sherry L. Murphy, *National Vital Statistics Report*, July 24, 2000.

---

5. *A seriously motivated suicide attempter who otherwise would have used guns is forced by their unavailability to substitute another method that is somewhat less lethal. He survives and makes no subsequent suicide attempts.* This scenario illustrates the most obvious reason to hope for some savings of lives if gun availability among serious prospective suicides could be reduced. Even if such persons substituted other common, frequently fatal means of suicide, deaths might not occur as often if the other methods are not quite as lethal as shooting. . . .

Even if one believes that the fatality rate of gun suicide attempts remains still higher than with other methods, the critical question remaining is the same . . . in connection with assault fatality rates: To what degree are the differences in suicide fatality rates across method categories attributable to differences in the technical lethality of the methods/weapons themselves, as opposed to differences in the seriousness of their users' intentions or motivations to inflict serious harm? Suicide attempters who use guns may be more serious and less ambivalent about dying than users of other common methods. Both [researchers] Jacob Tuckman and William Youngman and Sherman Eisenthal, Farberow, and Shneidman found that survivors of nonfatal suicide attempts who had used the "most serious" methods, including shooting, were more likely to subsequently commit suicide. [Researchers] K. Fox and M. Weissman found suicide attempts with more serious methods were less likely to be impulsive. They also found that among survivors of nonfatal suicide attempts, those who used the more violent or active methods (including shooting) were more likely to say in interviews that their intentions were serious and that they truly wanted to die. And common sense suggests that mentally unimpaired persons who did not want to die but rather wanted only to make a "cry for help" are unlikely to shoot themselves in the head or chest, given the nearly universal perception of guns as highly lethal devices. Finally, direct measures of "suicidal intent" have indicated that suicide completers and attempters with guns in their homes had higher suicidal intent scores than those without guns. Consequently there is strong a priori reason to believe that at least some of the difference in fatality rates between gun suicide attempts and those involving the less frequently fatal methods (or methods with less of a reputation for lethality) is attributable to differences in the "seriousness" of their users. However, it is not clear whether this argument would hold as well for a comparison of gun attempts with those involving other frequently fatal methods, such as hanging or carbon monoxide (CO) poisoning.

Temporarily Serious Attempters

6. *A suicide attempter is only temporarily intent on dying. Denied a gun, he substitutes a slow-acting method. This allows others to intervene to prevent death, without the attempt being followed by later attempts.* Most suicide attempts that do not result in death are never followed by subsequent suicide. Therefore, preventing suicide on the first attempt is usually tantamount to preventing it permanently. More relevant to the issue at hand, [social psychology professor] Josefina J. Card found that only 6.25% of suicide survivors who used guns subsequently killed themselves. Interpretation of these facts, how-

ever, is complicated by an obvious problem with sample censoring: only survivors of the initial attempts were "eligible" for a subsequent suicide. If those who killed themselves on the initial attempt were more lethal in their intentions than those who survived, the survivors would not be representative of all attempters and certainly not of serious attempters. It is possible that if one could somehow separately identify those attempters who had a serious and persistent intent to die, one would find that all of the survivors among this group did subsequently kill themselves. Perhaps the 93.75% of survivors of initial gun attempts who did not subsequently suicide were never serious in the first place, and had only shot themselves in nonvital areas of their bodies. Eliminating gun availability among this group would not reduce suicide since none of its members would ever have killed themselves anyway. And reducing gun availability among the "serious" attempters (those who died in the initial attempt and the 6.25% of survivors who later committed suicide) would not reduce suicide since all of these would have made subsequent successful suicide attempts had the initial attempt failed. Nevertheless it is possible that some attempters who use guns are seriously intent on self-destruction, but only temporarily so, and thus preventing suicide on the initial attempt could prevent it permanently.

Temporarily serious attempters who otherwise would have used guns would, if unable to get a gun, substitute other methods, some of which are about as lethal as guns. How then could lives be saved? Newton and Zimring argued that some of the methods substituted would be, even if of roughly equal technical lethality, somewhat slower acting, increasing the chances of others intervening to save the attempter's life. Among persons who currently use guns to make serious suicide attempts, would the substitution of slower methods result in increased successful intervention?

Intervention is possible only when the suicide does not isolate himself from others so as to preclude such an eventuality. [Forensic expert] Bruce L. Danto's evidence on Detroit gun suicides indicates that persons who used guns made intervention very difficult regardless of the method they had ended up using. He found that in twenty-eight of twenty-nine cases (97%), the gun suicide victim was home alone at the time of the event. Nevertheless, in a general sample of completed suicides using a variety of methods, [suicide expert] Donald W. Maris found that death occurred within an hour of the suicidal act in 66% of the cases in which the time interval was known, leaving a third of the cases in which there was over an hour of potential intervention time. Unfortunately, it was not possible to know how many lingering deaths involved seriously motivated attempters or the more lethal nongun methods. However, the Danto evidence on this matter indicates that causing substitution of slower methods would rarely result in successful intervention. Further, the other methods available as substitutes are all quieter than shooting; thus their use would reduce the chances of others becoming aware of the attempt or being drawn to the scene due to noise.

The Time Between Action and Death

7. *Substituting a method requiring longer preparation increases the chances of a temporarily serious attempter changing his mind.* This scenario involves a different time issue than the previous one, pertaining to the span between when a person decides to commit suicide and actually takes the first suicidal action (swallowing pills, breathing car exhaust fumes, pulling a trigger, etc.), rather than the time between this action and death. Many suicide attempts are impulsive, with the attempt being made shortly after the idea was first seriously considered, or at least this is the case among some survivors of nonfatal attempts. [Researcher] Neil Kessel reported that 66% of the nonfatal self-poisoning cases he studied were impulsive, although he did not precisely define impulsivity. However, there is evidence that few of Kessel's attempters were serious about dying, suggesting that they may have been different from the average gun user. For example, very few of the studied survivors said, after recovery, that they still wished to take their lives. Likewise, Fox and Weissman found that self-poisoners were more impulsive and less intent on dying than those using other methods, including guns.

Nevertheless, there are probably some gun users who attempt suicide impulsively. If guns had not been available, they would have had to substitute methods of suicide that required somewhat longer preparation time. [Some] studies concluded that most gun suicide victims had owned their guns for protection, and guns owned for protection, in turn, are especially likely to be kept loaded and in a location where they can be used quickly. Therefore, if a gun owner were home when he experienced a suicidal impulse, he usually could bring a loaded firearm to bear on a vital area of his body very quickly. In contrast, the methods likely to be substituted for guns all require at least a few more minutes of preparation time, for at least some of their users. Hanging oneself entails locating an exposed pipe, a roof rafter, a tree limb, or other strong support from which a noose can be suspended. For those without a sufficient existing supply of drugs, self-poisoning might entail acquiring them from friends or using prescriptions to accumulate a lethal stockpile from pharmacists. For those without a garage or similar enclosed space, CO poisoning would necessitate locating a hose of suitable diameter with which to direct exhaust fumes into the interior of a vehicle. For those who do not work or live in tall buildings with openable doors or windows on the upper floors, a fatal jump would require at least a short trip to a suitable jumping place. And drowning would often entail a similar trip to a large enough body of water. In short, for at least some prospective suicides, lethal alternatives to guns would not be instantly available, increasing the time in which suicides could reconsider their actions and decide not to attempt suicide at all, perhaps by as much as an hour.

Logically Plausible

The Fox and Weissman findings suggested that gun users are less impulsive than drug users but left open the possibility that even among seriously intended gun users there may be some whose suicidal intentions are serious for only a short time. This leaves open the possibility of preventing some suicides by reducing gun availability, delaying the execution of suicidal actions, and allowing temporarily suicidal persons to reconsider.

Ordinarily, when suicide scholars speak of "transitory" suicide impulses, they seem to mean those lasting a few weeks or days. However, an impulse lasting even as long as an hour would provide sufficient preparation time for using any of the major alternatives to shooting. Existing evidence does not give any indication as to how many gun suicides experience a serious suicidal impulse that lasts for less than an hour.

To summarize, some of the foregoing "preventable gun suicide" scenarios are logically plausible and not contradicted by available evidence. Although there is no evidence that any of them is very common in real life, there is also little solid evidence to the contrary. At best, one can say there is some a priori reason to hypothesize that gun control measures that reduced gun availability among suicide-prone persons might save at least a few lives.

"Buying a gun does not mean that you're more likely to go from being content to being suicidal."

Restricting Access to Guns Will Not Prevent Suicides

Angel Shamaya

Angel Shamaya is founder and director of KeepAndBearArms. com, an Internet-based grassroots organization that works to protect the right to gun ownership. In the following viewpoint, he argues that gun restrictions will not prevent suicide. To illustrate his point, Shamaya claims that gun-free Japan has much higher suicide rates than the United States. Shamaya insists that the person who commits suicide is solely responsible for the act and contends that it is illogical to blame the means that was used.

As you read, consider the following questions:
1. According to the author, why are guns blamed for suicides?
2. In Shamaya's view, why do those who lose someone to suicide advocate stricter gun control?
3. How does Shamaya support his claim that a determined person will commit suicide whether or not he or she has access to a gun?

Angel Shamaya, "Suicide in the Gun Debate," www.keepandbeararms.com, November 27, 2000. Copyright © 2000 by Keep and Bear Arms. Reproduced by permission.

Many anti-self-defense leaders today are bolstering the numbers of people dying by gunshot with the suicides that are taking place—increasing the legitimate "death by criminal misuse of gun" tally in hopes the larger numbers will further their pre-confiscation agenda. (Yes, pre-confiscation. The licensing of rights and registration of guns—now en vogue for anti-rights people—are the two major ways in which guns have consistently throughout history—on American soil and abroad—become the easy targets of successful confiscations.) In many cases—some of them widely publicized by gun control organizations and the liberal media—people enduring the pain of having lost a loved one through death-by-choice-with-firearm are now screaming for restrictive gun controls and even gun bans. . . .

Blaming Guns

When something goes wrong, people tend to want to blame something, anything, and this is never truer than when a great deal of pain is experienced. And, arguably, the deepest pain we as human beings will ever feel involves losing someone very close to us. When [my brother] Michael took his own life, the poetry that tore its way through my pen was so steeped in heartache, confusion, shock, horror and other powerful emotions, the very paper upon which I wrote was many times covered in tears. I hurt really really bad. I went through a rich variety of "blamings." I blamed myself and my parents, his teachers, society, and even God. And, for a time, I blamed "that damned shotgun."

I needed to pin that awful, gut-wrenching pain on something, anything, in my seemingly downward spiral of agony, if only to have some target upon which I could focus all of my aching, gnawing sense of loss and despair. I felt victimized, and I needed to vent that tremendous sense of helplessness upon whatever must be the *real* cause of my anguish. So overwhelmed by the rich flood of seemingly endless and unrelenting emotions, I needed to lock onto an "enemy" and tear its flesh, lashing out for what felt at the time like the gravest injustice I could ever or would ever feel.

Such is human nature. Ask any psychologist, psychiatrist or even a second year psych major, or just ask yourself about your own experience as a blamer. When the harder road is the one that requires personal, mental, physical, emotional and spiritual responsibility, underdeveloped or pain-stricken human beings sometimes falter for a time until they see and then rise above the pattern. We have all blamed, and that does include yours truly.

Gun-blamers who've suffered through a suicide, however, are advised to dig deeper—if their goal is truly to save lives. . . .

Responsibility

Responsibility means many things to many people. In this context, the definition to which I refer is: accountability.

[Entrepreneur] John D. Rockefeller said, "Every right requires a responsibility." When we as individuals within a free society exercise our rights regarding firearms, we possess in equal measure an accountability for the safe exercise of these rights. We are free to make choices, and that includes what others will see as "bad" choices or "wrong" choices. One could argue that free will—choice—is at the very root of human nature. We choose. And we suffer the consequences of our choices. And we bear the fruit of our choices, as well. The road forks, and we pick our paths and walk to the best of our abilities to the next fork in our road, making choices all along the way.

Some people come to a fork in the road where they perceive it to be a literal dead end. Suicide is a choice. Someone, for whatever reason, says, "goodbye," and they leave. Be it pills, rope, slashed wrists, tall buildings, reckless driving, alcohol or drugs, or by gun, a free will choice is engaged, and off they go. They "infringe"—to the extreme—their own right to life, by choice. . . .

My Brother Pulled the Trigger

What I finally had no other choice but to simply accept was that Michael pulled the trigger. My dear brother—loved by many and with whom I'd invested countless hours—took his own life. *He* did it. The gun was simply the vehicle; that is all. What I came to realize—through emotional trial and error—was that my unwillingness to accept and deal with that painful fact was what "pushed me" to seek other things to blame. I was, for a time and understandably, being immature and irrational under the weight of losing my little brother. And, though I didn't go to the extreme now exhibited by many anti-self-defense/anti-gun people who are calling for restrictions and in some cases complete usurpations of other citizens' God-given, constitution-recognized right to self-defense and liberty-defense, I can certainly speak from a place of authority about what they are doing and why. I walked a thousand miles in their mocassins.

People who've lost someone to suicide with a gun and now work to strip other citizens of their rights don't want to admit that the gun didn't do it to him/her, because then they'd have to look at what they are avoiding dealing with: guilt. I felt guilty as Hell Itself, deep down inside where it hurt like fire. What could I have done to change his mind? Why didn't I give him more of this or that? Why'd my brother leave me? Was it so bad that he couldn't talk to me. Did I not leave an opening for him to come to me? Etc. etc. ad painful nauseum. God knows I know all those questions and a thousand more, and I had to ask them, be with them, and move through it, and so do you.

But not at the expense of the right of a little old granny who doesn't want her last breath to be mixed with the sweat of a violent ex-convict the government let out of jail a few years too soon.

Excuses for Gun Restrictions by Suicide Survivors

Following are a few excuses being used by suicide survivors who now call for gun restrictions and gun bans, along with my observations: . . .

"Easy access is the cause." This is one of the two loudest arguments in the "control guns because of suicide" conversation. You don't have to look far to find someone who lost a loved one to suicide blaming easy access to guns. "If guns weren't so prevalent in our society, my son would still be here," says one very vociferous, grieving mother whose son shot himself in the family garage. She didn't mention if it was her own gun to which she provided access, nor did she tell us if she watched for warning signs, but I can tell you from experience that warning signs are not blinking neon,

and the fact is that some kids are going to kill themselves no matter what they use. . . .

The biggest problem with embarking on a "reduce gun access" crusade is that, in reducing access to guns to prevent the suicidal from gaining access, you're also reducing access to guns for self-defense, family-defense and liberty-defense for the other 99.9% of us, and that just isn't a very nice thing to do. In fact, when it comes to reducing access such that little old granny can't get one and must therefore submit to a knife-wielding rapist, it's downright ruthless—all in the name of working out your own issues.

I know it hurts, but do you really want to hurt more people in your own measured moves to do what you think is right—when it isn't?

Gun Purchases and Suicide

[A 1999] study looked at whether recent (legal) gun purchasers in California—an overwhelmingly prosperous, young, white, male sample—killed themselves shortly after buying a gun.

The actual number of suicides among recent purchasers was very small—only 114 out of 238,292 purchasers in the survey period killed themselves with a handgun (and we do not know whether it was with the particular handgun purchased).

Iain Murray, *St. Louis Post-Dispatch*, December 14, 1999.

"We've got to do *something* to stop suicides."

"I just *had* to do something." This one is as common as lying politicians. That vague little statement has come up in numerous interviews I've done with anti-gun people who've lost someone to a bullet—especially with suicide survivors—so many times I lost count long ago. And the "something" anti-gun voters and/or activists choose is that "something" that makes it easier for criminals to prey on people. When you take a gun away from a frail woman and put her up against a large, strong man, without a weapon or some serious training, she's going to lose every time. So your "something" you're doing is something, indeed, isn't it? Rational, logical people find that "something" is wrong when it strips a grandmother of her right to stop a murderer who wants her gold teeth. (That *happened* to a little old lady down the street from my own grandmother, and he raped her and ran over her 89-year-old body with her own car *before* he took her gold teeth, too. Houston, Texas, in the Heights area, several years ago, look it up.)

Guns hold self-defense empowerment for the grannies of the world, and your loved one choosing to step out of life prematurely is not a valid excuse for taking away that self-defense empowerment while you "do something." I implore you to seek higher moral ground.

If you really want to "do something," heal your own pain without inflicting more unnecessary pain and loss of life on other people's families, please. . . .

Facts, Statistics and Studies

Maybe some facts will help you get logical about this situation. Sometimes, after losing someone we love with all our hearts, so many emotions run so wildly and deeply, turning the lights on in our rational minds is an exceptionally productive exercise. Try some of these on for size . . .

Real Numbers and Common Sense According to the Center for Disease Control (who I have no reason to believe any more than I believe any federal government agency, but I am willing to use their statistics because they are accepted widely),

> In the United States, there were 32,436 gun deaths in 1997. Of these: 41.7% (13,522) were homicides/legal intervention [killed by law enforcement]; 1.1% (367) were of undetermined intent; 54.2% (17,566) were suicides; and 3.0% (981) were unintentional.

Taking the commonly used number of gun owners of 83,000,000 and dividing it by the number of suicides in the above year, we find that only 1 in every 4,727 gun owners committed suicide that year in America. Keeping in mind that they all did it *by choice*, and considering that the other 82,982,434 gun owners had nothing at all to do with that *choice*, can you understand how it's not very balanced or even sane to ask them to bear the responsibilities and burdens of those dead people's choices? Punishing 4,727 people for the actions of 1 person who made a choice you don't agree with is not only irrational, it is bizarre. . . .

Then you might look to the fact that people who are *committed* to dying are going to go through with it, whether they have a gun or not. Among many studies, Gary Kleck's *Targeting Guns: Firearms and Their Control*, offers the following:

> The full body of relevant studies indicates that firearm availability measures are significantly and positively associated with rates of *firearm* suicide, but have no significant association with rates of *total* suicide.

> Of thirteen studies, nine found a significant association between gun levels and rates of *gun* suicide, but only one found a significant association between gun levels and rates of *total* suicides. The only study to find a measure of "gun availability" significantly associated with total suicide . . . used a measure of gun availability known to be invalid.

> This pattern of results supports the view that where guns are less common, there is complete substitution of other methods of suicide, and that, while gun levels influence the choice of suicide method, they have no effect on the number of people who die in suicides.

If someone is going to kill him or herself anyway, why does it make sense to make an arthritic old man easier to accost by removing his right and means to defend himself with the same measure of effectiveness used by criminals? Unless you are going to ban all death-producing pills, all tall buildings, all knives or other wrist-slashing devices, all access to enclosed places where car exhaust can be accumulated . . . you'll not be stopping suicide with laws.

If you do see your anti-self-defense crusade being carried to that unfathomable extreme, please include rocks, beer bottles, pool cues, axe handles, shovels, pencils, and any other hard or sharp objects to legislate your "safe society." Then explain why gun-banned Britain has a violent crime rate with weapons other than guns that surpasses that of the United States as reported by the stridently anti-gun Dan Rather on CBS News. And I quote:

> The UK has a crime problem and, believe it or not, except for murder, theirs is worse than ours. Dan Rather, CBS Special Report, July 2000

The resolution to suicide is psychological, emotional and spiritual, not legislative.

Japan's example destroys the "guns and/or their availability cause suicide" myth. In Japan, less than 1% of the households have a gun, but total suicide is higher than in the

United States where 25–50% of the households have a gun. If guns and/or their presence in our society are causal in those unfortunate and painful losses, how can you explain Japan and still hold your rationale? . . .

And if you compare suicide rates and suicide-by-gun rates in various countries alongside those of the United States, an even more obvious reality emerges: people kill themselves at rates, in some countries, significantly higher per capita than here in America—including in places where gun ownership is so strictly prohibited you will go straight to jail (or the morgue) for having one. In other words, less guns in those societies but more people per capita dying of suicide deflates the "guns and/or their availability cause suicide" myth even further. No, actually, it annihilates it.

[Journalist] Iain Murry said a mouthful when he said:

> It is safe to say that buying a gun does not mean that you're more likely to go from being content to being suicidal. . . .

Unfair and Unrealistic

Not only is the use of suicides in addressing the issue of violence an unfair and unrealistic tactic, it is a blatant disregard for the true need to reduce preventable deaths and injuries, by gun or any other means, and is an irrational and emotionally immature place from which to "deal with" losing a loved one. Furthermore, punishing 4,727 people for each unhappy member of our society who chose to stop exercising his or her right to life is not only rude and irresponsible, when it costs women their sexual dignity or their very lives and when it costs families their precious loved ones, it is socially unacceptable to the point of being criminal. . . .

Blaming a gun is a simple scapegoat during an emotionally trying healing process, but as I believe I have shown, attacking guns and self-defense/liberty-defense rights is not a reasonable answer, nor a valid one. I have yet to hear someone blame a razor blade or a rope for their loved one's death. And I don't think the families of suicide "victims" who chose a rope, pills, a sharp object or a long fall really cared what method they used; the result was still the same. If my brother had jumped off of a tall building, he would not be any less dead. Guns are a politically-correct target, not a sensible one.

> *"Schools can drive down the youth-suicide*
> *rate if they employ very specific methods."*

Schools Can Help Prevent Suicide

Jessica Portner

Jessica Portner writes for the *San Jose Mercury News*. In the following viewpoint, she contends that schools can play an important role in preventing suicide among children and adolescents. She suggests that school personnel can aid in suicide intervention if they are trained to recognize and act upon the behavioral clues of students at risk for suicide. Moreover, students who practice problem-solving through group role-playing sessions at school are less likely to exhibit suicidal behavior, according to Portner. She also asserts that conducting detailed interviews that evaluate students' emotional and mental health and addressing bullying and academic pressures in schools may prevent suicide.

As you read, consider the following questions:
1. How does the author describe the typical school suicide prevention program?
2. According to Portner, what is a "calling tree"?
3. In the author's opinion, how can schools avoid glamorizing suicide?

Jessica Portner, "Suicide: Many Schools Fall Short on Prevention," *Education Week*, vol. 19, April 19, 2000, pp. 20–22. Copyright © 2000 by *Education Week*. Reproduced by permission.

All schools conduct fire drills, and many have detailed plans for coping with floods, hurricanes, or earthquakes. They employ nurses to vaccinate students against diseases. These days, some even practice for the one-in-a-million chance that an armed intruder will go on a shooting spree.

But most schools are unprepared to deal with a far more common threat to their students: Suicide is the third-leading killer of 10- to 19-year-olds in the United States, yet only one in 10 schools has a plan to prevent it.

More Harm than Good?

Most schools that teach suicide prevention generally opt for quick units in health class or school assemblies. Typically, they show videos of healthy-looking adolescents who have survived a suicide attempt. But psychologists warn that such an approach can do more harm than good.

Whether owing to a lack of financial resources or to ignorance or denial of the problem, few schools are tackling suicide prevention in a comprehensive way that research suggests can save lives and help school districts avoid legal liability.

And there are lives to be saved. Youth suicide rates have tripled in the past 30 years, reaching an all-time high of 2,700 fatalities in 1997. On average, one out of every three districts loses a student to suicide each year—sometimes on their own campuses.

In May 1999, a 14-year-old girl hanged herself in the restroom of her New York City middle school. In March 1999, the 17-year-old captain of the football team in a small Connecticut town doused his body with gasoline and ignited himself on the practice field.

"It usually takes multiple deaths on school grounds to grab administrators' attention," said Scott Poland, the psychological services director for the Cypress Fairbanks, Texas, public schools and the author of the book *Suicide Intervention in Schools.* . . .

No Simple Task

It's no simple task to detect a child's suicidal intent. Metal detectors and surveillance cameras may nab gun-toting teenagers, but they don't pick up inner turmoil.

Most U.S. schools—58 percent—discuss suicide prevention in some academic course during the school year, according to a 1995 survey of school health programs published in the *Journal of School Health*. Those units, which typically last three hours or less, usually include video docudramas of teenagers who survived a suicide attempt, use shocking statistics designed to get students' attention, and provide information on where teenagers should go for help.

Publications now on the market range from mail-order suicide-prevention kits at $6.65 apiece to higher-priced textbooks. To fulfill their suicide-prevention requirement, many schools hire lecturers to speak to large assemblies on the subject. Like the ubiquitous drug-awareness programs in which police officers try to "scare kids straight" with the gritty realities of addiction, many suicide-prevention programs now employ medical experts to deliver a similar jolt of shock therapy.

In his presentations to high school students, Dr. Victor Victoroff, the chairman emeritus of psychiatry at Huron Road Medical Center in Cleveland, shows slides of teenagers who attempt suicide and end up in emergency rooms: a girl who had her stomach pumped, a boy with his face blown off by a gunshot blast, a girl with her wrists carved up. "I'll use any means to cut through the romantic haze. I want them to know suicide is a painful experience," Dr. Victoroff said.

Working Toward Prevention

The general view among mental-health professionals is that talking about suicide can help prevent teenagers from doing it. But there is no evidence that short lectures in classrooms or heavily attended school assemblies, or even visits to the morgue have any measurable effect on preventing teenagers from killing themselves. And some of the approaches may actually aggravate the situation for the most vulnerable students.

In one of the most rigorous evaluations of suicide-prevention programs, Dr. David Shaffer, a professor of psychiatry at Columbia University, found that the most commonly used suicide-awareness programs in schools often did more harm than good.

In his 1987 study, Dr. Shaffer evaluated several widely

used programs with 1,000 students in six New Jersey high schools. While there was no evidence that the didactic classroom discussions caused emotional distress among students as a whole, neither did the course alter the disturbing attitudes of those students who said that "in certain situations, suicide was a reasonable solution to one's problems."

Moreover, the study found, those students who were already contemplating suicide were more distressed after being exposed to the lessons. "At any one time in any classroom, there are going to be one in four kids who have thought about suicide," Dr. Shaffer said recently. "Talking about it might stimulate what has been bottled up, and that's not necessarily a good thing."

Such findings have provided support for critics who believe suicide-prevention courses ought to be dropped. "These death-and-dying courses can have dangerous consequences," said Ms. Schlafly of the Alton, Ill.-based Eagle Forum. "Some children may be tripped over the edge."

But schools can drive down the youth-suicide rate if they employ very specific methods, researchers say.

Preliminary findings from a study by University of Washington researchers suggest that students who practice solving difficult dilemmas in their lives through role-playing in group sessions with other students twice a week are less likely to be depressed or to exhibit suicidal behavior than those who do not take part in such programs.

Recognizing Behavioral Clues

The American Association of Suicidology, a nonprofit organization based in Washington dedicated to understanding and preventing suicide, suggests that one way to curb suicides is to train school personnel from bus drivers to custodians to teachers to recognize certain behavioral clues that a student is at risk. A sustained case of the blues, discarding valuable possessions, emotional volatility, or suicidal statements all hint at trouble.

Teachers might also read student essays for more than their literary value. A 1986 study of students' work in several schools found 500 poems that contained suicidal references but that were returned to students without comment or follow-up.

One of the students, an 11-year-old boy, turned in an essay titled "Suicide Mistake" in which he outlined his own death in detail. That night, he killed himself just as he'd described.

Teachers are often reluctant to talk to their colleagues about students for fear that they will violate a student's privacy rights, [Julie] Underwood of the National School Boards Association (NSBA) said: "Students' privacy gets so drilled into their heads, and unfortunately they sometimes get snagged by it."

If teachers detect morbid preoccupations, however, they should be discreet about revealing them, Mr. Poland said. In his book, Mr. Poland cites the case of a Denver teacher who intercepted a note written by a 12-year-old 7th grader and read the personal details about his melancholy state to the class. The boy committed suicide later that day.

Another way to put a dent in the youth-suicide rate is to persuade teenagers to tell adults when they know other students have such intentions, even though it might be seen as tattling.

From Stigma to Support

The unwritten code of silence among students has to be broken, said Clark Flatt, whose youngest son shot himself in 1997. "In 70 percent of all teen suicides, another teen knew about it and did nothing," said Mr. Flatt who, through the Nashville-based Jason Foundation, named for his dead son, trains teenagers to take their friends' morbid musings seriously.

Though no formal research has been done, Mr. Flatt is encouraged by the results so far: Since he launched the Teens Helping Teens program three years ago, Mr. Flatt has received 42 letters from young people who said their friends' "snitching" had saved their lives.

Many experts say the subject is particularly difficult to teach about—even more sensitive than AIDS, sex, or drugs—because talking about suicide has long been considered taboo.

Greeks and Romans condemned suicide as an offense against the state because suicide deprived society of a productive member. Many religious denominations have held that suicide victims are condemned to hell, and have barred their burial in sacred ground and shrouded their memory in shame.

A more compassionate view of suicide victims has emerged in recent years. For example, the Reverend Arnaldo Pangrazzi, a Roman Catholic priest in Italy, expressed the current official Catholic teaching in a 1984 newsletter article: "Churches should teach compassion toward those who take their own lives and judgment should be left to God."

But the overarching taboo remains, [former] U.S. Surgeon General David Satcher said at a suicide-prevention conference in Nashville in fall 1999. In a year in which 30,000 Americans would commit suicide and half a million would attempt it, Dr. Satcher argued that the country should see suicide as a public-health epidemic.

"It's time for us to move from shame and stigma to support," said Dr. Satcher, who is expected to unveil an ambitious plan this spring to increase federal financial support for mental-health services. Because a majority of teenagers who kill themselves suffer some type of diagnosable mental-health problem, Dr. Satcher said, the best way schools can ward off more suicides is to usher troubled children to the nearest mental-health professional. The dip in the teenage-suicide rate in the late 1990s is partly attributable to better screening of children for mental-health problems, some experts say.

In the Nurse's Office

One of the most promising places in this country to thwart a suicide may be the school nurse's office.

In a 10-month University of Washington study in 14 Seattle schools, students who were deemed at risk for dropping out were interviewed in two-hour sessions by a nurse or social worker who asked them a series of questions about their mood and called their parents or a hospital if they expressed suicidal inclinations.

Those who participated in the psychological-interview program were 54 percent less likely to have suicidal thoughts or act on them in the months following the session than those who did not participate, the study found.

The potential for preventing teenage suicide through screenings like those is huge, experts say, simply because of the volume of visitors to a school nurse's office.

Of all the children in the United States who seek mental-health services, half get them at school. But states spend less than 1 percent of their education budgets on mental-health services in schools. With limited funds to hire psychologists and social workers, most schools don't have staff members who are trained to diagnose mental-health conditions.

Recognizing the Warning Signs

Four out of five teens who attempt suicide have given clear warnings. Pay attention to these warning signs:

- Suicide threats, direct and indirect
- Obsession with death
- Poems, essays and drawings that refer to death
- Dramatic change in personality or appearance
- Irrational, bizarre behavior
- Overwhelming sense of guilt, shame or reflection
- Changed eating or sleeping patterns
- Severe drop in school performance
- Giving away belongings

National Mental Health Association Mental Health Information Center
Fact Sheet, 1997.

"You have to know the difference between a joking teen and one who has a knife under their bed or has already counted out the pills," said Leslie Kraft, who runs Columbia University's well-regarded Teen Screen program, in which social workers and nurses are trained to identify teenagers in four New York City high schools in the Bronx who are at risk for suicide. About a quarter of the more than 800 students identified as being at risk were referred for further evaluation last year. "We have kept a lot of these kids alive," Ms. Kraft said.

Experts say that in the best of all possible worlds, children's emotional deficits would be catalogued in kindergarten. Spotlighting and giving early treatment to children with short attention spans, school phobias, or short fuses could greatly reduce problems in later grades, they say.

Reaching the Numbers

In addition, advocates of smaller schools and classes say, responding to individual students' needs is harder when buildings and classrooms are packed.

"The larger you get, the harder it gets. You have to have numbers that are reachable," said Stephen Mulligan, a former counselor for the 9,000-student Smithtown, N.Y., public schools, who recently retired after 28 years. "If you have a teacher teaching 150 kids a day, you don't know them as well."

And not every suicide-prevention plan that works costs money: Just knowing how to react after a suicide can help prevent future ones, experts say.

The National Association of School Psychologists suggests that schools take certain steps immediately after a student kills himself: construct a "calling tree" to spread the news to school staff members, alert the parents of the friends of the deceased, assign a counselor to talk to students in his class, call the family to offer assistance, and keep the superintendent informed.

Another important rule is not to glamorize the act by constructing elaborate shrines to the dead. Experts advise that establishing a fund in the student's memory is preferable to even the most modest memorial.

Minimizing exposure to media reports of the tragedy can also reduce the chances of "copycat" suicides, some experts say. In the weeks after the April 1999 highly publicized Columbine High School shootings in Colorado, in which the two assailants turned their guns on themselves after killing 13 others, suicide attempts peaked in several districts nationwide.

The Welcoming School

Schools can play a role in reducing youth suicide simply by making their schools as welcoming as possible, many educators say.

Most school employees may labor to provide happy environments for students, but some observers warn that many schools are places where bullying is rampant, cliques are ruthless, and teachers are too harried to care.

In a 1999 survey of 558 6th, 7th, and 8th graders at a suburban Indianapolis middle school, researchers from the University of Illinois at Urbana-Champaign found that 80 percent of the students reported they had bullied another classmate in the past 30 days. Children who are repeatedly harassed are more likely to kill themselves, studies have found.

The national push to raise academic standards and hold schools more accountable for their students' performance has also placed new pressures on children, some health educators say. Performing well on new, high-stakes tests can be just as stressful for some students as a verbal assault by the class bully.

"They don't give awards to the mediocre," Mr. Mulligan said.

Gifted students who are competing for slots at top colleges can just as easily be overwhelmed by pressures for them to succeed, said Mr. Lieberman, who points to a Los Angeles high school senior with a 4.0 grade point average who killed himself [in fall 1999] after he was rejected by the University of California, Los Angeles.

In a survey of teenagers on the reasons why they attempted suicide, school pressures ranked in the top three, along with a romantic split and family problems. "You can't separate out students' emotional report card from their academic report card," said Dr. William Pollack, a professor of psychiatry at the Harvard Medical School and an expert on adolescent health.

Dr. Pollack and others suggest a fairly straightforward solution to improving students' mental health: expressing affection. Studies dating to the 1960s have shown that animals that are deprived of physical affection when they are young tend to exhibit more aggressive and violent behavior later in life.

Tiffany Field, a University of Miami researcher who runs the Touch Institute, applied that theory to the classroom in her study of interactions between teachers and students in France and the United States. Ms. Field found that the French students, whose teachers were more physical with them (whether to show discipline or affection), were better behaved and less aggressive than American students, who had less physical contact with their teachers.

Ms. Field laments reports that many U.S. teachers are reluctant to hug students for fear that their gestures will be misinterpreted as sexual. "We are less touchy-feely because there are more lawyers around," she said, "even though setting limits with affection is the best way to be a teacher or a parent."

Of course, suicide-prevention experts acknowledge, many measures that might reduce the youth suicide rate are out of educators' hands.

Researchers often cite a British study to show that reducing access to deadly means can greatly drive down the rate. In 1957, the carbon monoxide content of domestic cooking gas in Britain was 12 percent, and self-asphyxiation accounted for 40 percent of all suicides there. By 1971, a year after the introduction of natural gas reduced the carbon monoxide levels to 2 percent, asphyxiation accounted for less than 10 percent of suicides, and the overall suicide rate in Britain plummeted by 26 percent.

In the United States, two-thirds of people under 18 who commit suicide use a firearm.

Diagnosis and Treatment

[The head of the Suicide Prevention Research Center] Thomas Shires prescribes a multipronged approach to fighting suicide: If physicians were better trained, more students had caring adults in their lives from infancy on, and schools were better prepared to identify and get troubled children the help they needed quickly, the youth-suicide rate would surely plummet, he said.

In light of the societal forces driving children to suicide, Linda Taylor says, schools that take up the challenge have to be warned that they can't save every child.

Ms. Taylor, a counselor at the Los Angeles public schools' well-respected mental-health clinic, tells the story of a rambunctious 10-year-old girl she was treating years ago for attention deficit hyperactivity disorder. One evening, the child's mother told the 5th grader to clean up her room and not to come out until it was clean. The girl hanged herself from a belt in her bedroom closet.

"Everyone was devastated," said Ms. Taylor, who added that though the girl's father had recently died, the family was close and there was no clear sign the child had serious emotional problems. "We felt, my God, what did we miss? How did we not see what was coming?"

"Long-term lithium treatment may have an antisuicidal effect."

Lithium Treatment May Prevent Suicide

M.J. Friedrich

In the following viewpoint, M.J. Friedrich asserts that studies have shown that treatment with the drug lithium may prevent suicides that are the result of bipolar disorder. Unlike other mood-stabilizing drugs, the author claims that lithium has unique antisuicidal properties that affect the brain's serotonin levels, which are thought to play a major role in clinical depression and bipolar disorder. Therefore, expanding lithium treatment could reduce suicide rates. Friedrich is a frequent contributor to the *Journal of the American Medical Association*.

As you read, consider the following questions:

1. According to Friedrich, who revitalized interest in lithium for the treatment of mood disorders? How?
2. In the author's opinion, why did lithium fall out of favor in the medical community?
3. According to the author, which other drug besides lithium is prescribed as a mood stabilizer?

M.J. Friedrich, "Lithium: Proving Its Mettle for 50 Years," *The Journal of the American Medical Association*, vol. 281, June 23–30, 1999, pp. 2,271–73. Copyright © 1999 by the American Medical Association. Reproduced by permission.

In 1949, Australian psychiatrist John Cade published a paper detailing the value of using lithium salts to treat acute mania. Half a century later, lithium is still used in the treatment of mood disorders, particularly bipolar illness, and ongoing research is providing evidence for other benefits of the drug, including an antisuicidal effect. . . .

The therapeutic benefits of lithium were appreciated prior to Cade's research, said James W. Jefferson, MD, of the Lithium Information Center at Madison Institute of Medicine in Wisconsin. Lithium, an alkali metal and the lightest of the solid elements, was discovered in 1817. Not long after its discovery, physicians began to use the drug in the treatment of diseases such as gout, and in the latter part of the 1800s, British physician Sir Alfred Garrod detailed lithium's therapeutic merits in treating mood disorders, which he believed were caused by "gout retroceding to the head."

Claims for lithium's healing powers expanded in the late 1800s and early 1900s. Natural waters purported to contain high concentrations of this element were bottled and advertised as a cure for just about anything, said Jefferson. When these promises were not realized, lithium fell out of favor and came to be regarded as an "old and flourishing blunder in medicinal chemistry," as an anonymous pundit described it.

Cade's publication revitalized interest in lithium, and the drug gained acceptance worldwide in the next two decades. A delayed endorsement in the United States—the drug did not win US Food and Drug Administration approval until 1970—resulted in part from reports of lithium chloride's toxicity when used as a salt substitute for patients on low sodium diets. Although the therapeutic armamentarium of psychiatry had grown by this time, lithium was considered the most effective medication for stabilizing patients with bipolar disorder. . . .

Lithium's Antisuicidal Effect

Several researchers [have] discussed the problem of suicide and the possibility that long-term lithium treatment may have an antisuicidal effect. Kay Redfield Jamison, PhD, of Johns Hopkins University School of Medicine, pointed out the tremendous extent of suicide as a public health problem.

"World Bank studies on deaths in the world among men and women between the ages of 15 and 44 show that in women, suicide is the second leading cause of death, and in men it is fourth," she said. In the United States, suicide recently became the second most common cause of death among persons 15 to 24 years of age.

"Manic depression and depression carry with them elevated rates of suicide over the general population," said Jamison. "At least 90% of people who commit suicide have a diagnosable major psychiatric illness." However, illnesses that lead to suicide are consistently undertreated—a major problem that must be remedied by better diagnosis and aggressive treatment of these conditions.

But does aggressive treatment of affective disorders, regardless of the type of medication used, reduce the risk of suicide? "For many years it was a silent, self-evident assumption that rigorous treatment of depressive episodes would reduce suicide risk," said Bruno Müller-Oerlinghausen, MD, of the Free University of Berlin. "However, epidemiological studies, in spite of worldwide use of antidepressants, did not support such hope, which was a sobering and disappointing message."

Although evidence for an antisuicidal effect of antidepressants may be lacking, a number of findings accumulated in the last 15 years provide evidence that long-term lithium prophylaxis decreases the risk of suicide and normalizes mortality in patients with affective disorders, he said. An ad hoc analysis of findings from a German study called the Multicenter Study of Affective Psychoses (MAP) shows that lithium is superior to carbamazepine[1] in preventing suicide. In this large, prospective controlled trial, the prophylactic efficacy of these two mood stabilizers was studied for 2.5 years in 378 patients with bipolar, schizoaffective, and unipolar disorders. Among these subjects, 146 were randomized to take lithium and 139 took carbamazepine.

Although the protocol of MAP did not include an analysis of suicides and suicide attempts as end points, said Müller-Oerlinghausen, he and his colleagues analyzed suicidal acts in these groups after the study was completed. "A total of nine

1. An anticonvulsant used to treat epilepsy and depression.

suicide acts—four suicides and five suicide attempts—were observed," he said. "None occurred in the patients on lithium, and all occurred with patients taking carbamazepine, which is a statistically significant difference."

Unique Properties

Müller-Oerlinghausen speculated that if it is true that lithium alone among psychotropic compounds counteracts suicide risk in patients at high risk, it may be because lithium has unique serotoninergic[2] and antiaggressive properties. Lithium is marked by a combination of specific pharmacological properties, in particular serotonin agonistic effects, that other mood stabilizers and most antidepressants do not share, he explained. "It seems very likely that this serotoninergic action, possibly in connection with other brain effects, is related to lithium's very well-established antiaggressive effects in animals as well as humans. Such an effect would fit very well with the notion of suicidality and aggressivity as behavior caused by or related to deficits in serotoninergic neurotransmission."

Another more difficult question, said Müller-Oerlinghausen, is whether the antisuicidal effect of lithium acts independently of its general episode-reducing effect. He and his colleagues have found evidence for an independent suicide-preventive action of lithium in an analysis of patients at high risk for suicide seen at the Berlin Lithium Clinic. Although some patients were not classified as good responders in

---

2. Irregular serotonin levels in the brain are thought to cause depression and bipolar disorders.

terms of episode prevention, they did show reduced suicide rates, which investigators attributed to lithium, he said.

These findings, said Müller-Oerlinghausen, were replicated in a recent analysis of a high-risk subgroup of lithium-treated patients taken from the International Group for the Study of Lithium-Treated Patients (IGSLI) data pool. For this analysis, only patients with at least one suicide attempt before beginning lithium medication were selected. Patients were separated into three groups—excellent, questionable, and poor responders—on the basis of their response to the drug in terms of reduction of depressive inpatient episodes. Researchers found a statistically significant decrease in suicide attempts in all three groups, which, he said, supports the idea that lithium exerts a specific antisuicidal effect, independent of its episode-prevention effect. "Thus," said Müller-Oerlinghausen, "discontinuing lithium or switching to other medications in apparently nonresponding patients may be considered a rational step toward optimizing medication, but it may result in the death of the patient."

Major Implications for Suicide

Evidence supporting the suicide-preventive effect of lithium is important to consider, particularly in light of the changes in prescription patterns for [mood-stabilizing drugs such as] lithium, carbamazepine, and the anticonvulsant drug divalproex sodium that are occurring in the United States. According to Hopkins' Jamison, divalproex sodium recently became the number-one prescribed drug for bipolar illness in the United States. Such a change, she said, "has major public health implications for suicide, since we don't have any data that suggest that anticonvulsants have any effect against suicide."

Periodical Bibliography

The following articles have been selected to supplement the diverse views presented in this chapter.

Fox Butterfield	"Guns Used More for Suicide than Homicide," *New York Times*, October 17, 1999.
Thomas Curwen	"Psych-ache," *Los Angeles Times Magazine*, June 2, 2001.
David C. Helsel	"Does Your School Track the Suicidal Student?" *Clearing House*, November 1, 2001.
Randi Henderson	"Out of the Blues," *Common Boundary*, January/February 1998.
Linda Marsa	"Addicted to Suicide," *Self*, March 2002.
Iain Murray	"When It Comes to Suicide, Gun Control Is Not the Answer," *St. Louis Post-Dispatch*, December 14, 1999.
Dinitia Smith	"Evolving Answers to the Why of Suicide," *New York Times*, July 31, 1999.
Aparna Surendran	"Suicidal Behavior May Not Be Contagious After All," *Los Angeles Times*, July 23, 2001.
Julie Thomerson	"Violent Acts of Sadness: The Tragedy of Youth Suicide," *State Legislature*, May 2002.
Washington Post	"For Those Who Want Help, Treatment Can Be Effective," January 23, 2001.
Jan Marie Werblin	"The Link Between Depression and Suicide," *Professional Counselor*, June 2000.
Cheryl Wetzstein	"Preventing Suicide," *Insight on the News*, May 1, 2000.
Joni Woelfel	"Stars on the Blackest Night," *National Catholic Reporter*, December 8, 2000.

For Further Discussion

Chapter 1

1. Of the religious, philosophical, and traditional objections to suicide that Ernest van den Haag presents, which, in your opinion, is the most persuasive? Explain your answer.

2. Charles F. McKhann contends that rational suicide may be a sound and reasonable choice for some individuals suffering from terminal illness. However, Adina Wrobleski argues that rational suicide is a name given to the coerced suicides of the elderly, the seriously ill, and other individuals perceived as burdens on society. Who makes the more compelling argument? Use examples from the viewpoints in support of your answer.

Chapter 2

1. Jessica Portner asserts that many factors contribute to teen suicide. Which of the factors she discusses seem most important? Use specifics from the viewpoint and your own personal experiences to construct your answers.

2. Concerned Women for America (CWA) argues that homosexual activists manipulate statistics on homosexual teen suicide to promote their alternative lifestyle. Does Gary Remafedi's use of statistics convince you that teen suicide is a serious problem? Or, do you agree with CWA that such arguments merely exploit teen suicide as a way to promote homosexuality? Explain your answer, using specifics from the viewpoints.

3. David Satcher claims that depressed children and adolescents share a pessimistic mind-set in which they assume personal blame for negative events, expect that one negative event is part of a pattern of many other negative events, and interpret positive events in a negative fashion. Using specifics from the viewpoints and your own personal experiences, describe ways that children and adolescents can be influenced or encouraged to adopt such a mind-set.

4. Julian Guthrie states that although they may be academically successful, athletic, and popular, high-achieving teens are at risk for suicide because they are prone to be self-critical. In your opinion, does he adequately address the pressure that high-achieving teens may experience from their parents to succeed? Cite the viewpoint and examples from your own life to construct your answer.

Chapter 3

1. Faye Girsh argues that banning physician-assisted suicide harms terminally ill patients by driving desperate patients to end their lives in violent, traumatic ways. Marilyn Golden contends that lifting the ban on physician-assisted suicide would harm terminally ill patients because for-profit health care organizations would pressure doctors to deny treatment to the terminally ill and suggest assisted suicide instead. In your opinion, which author is more persuasive? Explain your answer.

2. Tom L. Beauchamp asserts that there is no difference between allowing patients to die by discontinuing medical treatment and actively helping them die by administering a lethal dose of medication because, in either case, the patient does not die from the underlying disease or condition. Kerby Anderson objects to Beauchamp's argument and claims there is a difference between letting death run its course and hastening death with a lethal drug because deliberately ending life is murder. In your opinion, who makes the more persuasive argument? Use examples from the viewpoints to support your answer.

3. Trudy Chun and Marian Wallace allege that proponents of physician-assisted suicide manipulate words such as "compassion" and "mercy" to advance their agenda. In your view, does Peter Rogatz manipulate language in his arguments for physician-assisted suicide? Use examples from the viewpoints to support your answer.

Chapter 4

1. The Evangelical Lutheran Church in America argues that suicide is a public health issue. On the other hand, Thomas Szasz claims that suicide is a personal action and not a public health concern. In your opinion, who makes the more persuasive argument? Use examples from the viewpoints to support your answer.

2. Gary Kleck presents several hypothetical scenarios in which a person is prevented from carrying out or dying from a suicide attempt because a gun was not available. In your view, which scenario is the most compelling? Which is the least compelling? Explain your answer.

3. This chapter lists several possible methods of preventing suicide. Of these possible methods, choose the one that you believe would most effectively prevent suicide and explain why. Use specifics from the viewpoints to support your answer.

Organizations to Contact

The editors have compiled the following list of organizations concerned with the issues debated in this book. The descriptions are derived from materials provided by the organizations. All have publications or information available for interested readers. The list was compiled on the date of publication of the present volume; the information provided here may change. Be aware that many organizations take several weeks or longer to respond to inquiries, so allow as much time as possible.

American Association of Suicidology (AAS)
4201 Connecticut Ave. NW, Suite 408, Washington, DC 20008
(202) 237-2280 • fax: (202) 237-2282
e-mail: info@suicidology.org • website: www.suicidology.org
The association is one of the largest suicide prevention organizations in the United States. It promotes the view that suicidal thoughts are almost always a symptom of depression and that suicide is almost never a rational decision. In addition to prevention of suicide, the group also works to increase public awareness about suicide and to help those grieving the death of a loved one to suicide. The association publishes the quarterly newsletters *American Association of Suicidology—Newslink* and *Surviving Suicide*, and the quarterly journal *Suicide and Life Threatening Behavior*.

American Foundation for Suicide Prevention (AFSP)
120 Wall St., 22nd Fl., New York, NY 10005
(888) 333-AFSP • fax: (212) 363-6237
e-mail: inquiry@afsp.org • website: www.afsp.org
Formerly known as the American Suicide Foundation, the AFSP supports scientific research on depression and suicide, educates the public and professionals on the recognition and treatment of depressed and suicidal individuals, and provides support programs for those coping with the loss of a loved one to suicide. It opposes the legalization of physician-assisted suicide. AFSP publishes a policy statement on physician-assisted suicide, the newsletter *Crisis*, and the quarterly *Lifesavers*.

American Life League (ALL)
PO Box 1350, Stafford, VA 22555
(540) 659-4171 • fax: (540) 659-2586
e-mail: whylife@all.org • website: www.all.org
The league believes that human life is sacred. It works to educate Americans about the dangers of all forms of euthanasia and op-

poses legislative efforts that would legalize or increase its incidence. It publishes the bimonthly pro-life magazine *Celebrate Life*, and distributes videos, brochures, and newsletters monitoring euthanasia-related developments.

American Psychiatric Association (APA)

1400 K St. NW, Washington, DC 20005
(888) 357-7924 • fax: (202) 682-6850
e-mail: apa@psych.org • website: www.psych.org

An organization of psychiatrists dedicated to studying the nature, treatment, and prevention of mental disorders, the APA helps create mental health policies, distributes information about psychiatry, and promotes psychiatric research and education. It publishes the *American Journal of Psychiatry* and *Psychiatric News* monthly.

American Psychological Association (APA)

750 First St. NE, Washington, DC 20002-4242
(800) 374-2721 • fax: (202) 336-5708
e-mail: public.affairs@apa.org • website: www.apa.org

This professional organization for psychologists aims to "advance psychology as a science, as a profession, and as a means of promoting human welfare." It produces numerous publications, including the book *Adolescent Suicide: Assessment and Intervention*, the report "Researcher Links Perfectionism in High Achievers with Depression and Suicide," and the online guide *Warning Signs—A Violence Prevention Guide for Youth*.

Compassion in Dying Federation

PMB 415, 6312 SW Capitol Hwy., Portland, OR 97201
(503) 221-9556 • fax: (503) 228-9610
e-mail: info@compassionindying.org
website: www.compassionindying.org

The mission of Compassion in Dying Federation is to provide national leadership for client service, legal advocacy, and public education to improve pain and symptom management, increase patient empowerment and self-determination, and expand end-of-life choices to include aid-in-dying for terminally ill, mentally competent adults. It publishes periodic newsletters, press releases, and testimonials.

Depression and Related Affective Disorders Association (DRADA)

Meyer 3-181, 600 N. Wolfe St., Baltimore, MD 21287-7381
(410) 955-4647: Baltimore, MD
(202) 955-5800: Washington, DC
e-mail: drada@jhmi.edu • website: www.drada.org

DRADA, a nonprofit organization that works in cooperation with the Department of Psychiatry at the Johns Hopkins University School of Medicine, seeks to alleviate the suffering arising from depression and manic depression by assisting self-help groups, providing education and information, and lending support to research programs. It publishes the report "A Look at . . . Suicide, a Relentless and Underrated Foe" and the book *Night Falls Fast— Understanding Suicide*.

Euthanasia Prevention Coalition BC
103-2609 Westview Dr., Suite 126
North Vancouver, BC V7N 4N2 Canada
(604) 794-3772 • fax: (604) 794-3960
e-mail: info@epc.bc.ca • website: www.epc.bc.ca

The Euthanasia Prevention Coalition opposes the promotion or legalization of euthanasia and assisted suicide. The coalition's purpose is to educate the public on risks associated with the promotion of euthanasia, increase public awareness of alternative methods for the relief of suffering, and to represent the vulnerable as an advocate before the courts on issues of euthanasia and related subjects. Press releases from the coalition are available at its website.

Foundation of Thanatology
630 W. 168th St., New York, NY 10032
(212) 928-2066 • fax: (914) 793-0813

This organization of health, theology, psychology, and social science professionals is devoted to scientific and humanist inquiries into health, loss, grief, and bereavement. The foundation coordinates professional, educational, and research programs concerned with mortality and grief. It publishes the periodicals *Advances in Thanatology* and *Archives of the Foundation of Thanatology*.

The Hemlock Society
PO Box 101810, Denver, CO 80250
(800) 247-7421 • (303) 639-1202 • fax: (303) 639-1224
e-mail: hemlock@hemlock.org • website: www.hemlock.org

The society believes that terminally ill individuals have the right to commit suicide. The society publishes books on suicide, death, and dying, including *Final Exit*, a guide for those suffering with terminal illnesses and considering suicide. The Hemlock Society also publishes the newsletter *TimeLines*.

International Anti-Euthanasia Task Force (IAETF)
PO Box 760, Steubenville, OH 43952
(740) 282-3810
e-mail: info@iaetf.org • website: www.internationaltaskforce.org
The task force opposes euthanasia, assisted suicide, and policies that threaten the lives of the medically vulnerable. IAETF publishes fact sheets and position papers on euthansia-related topics in addition to the bimonthly newsletter, *IAETF Update*. It analyzes the policies and legislation concerning medical and social work organizations and files *amicus curaie* briefs in major "right-to-die" cases.

National Depressive and Manic-Depressive Association (NDMDA)
730 N. Franklin St., Suite 501, Chicago, IL 60610-7204
(800) 826-3632 • (312) 642-0049 • fax: (312) 642-7243
e-mail: questions@ndmda.org • website: www.ndmda.org
The association provides support and advocacy for patients with depression and manic-depressive illness. It seeks to persuade the public that these disorders are biochemical in nature and to end the stigmatization of people who suffer from them. It publishes the quarterly *NDMDA Newsletter* and various books and pamphlets.

National Foundation for Depressive Illness (NAFDI)
PO Box 2257, New York, NY 10116
(800) 239-1265
website: www.depression.org
NAFDI informs the public, health care providers, and corporations about depression and manic-depressive illness. It promotes the view that these disorders are physical illnesses treatable with medication, and it believes that such medication should be made readily available to those who need it. The foundation maintains several toll-free telephone lines and distributes brochures, bibliographies, and literature on the symptoms of and treatments for depression and manic-depressive illness. It also publishes the quarterly newsletter *NAFDI News*.

National Hospice Foundation (NHF)
1700 Diagonal Rd., Suite 625, Alexandria, VA 22314
(703) 516-4928 • fax: (703) 837-1233
e-mail: info@nhpco.org • website: www.hospiceinfo.org
The organization works to educate the public about the benefits of hospice care for the terminally ill and their families. It seeks to promote the idea that with the proper care and pain medication, the terminally ill can live out their lives comfortably and in the

company of their families. The organization opposes euthanasia and assisted suicide. It conducts educational and training programs for administrators and caregivers in numerous aspects of hospice care. It publishes the quarterlies *Hospice Journal* and *Hospice Magazine*, as well as books and monographs.

Partnership for Caring (PFC)
1620 Eye Street NW, Suite 202, Washington, DC 20006
(800) 989-9455 • fax: (202) 296-8352 • (202) 296-8071
e-mail: pfc@partnershipforcaring.org
website: www.partnershipforcaring.org

Partnership for Caring (formerly Choice in Dying) is a national, not-for-profit organization dedicated to fostering communication about complex end-of-life decisions among individuals, their loved ones, and health care professionals. The organization invented living wills in 1967 and provides the only national hotline to respond to families and patients during end-of-life crises. PFC also provides educational materials, public and professional education, and ongoing monitoring of changes in state and federal right-to-die legislation.

SA\VE—Suicide Awareness\Voices of Education
PO Box 24507, Minneapolis, MN 55424-0507
(612) 946-7998
e-mail: save@winternet.com • website: www.save.org

SA\VE works to prevent suicide and to help those grieving after the suicide of a loved one. Its members believe that brain diseases, such as depression, should be detected and treated promptly because they can result in suicide. In addition to pamphlets and the book *Suicide: Survivors—A Guide for Those Left Behind*, the organization publishes the quarterly newsletter *Voices*.

Suicide Information and Education Centre (SIEC)
#201, 1615 10th Ave. SW, Calgary, AB T3C 0J7 Canada
(403) 245-3900 • fax: (403) 245-0299
e-mail: siec@suicideinfo.ca • website: www.suicideinfo.ca

The Suicide Information and Education Centre acquires and distributes information on suicide prevention. It maintains a computerized database, a free mailing list, and a document delivery service. It publishes the quarterly *Current Awareness Bulletin* and the monthly *SIEC Clipping Service*.

Bibliography of Books

Leroy Aarons — *Prayers for Bobby: A Mother's Coming to Terms with the Suicide of Her Gay Son.* San Francisco: Harper, 1996.

David Aldridge — *Suicide: The Tragedy of Hopelessness.* London: Jessica Kingsley, 1998.

Bev Cobain — *When Nothing Else Matters Anymore: A Survival Guide for Depressed Teens.* Minneapolis, MN: Free Spirit, 1998.

Timothy J. Demy and Gary P. Stewart, eds. — *Suicide: A Christian Response: Crucial Considerations for Choosing Life.* Grand Rapids, MI: Kregel, 1998.

John Donnelly, ed. — *Suicide: Right or Wrong?* 2nd. ed. Amherst, NY: Prometheus Books, 1998.

Carla Fine — *No Time to Say Goodbye: Surviving the Suicide of a Loved One.* New York: Main Street Books, 1999.

Kathleen Foley and Herbert Hendin — *The Case Against Assisted Suicide: For the Right to End-of-Life Care.* Baltimore, MD: Johns Hopkins University Press, 2002.

Louise Harmon — *Fragments on the Deathwatch.* Boston: Beacon Press, 1998.

Keith Hawton and Kees van Heeringen — *The International Handbook of Suicide and Assisted Suicide.* New York: Wiley, 2000.

Herbert Hendin — *Seduced by Death: Doctors, Patients, and the Dutch Cure.* New York: W.W. Norton, 1998.

James Hillman — *Suicide and the Soul.* Woodstock, CT: Spring Publications, 1997.

Derek Humphry and Mary Clement — *Freedom to Die: People, Politics and the Right-to-Die Movement.* New York: St. Martin's Press, 1998.

Kay Redfield Jamison — *Night Falls Fast: Understanding Suicide.* New York: Vintage Books, 2000.

Wanda Y. Johnson — *Youth Suicide: The School's Role in Prevention and Response.* Bloomington, IN: Phi Delta Kappa, 1999.

David Lester — *Why People Kill Themselves: A 2000 Summary of Research on Suicide.* 3rd ed. Springfield, IL: C.C. Thomas, 2000.

Roger S. Magnusson and Peter H. Ballis — *Angels of Death: Exploring the Euthanasia Underground.* New Haven, CT: Yale University Press, 2002.

Eric Marcus	*Why Suicide? Answers to 200 of the Most Frequently Asked Questions About Suicide, Attempted Suicide, and Assisted Suicide.* San Francisco: Harper, 1996.
Ronald W. Maris et al.	*Comprehensive Textbook of Suicidology.* New York: Guilford Press, 2000.
Charles F. McKhann	*A Time to Die: The Place for Physician Assistance.* New Haven, CT: Yale University Press, 1999.
James M. Murphy	*Coping with Teen Suicide.* New York: Rosen Publishing, 1999.
Paul R. Robbins	*Adolescent Suicide.* Jefferson, NC: McFarland & Co., 1998.
Jay F. Rosenberg	*Thinking Clearly About Death.* 2nd ed. Indianapolis, IN: Hackett Pub. Co., 1998.
Edwin S. Shneidman	*Comprehending Suicide: Landmarks in Twentieth-Century Suicidology.* Washington, DC: American Psychological Association, 2001.
Edwin S. Shneidman	*The Suicidal Mind.* New York: Oxford University Press, 1998.
Margaret Somerville	*Death Talk: The Case Against Euthanasia and Physician-Assisted Suicide.* Ithaca, NY: McGill-Queen's University Press, 2001.
Elsebeth Steganer and Egon Steganer	*Disease, Pain, and Suicidal Behavior.* New York: Haworth Medical Press, 1998.
Geo Stone	*Suicide and Attempted Suicide: Methods and Consequences.* New York: Carroll & Graf, 2001.
Lois Syder and Arthur L. Caplan, eds.	*Assisted Suicide: Finding Common Ground.* Bloomington: Indiana University Press, 2002.
Thomas Szasz	*Fatal Freedom: The Ethics and Politics of Suicide.* Westport, CT: Praeger, 1999.
Michael Uhlmann, ed.	*Last Rights? Assisted Suicide and Euthanasia Debated.* Grand Rapids, MI: William B. Eerdmans, 1998.
Danuta Wasserman, ed.	*Suicide: An Unnecessary Death.* London: Martin Dunitz, 2001.
James L. Werth Jr., ed.	*Contemporary Perspectives on Rational Suicide.* Philadelphia: Taylor and Francis, 1999.
Sue Woodman	*Last Rights: The Struggle over the Right to Die.* New York: Plenum Trade, 1998.

Index

JIM THORPE
20TH-CENTURY JOCK

ROBERT LIPSYTE

HarperCollins*Publishers*

Acknowledgments

Every effort has been made to locate the copyright holders of all copyrighted materials and secure the necessary permissions to reproduce them. In the event of any questions arising as to their use, the publisher will be glad to make changes in future printings and editions.

In addition, the publisher acknowledges the following institutions and individuals for the illustrations provided to us: Page viii: Courtesy of Southwest Museum, Los Angeles, California; page 8: The Warner Collection of Gulf States Paper Corp., Tuscaloosa, Alabama; page 12: Woolaroc Museum, Bartlesville, Oklahoma; page 19: Francis G. Mayer/Photo Researchers; page 26: The Bettmann Archive; pages 32, 33, 41, 48, 57, 59, 61, 64, 66, 74, 75, 79: Cumberland County Historical Society, Carlisle, Pennsylvania; pages 40, 63, 81, 84, and 87: Hall of Fame/NFL Photos; page 92: UPI/Bettmann; page 94: Rick Hill/Lacrosse USA, Inc.

Jim Thorpe
20th-Century Jock

Library of Congress Cataloging-in-Publication Data
Lipsyte, Robert.
  Jim Thorpe : 20th-century jock / by Robert Lipsyte.
    p.   cm. — (Superstar lineup)
  Summary: A biography of the American Indian known as one of the best all-round athletes in history for his accomplishments as an Olympic medal winner and as an outstanding professional football and baseball player.
  ISBN 0-06-022988-8. — ISBN 0-06-022989-6 (lib. bdg.)
  1. Thorpe, Jim, 1887–1953—Juvenile literature.   2. Athletes—United States—Biography—Juvenile literature.   3. Indians of North America—Biography—Juvenile literature.   4. Athletes, Indian—United States—Juvenile literature.
  [1. Thorpe, Jim, 1887–1953.   2. Athletes.   3. Indians of North America—Biography.]   I. Title.   II. Series.
GV697.T5L57   1993
796'092—dc20   92-44069
[B]   CIP
                                                                         AC

Typography by Tom Starace
1   2   3   4   5   6   7   8   9   10

First Edition

★

This page is for my team.

Robert Warren, my editor, and Theron Raines, my agent, were smart and steady coaches.

Kathy Sulkes, my wife, was the photo researcher who never quit.

Professor Peter Levine of Michigan State University checked the manuscript with his Captain History eye.

Benjamin Kabak, a student at the Horace Mann–Barnard School in New York, was a very helpful reader.

And without the editing, writing and research of Sam Lipsyte, there would be no pages after this one.

★

Jim Thorpe

In 1884, three years before Jim was born, this Yuman Runner of the Southwest was poised to run a marathon at a moment's notice and deliver a message that could save his Nation.

Prologue

The first athletes of America were the Runners of the native Nations, the people who have come to be called Indians. These Runners were fast and dependable and smart. They memorized messages that might take hours to tell, and they remembered them for days at a time, while running through unfamiliar, sometimes hostile territory. Then, after delivering the long message, a Runner might even be expected to help negotiate a peace treaty, work out an alliance for war, offer advice in a sensitive political situation or take another long message back home.

The Runners were heroes, admired for their intelligence, their dedication and their athletic skills, which they kept at peak performance by regular training. It was a full-time job; they ran thousands of miles in preparation for their journeys, studied with their tribal wisdom keepers and ate vegetables, grains and the meat of swift

creatures such as antelope and quail.

Sometimes they competed against each other in public races, betting clothes and jewelry. In their daily lives of exercise and careful nutrition and relaxation, of listening to older Runners and to the Chiefs, they were like modern athletes. Yet the importance of their duties made them similar to modern diplomats and journalists. They bound their world together with their savvy and their speed.

They ran the Iroquois Trail in what is now upstate New York. They found ways to ford the swollen spring rivers of the Midwest, and they made their own paths through dense southern forest. They clawed up the sheer rock cliffs of the Pacific Coast.

In 1680, in the cool of the Southwest night, pairs of Pueblo Indian Runners coursed over the high desert in what is now northern New Mexico, carrying messages coded into carved sticks and knotted strings. Their mission was to signal the Pueblo Indians to rise up against the Spanish colonists who had taken control of their villages, burned their sacred masks and flogged their religious leaders. For the Runners, discov-

ery meant instant death. But timidity was worse; if they were late, if the attack wasn't precisely coordinated, the revolt would fail and thousands of Indians would be killed. The Runners were successful, and so was the Pueblo uprising; it was an American revolution a century before *the* American Revolution.

Sometimes Indian Runners carried heroic messages, and sometimes they tried to stop foolish slaughter. In 1790, the Creeks and the Choctaws, in an attempt to decide who had the rights to trap beaver on a pond of the Noxubee River in Mississippi, played winner-take-all "bump hips," the game that became lacrosse. As the game was often played in those days, there were hundreds to a side, and the goals were miles apart. The brawling contest soon became a bloody riot; hundreds might have died except for the speed of couriers who brought the head Chiefs to settle the dispute.

In 1890, Runners made their way to Washington, D.C., to tell the Indian version of the massacre at Wounded Knee. More than a hundred Indians, including many women and children, were killed at the Pine Ridge Reservation

in South Dakota when U.S. cavalry troopers began firing into the spiritual gathering called "Ghost Dancing."

Indian athletes competed against whites, and because Indians had been hyped by newspaper reporters and cavalrymen as such powerful savages, it was big news when a white athlete beat an Indian. In 1844, in Hoboken, New Jersey, 30,000 whites cheered the New York carpenter who beat John Steeprock, a Seneca, in a $1,000 long-distance run. The sportswriter who covered the story declared the victory a triumph of white superiority.

Tom Longboat, an Onondaga (known as "The Bronze Mercury" when he won the 1907 Boston Marathon), and Louis Tewanima, a Hopi, ran in the 1908 Olympics. Ellison ("Tarzan") Brown won the Boston in 1936, and then went on to the Berlin Olympics as a member of the U.S. team. In 1964, Billy Mills, an Oglala Sioux, became the first American to win the 10,000-meter Olympic championship. There were fine major-league baseball players as Louis Sockalexis (it is said that the Cleveland Indians were named after him); Charles Bender, who

was elected to the Hall of Fame; John Meyers; and Allie Reynolds.

But the most famous Indian athlete, and perhaps the greatest all-around male athlete in American history, was more than a sporting hero, and his victories were more than marks in a record book.

Jim Thorpe was a spirit of his time, a symbol of a country flexing its muscles in the world arena, a person who would not be beaten down; he was an athletic pioneer, but he also followed a path blazed by centuries of Runners for the Nation. The message he carried was his own story.

1

An Indian who is as bad as a white man could not live in our Nation. . . .

—BLACK HAWK

The graceful, restless boy Bright Path had hair as black and glistening as a raven's wing. His eyes were merry and bold. His jutting chin was square and strong. The old people watched him roam the reservation and reminded each other that this boy carried the blood of Black Hawk, their legendary warrior chief. The boy was half white, and his parents, the Thorpes, called him Jim more often than they called him Bright Path. But the old people filled the boy's head with tales of his great-uncle, who had led them against United States soldiers in the most painful, the proudest time in their history.

The Black Hawk War was short and bloody, a disaster for the Sac and Fox Nation. The natives lost the land they farmed and hunted along

the Mississippi River in what is now Illinois and Iowa.

The war began in 1832 after some members of the Nation sold land to the white American government without permission of the Sac and Fox council, which had ruled that land was not an individual's to sell—all the land belonged to all the people together. There were reports that the sellers had been bribed with whiskey.

The Nation split. Some argued for peaceful acceptance of what had unfortunately happened; after all, the U.S. Army had the firepower. These people were considered sellouts by others, who begged their most famous combat veteran, Black Hawk, to lead their resistance.

Black Hawk, black-haired, jut-jawed, was wary of more battle. He had fought alongside Tecumseh, the visionary Shawnee leader who had tried to unite all American natives into one great army. Black Hawk knew that the troopers had the guns and that too many Indians were ready to make a separate peace. But in the end, he listened to the war drums and fought for his homeland.

The great Sac and Fox chief Black Hawk died a half century before Jim was born, but old-timers on the reservation saw the warrior's pride in the boy's eyes and his wiry strength in the boy's body. They believed Jim was a blood descendent.

Even though he was betrayed by allies who promised assistance, and hampered by mutiny and conflict in his own camp, Black Hawk won

minerals, housing space. Toward the end of the nineteenth century, the U.S. government didn't even bother bribing Chiefs or getting them drunk enough to sign bad treaties; it just took the land.

The Sac and Fox Nation was dispersed. Some families found ways to stay in Kansas, while others wound their way back to the original homelands along the Mississippi and moved in with local tribes. The most adventurous, including the Thorpes, set out for Indian Territory, in what is now Oklahoma.

Hiram P. Thorpe grew up as raw and hard as the frontier, a top rider, hunter, fighter, drinker. He had a short temper and a big heart. He liked to invite his neighbors over for summer picnics behind the family cabin. Years later, Jim Thorpe would remember sitting in the cool twilight with the other children as the men raced horses and wrestled. Hiram was astonishingly quick and strong and daring. The games grew fierce, and Hiram usually won.

Hiram became a trader and sold whiskey to other Indians. This was illegal. Heavy drinking was already a serious problem in many Indian

communities. If Hiram was as greedy as most traders, he probably watered the booze and added spices and tobacco juice to give it bite. It was called "firewater."

Hiram fathered at least nineteen children. His third wife, Charlotte Vieux, was also of "mixed blood," the large, strong daughter of a wealthy merchant of French descent and a Potawatomie woman. A devout Roman Catholic, Charlotte demanded that her children be baptized and attend Mass.

On May 22, 1887, she gave birth to twin boys. Disease was rampant and medicine scarce in Indian Territory (now Oklahoma)—several years earlier, Hiram and Charlotte's twin baby girls had died—but Jim and Charlie seemed healthy and strong.

Moments after James Francis Thorpe was born, his mother glanced out the window as the morning sun cut a trail of light toward the cabin door. That's how the world's greatest athlete got his Indian name: Wa-tho-huck, Bright Path.

2

"Extermination" is the battle cry now.
—THE NEW YORK TIMES

Wa-tho-huck was an optimistic name for a Native American born near the end of the nineteenth century. White America was pushing west, clearing the land to lay railroad track, dig mines, build cities. Many whites considered Indians to be merely an annoying, even dangerous, form of wildlife in the way of growth and profit.

Newspapers and cheap magazines were filled with fantasies of the "bloodthirsty Redskins" who roamed "wild" in the western paradise, worshipping birds and kidnapping white children after murdering their parents. Imagine the readers back east, many of them immigrants from Europe crammed into tiny rooms in crowded cities, scrabbling to survive by working

in locked sweatshops and filthy factories. How could they understand the lives of the Thorpes, also working hard to survive, but on vast stretches of land under a big sky? No wonder so many otherwise decent Americans had no argument with local policies on the "Indian problem," which at one time included a $500 reward in Arizona for each "buck Indian's scalp."

"This reward system," *The New York Times* explained to its readers,

> *while it may seem savage and brutal to the Northern and Eastern sentimentalist, is looked upon in this section as the only means possible of ridding Arizona of the murderous Apache. . . .*
>
> *From time immemorial all border countries have offered rewards for bear and wolf scalps and other animals that destroyed the pioneer's stock or molested his family. . . . 'Extermination' is the battle cry now. . . .*

Actually, the so-called "exterminationists" were a small minority, and many white Americans did protest the inhumane treatment of natives. But most whites were conditioned to

believe that Indians were a subhuman species who would die out because their time was over. Many politicians, business leaders and homesteaders believed in the "humane" way of wiping out the Indians, and that was to turn them into coppery-tinted white people—shorthaired, English speaking, churchgoing. Although the Indian school movement included exploiters who thought the savages could be tamed into cheap labor—maids, farmhands—for local settlers, the best of the schools were run by serious educators who thought the Indians' "native intelligence" could be productively channeled.

As more schools were set up, and more settlers and financiers poured into Indian Territory to gear up for Oklahoma statehood, Indians grew more concerned that their old ways would be completely forgotten and that the strength of the Indian community, extended families taking care of their own, would be destroyed.

Hiram and Charlotte apparently tried to give their children the best of both Indian and white cultures; they made sure they could read and write English, but also know about their Indian customs and languages. In later years, Jim

would be able to move easily in both worlds.

Jim and Charlie, inseparable friends in the way twins often are, also learned the skills and games their father had mastered. They spent long days hunting and fishing, and some nights Hiram would take them deep into the woods so they could learn to live off the land. Jim became a good trapper and sometimes would disappear for a day or two alone, hunting and wandering through the forest.

They learned Indian games such as "fox and geese," a contest like jacks, and "crooked path," which was like "follow the leader." Jim and Charlie heard stories about the Indian Runners, those first great athletes of America, and about the old days when hundreds to a side played the ball game called "tewaarathon" by the Haudenosaunee (Iroquois) and "baggataway" by the Algonquins, the game the French would later name "lacrosse" because the shape of the "otchi," or stick, reminded them of a bishop's crozier.

But because Hiram and Charlotte wanted their children to survive in both worlds, they sent the six-year-old twins to the nearest free In-

The game was called "bump hips" by the Iroquois, who believed it was a gift from the Creator. In early days, hundreds played on a side and the field might be miles long. A game played by many Indian Nations, it was the first team sport many Europeans ever saw. The French named it "lacrosse" because they thought the stick resembled a bishop's staff.

dian Agency boarding school, to learn "white ways." Charlie, smaller, darker and more reserved than his brother, was a careful student who earned high grades. Jim, energetic and playful, mainly excelled at recess.

The school was twenty-five miles away, and the students—more than fifty children of differ-

ent ages and from different tribes—lived in dormitories. Girls and boys were separated. They studied reading and writing, arithmetic, geography and history (the white man's version, from the Pilgrims on). Afternoons were spent in the woodworking or tailor shops, or doing farm chores.

Robert Wheeler, in his biography of Thorpe *Pathway to Glory,* quotes one of Jim's classmates, Art Wakolee:

> *It took us a long time to learn our lessons in kindergarten because most of the teachers had very little patience with the Indian children. Some of the teachers were kind while others were very mean. We got a licking many times when we could not spell a simple word. As a result, we could not learn very much because most of us were afraid of our teacher.*

Before they learned the white ways, however, they had to unlearn their Indian ways.

"They told us Indian ways were bad," Sun Elk, a Taos Pueblo, remembered of his days at the famous Carlisle Indian School in Pennsylva-

nia in Peter Nabokov's *Native American Testimony*.
"They said we must get civilized. I remember
that word too. It means 'be like the white man.'
I am willing to be like the white man but I did
not believe Indian ways were wrong."

Maybe Jim did not believe it either, or
maybe he was just bored in school; his backside
ached on the hard wooden chair; voices droned
stale facts and figures into his throbbing head
while outside the window the sun shone down
on the grass and the trees. Whatever the reason,
Jim was no teacher's pet. He shot at flies with
rubber bands, did somersaults in class, farted at
the teacher.

He escaped several times, sneaking out of the
three-story brick dorm and shedding his uniform as he ran home to an angry Hiram, who
would throw his sobbing son in the wagon and
drive him back to school. Once, after an escape,
Hiram returned to his farm after dropping Jim
off at the school only to find Jim had escaped
again and run the twenty-five miles to beat his
father home.

Jim eventually settled down. His older broth-
ers encouraged him to stay in school, and he be-

gan to enjoy some of the games they played in their free time, especially a new game that was becoming increasingly popular throughout the country, a Colonial cousin of cricket called "baseball." Jim was a deft fielder with a powerful throwing arm, speedy on the bases and a slugger at bat. The game had started as an upper-class sport, but immigrant groups took it over, and by the time Jim was playing, there were professional leagues and fans were arguing whether German Americans or Irish Americans were more "naturally suited" to the game.

But it was Jim's love for his brother Charlie, not baseball, that kept him in school. The twins were very different, yet they understood each other in ways no one else could. Jim, robust and adventurous, and Charlie, thoughtful and calm, seemed to complement each other. Jim protected Charlie from the bullies. Charlie helped Jim with his schoolwork. They shared secrets, they kept each other's spirits up.

Then pneumonia and smallpox swept through the school in the spring of 1897. Charlie died. Nothing could console Jim. Almost ten,

Bright Path grew dark and sad. Even the games were no longer fun. He ran away again.

When Jim was eleven, Hiram decided to send him to a distant boarding school. He is supposed to have said to his son: "I'm going to send you so far, you will never find your way home again."

3

I want him to go make something of himself, for he cannot do it here.
—HIRAM P. THORPE

Homesick and mourning Charlie, Jim was twelve when he arrived at the Haskell Indian School outside Lawrence, Kansas, in 1899. Haskell was renowned for its ethic of work, discipline and, most of all, assimilation into "white ways." Like all the government-run Indian boarding schools, Haskell was free. After Carlisle, in Pennsylvania, Haskell was the most famous Indian school in the country.

Jim kept his dark suit clean and his buttons shiny as he trudged from class in the morning to the shops in the afternoon, learning to bake bread, sew clothes and wire electricity. The rules were strict: no roughhousing, no tardiness, no romance between students. And never, ever, speak in your native language.

Students from the same tribe were not allowed to room together. Often, youngsters would return to their reservations after years at Haskell unable to talk with their families. Even if they relearned the old language, they were treated like aliens.

As the Pueblo Chiefs told Sun Elk's father: "He has no hair. He has no blankets. He cannot even speak our language and he has a strange smell. He is not one of us."

When Jim arrived at Haskell, the sports craze was football, which had begun thirty years before as a brutal, sometimes deadly game played at elite Eastern colleges. (President Theodore Roosevelt called for safety measures after his son was knocked unconscious in a game between Harvard and Yale.)

As football's popularity spread, so did a national debate; some said it built character, others that it taught violence. Its language was military; after all the quarterback was a "field general" and teams "crushed," "routed" and "demolished" their "foes."

What kind of character football builds is a question people still argue today. But in 1899,

By 1880 football was an established college sport, less organized than today but at least as brutal. Then as now, some people thought it had no place in higher education, while others saw it as a great way for less-privileged students to get ahead.

as Americans began to imagine themselves the greatest nation on earth, football was seen as a fierce and dramatic game that only Americans played. It was easy for Jim to catch the football fever. Haskell encouraged the sport as another way to turn Indians into Americans.

The hero of Haskell was Chauncey Archiquette, star quarterback and honor student. Chauncey shouted out pointers from the sidelines as Jim and the other younger boys fought over a rag-stuffed cloth ball, crashing into each other, mimicking the stances and moves of their varsity models.

For Jim, football was recess in a long, strange year of so many new faces and new routines. He missed Charlie, and he missed home. He kept himself busy with chores and schoolwork. He had just begun to settle into Haskell when he received word that his father had been badly wounded in a hunting accident.

Jim walked right off the Haskell grounds in his work clothes and hopped on a freight train, only the train was going in the wrong direction. When he realized his mistake, he jumped off and walked for two weeks back the other way.

He returned home to a healed and raging Hiram. "How could you run away again!" his father exploded, hurling his son to the ground. Hiram and Jim felt betrayed by each other; the father because his son had walked away from his future, and the son because his father reacted so angrily to his concerned love.

Jim hung around for a while, but the tension was thick. In the small house, Jim felt in the way of his younger brother and sister. His mother, Charlotte, was pregnant again. He helped with the chores and sometimes attended the one-room public school that had just opened nearby. But he was restless and bored.

One morning, Jim headed out for the Texas border. There were no uniforms or school bells out in cattle country, just hard work. Jim built fences and broke horses, skills Hiram had taught him. He was thirteen, scrawny but strong, and he was out on his own.

After a while, he grew tired of the range life. The days were long, the nights were cold and he was surrounded by lonely men who worked to exhaustion for liquor money. Being a cowboy was never glamorous work. He saved his wages

to buy a team of horses that he rode home and gave to Hiram as a peace offering and a way of showing his father that he was now a man who could take care of himself, who didn't need to go to school. Hiram invited Jim to stay and help with the family.

But the family had changed. While Jim was away, his mother had died in childbirth, along with the baby. Hiram soon married his fourth wife, a white woman named Julia. It was crowded in the house, and the relationship with his new stepmother was strained.

One of his few pleasures those days back in Oklahoma was baseball, marathon games played out in the fields on Saturdays or before supper during the week. Jim's months on the range had paid off; he was incredibly strong for his age. Recruiters from semipro teams and colleges came to see him blast the ball over barn roofs, fire pinpoint throws to home from deep center or pitch humming fastballs. He was only fifteen, and raw, but also smart and talented. He had a gift for games.

Hiram dreamed of something better than prairie baseball for Jim, and he wrote a letter to

the Carlisle Indian School in Pennsylvania asking for their help. It was even farther away than Haskell, and more prestigious. It was probably on the basis of Hiram's plea, which must have touched the school's sense of purpose, that Jim was accepted.

"I want him to go make something of himself," Hiram wrote, "for he cannot do it here."

4 I believe in immersing the Indians in our civilization, and when we get them under holding them there until they are thoroughly soaked.
—RICHARD HENRY PRATT

On Jim's first day at the Carlisle Indian School, in early February 1904, he and the other new students were herded into the barbershop for short haircuts. For some, it meant losing long traditional braids they had worn all their lives, symbols of their tribal identity. For Jim, who had been through all this before, it was probably just a haircut.

The students were issued military-style uniforms. Afterward, teachers handed out slates for the first test: Write your name. This meant, of course, your Christian name. If you didn't have one, the school would make one up for you. Maybe it should have been called a *de*-Indian school.

The Indian schools' first step in turning their young students into red-skinned white folks was to cut their hair and put them in uniforms. This is what a group of Chiricuhua Apaches from Florida looked like when they arrived at Carlisle in November of 1883.

Finally, boys and girls were separated and organized into military formations, with student officers in charge of marching them through the Carlisle campus, an old Army compound of abandoned barracks, to the main parade grounds, where Colonel Richard Henry Pratt, the founder and principal, addressed them.

Jim and his classmates had probably already heard stories about him from the older students. Pratt had been a famous Indian fighter. He might have hunted many of their relatives back

And this is what they looked like four months later.

in the 1860's and 1870's. Pratt had helped train and lead the Tenth Cavalry, the so-called Buffalo Soldiers, African-American troopers commanded by white officers. In 1879, he had opened Carlisle; there were now about one thousand students.

As Pratt explained to his new students, his experiences with his own black soldiers and their Indian scouts, and with captured Indian warriors, had convinced him that all people were created equal, that whites were not superior to blacks or reds. He believed that people of color, especially Native Americans, had not only

been treated unjustly but underrated as well.

Indians, he told the new students, because of their intelligence, character and adaptability, could flourish in the white world if given the chance. And the purpose of Carlisle was to give them that chance—their only hope of survival, according to Pratt.

"I believe in immersing the Indians in our civilization," he had written, "and when we get them under holding them there until they are thoroughly soaked. There is a great amount of sentiment among Indian teachers but in the work of breaking up Indian customs there is no room for sentiment."

Jim was no stranger to these notions—his old schools had been based on them, too—but he braced himself for an especially grueling first year. The awkwardness and uncertainty of being a new boy were familiar, but now there was the added intensity of this Pratt and his obsession for assimilation.

The rules were stricter here and the punishment for breaking them more severe, too. Students were kept occupied with class and chores all the time and very rarely allowed to leave the

campus. Even though some students were in their late teens and early twenties, sex was outlawed: Caught, you were sent home in disgrace.

In some ways, life was easier at Carlisle for Jim than for many of the other youngsters; he was physically strong and tough-minded, he had survived on his own out in the world and he was half white—there was less Indian that had to be drummed out of him.

Yet, for some of those same reasons, Carlisle life was harsher on Jim; he knew what freedom was—he had always rebelled against authority—and it must have been hard for him to accept the Carlisle credo that there was something wrong with him, his Indian side, that needed to be scraped away.

Later that year, his father, Hiram, died from a snakebite. Sad and lonely, Jim decided to stick it out in his new home.

One activity at Carlisle that Jim hated were the "outings." Colonel Pratt believed that to truly understand white ways, the students needed contact with whites in a close, daily environment. They were sent off for months at a time to live with and work for local families. It

would be a chance to perfect their English and learn how to deal with whites. Despite a screening process to make sure people wouldn't exploit the students, there were some reports of abuse by farmers who saw the Carlisle students only as a source of cheap labor.

Jim despised cooking and cleaning, and one time he just quit an outing assignment and returned to Carlisle. He spent a few days in the guardhouse for that. Another time, the outing family felt so sorry for him, they requested he be returned to school. But back at school, Jim was faced with textbooks, which he didn't much like either. There was only one solution: The "Athletic Boys" of Carlisle never had to go on outings, and their exploits on the field cut them slack in the classroom.

Years before Jim's arrival at Carlisle, Pratt had realized that the school would always need more money than it got from the government, and favorable publicity—there were too many people who thought teaching "savages" was a waste of time and taxes. Pratt knew one sure way to get cash and ink—winning sports teams. It's a technique that many universities use to-

day. By the time Jim arrived at Carlisle, Pratt had already picked the man to help keep his dream alive.

Glenn Warner, a big, young, gruff coach, was legendary at the school. He had been called "Pop" since his college days at Cornell, when he played football years past his eligibility. He was relentless in his drive to make Carlisle a football powerhouse. He could be nasty, abusive and profane. Once he hit a player for making a mistake. But he could also be very kind, and he respected the players and their abilities.

Indian athletes on the whole have always been less willing to be yelled at than most white athletes (even now, rather than complain about a coach's behavior, they will simply leave the team), but they are also more willing to put aside the quest for personal glory for the good of the group. According to both Indian and non-Indian coaches, Indian athletes tend to take criticism poorly, but because they have been trained as observers, they learn very quickly. These are cultural differences that good coaches learn to accept and even use. Pop Warner was a good coach—he toned down his foul language

and took advantage of his players' specialness, which happened to fit his own playful inventiveness. Pop's ideas were the wave of the future in a new game that did not yet have the technological precision of the NFL today. Pop would go on to coach for many years at major universities—Carlisle was his laboratory.

Pop came up with the "Indian block," in which a player led with his hips and used his whole body to hit, instead of just his shoulders. Pop taught his passers to throw perfect spirals. From discarded wood and cloth he built the first blocking sleds, and drilled his linemen in blocking techniques. He spent hours in the Carlisle shops designing new kinds of padding and gear.

Warner's most notorious play was the "hidden ball trick." During one game, the Carlisle team formed a giant wedge to receive a kickoff. Hidden from the opposing team but not from the giggles and shouts in the stands, the receiver slipped the ball into a special pouch sewn into the back of a blocker's jersey. The blocker practically walked in for a touchdown while the other team searched frantically for the ball.

Eventually, the play was outlawed, but Pop didn't mind. Football was still a young game

with flabby rules, and he had plenty of other tricks up his sleeve, most of which he invented out of necessity; in the days in which a 200-pound lineman was considered huge, Carlisle players rarely weighed more than 160.

Jim, who was small for his age as a teenager, was about 5 feet 5 inches and 120 pounds when he arrived at Carlisle not quite seventeen years old. Nevertheless, he played intramural football that year, on the tailor-shop team. Like everyone else, he worshipped the varsity players from afar. But it was track and field that first got him noticed, three years later.

One spring twilight on his way to a game, in 1907, Jim walked by the high-jump pit and sat down to watch the varsity jumpers practice. They set the bar higher and higher until one by one none of them could clear it. Jim, still in his bulky work overalls, asked for a try. The varsity jumpers laughed and shrugged.

He leaped the bar with ease. Nobody said a word, and Jim walked away. The next afternoon one of the jumpers found Jim in the dining hall.

"Do you know what you did?" the jumper supposedly asked.

It's not hard to imagine this cocky young Jim Thorpe as a jock hero today.

"What?" For a moment Jim might have been afraid he would be punished or, worse, sent on an outing.

"You broke the school record."

When Pop, who was the track coach as well as football coach and athletic director, heard the news, he issued Jim a team uniform. He asked his star, Albert Exendine, to whip Jim into

The 1909 Carlisle track team poses for its group portrait. That's Pop in the suit and tie, and Jim, already twenty-two years old, seated fourth from the left, under Pop's shoulder.

shape. The two became close friends, even after Jim's first season, when he broke all of Albert's records. Jim and Albert became the best known of all the Athletic Boys.

But what Jim really wanted was to play varsity football.

5

One afternoon in the fall of 1907, so the legend goes, Jim marched to the varsity football practice in a borrowed uniform two sizes too large and asked to try out for the team. Everyone chuckled except Pop Warner, who shouted something like "Take that uniform off!" He would not have wanted his new track star to get banged around.

"I want to play," Jim might have said, perhaps with that tough, stubborn look in his eye that teammates later remembered.

"If that's the way you want it," said Pop, tossing Jim the first real leather football he'd ever held. He pointed to the varsity players warming up on the field. "Give them some tackling practice."

Jim strolled to one end zone, hugged the ball and took off. He had an easy lope, a distance runner's stride, and the first player to reach him leaped like a wolf on a deer. He was shocked when all he grabbed was air before he hit the ground. Jim cut and spun and stopped short, leaving the heroes of Carlisle sprawled behind him on the grass. He sprinted the last twenty yards and no one was close.

Pop was speechless as Jim trotted back to the sideline.

"Nobody tackles Jim," he said, trying not to grin.

"You can't do that again," sputtered Pop.

Of course he could. It was a little harder this time—the varsity was ready and steamed—but Jim wove his way through the entire team, dodging tacklers, wriggling out of a grasp, now and then stiff-arming someone out of his way.

What could Pop say? "Get him a uniform that fits."

That first season, Jim practiced the fundamentals: blocking and tackling, how to read the opposing team, how to bring a ballcarrier down and shake the ball loose. He practiced drop and

place kicking until he could split the goal posts at every distance from nearly impossible angles.

But he didn't start right away. Carlisle was becoming a national football power behind quarterback Frank Mt. Pleasant, who had a rifle arm and a quick mind. While most teams used size and brute strength to win games that were more bar brawl than sport, Carlisle relied on what newspapers of the day described as a "wealth of marvelous plays" and "beautifully executed forward passes."

The team lost only one game that season, but it somehow got a reputation for not being tough in bad conditions like rain or snow or on a mud-soaked field. Journalists had a habit of writing that the Indians played for sheer pleasure rather than school pride, so when the weather killed the fun, they just gave up. Actually, many of their tricky plays simply didn't work on a slippery field with a wet ball.

The theories the sportswriters offered were part of the white mind-set that saw Indians as "noble savages," alternately childlike, barbaric, cunning, innocent, certainly too close to nature to be like other Americans. This attitude helped

rationalize either the massacre of Indians (they were "bloodthirsty redskins") or the taking control of their land and education (they needed to be protected). It was used to justify herding them into rural ghettoes and stripping away their language, clothes, religion.

This attitude made it impossible to treat Indians as fellow citizens, to respect their culture or to trust them to make their own decisions about their lives. In sports, this attitude made it impossible to see teams from Carlisle as hardworking, well-trained, motivated units. It was easier to see them as peaceful war parties of animalistic grace and power.

There is an enduring myth about Jim arriving alone at an out-of-town track meet and winning every single event. A one-man varsity. It simply wasn't true, but it fit into that white misconception of the primitive superman who never needed to train. It has followed Jim Thorpe to this day, that image of a great performing animal. It was hard for people to accept an Indian as hardworking, well-conditioned, smart.

A half century later, when African-American

athletes began to dominate major-league team sports, sportswriters and sportscasters often cast them as "natural" athletes rather than products of intelligent hard work, as were white athletes. It was the same kind of attitude at work.

But as far as Coach Warner was concerned, so long as his team was becoming nationally famous and bringing in money, the sportswriters could have their fantasies. And Pop's team soon became even more of a public relations machine than Colonel Pratt could have hoped. Raggedy little Carlisle, which was not even an accredited college, was playing the big college teams—Harvard, Yale, Pennsylvania, Syracuse, Princeton, Minnesota—and not only beating them but raking in a fortune on ticket sales. Later on, after Pratt had left, there would be a scandal that closed Carlisle: Investigations would show that Pop slipped some of the money into his own pocket.

But Pop took care of his Athletic Boys. Everything was easier for Jim the moment he pulled on the jersey with the big "C" on the front. He lived in a more comfortable dorm than other students, ate more and better food

How good was the 1912 Carlisle football team? Jim, Pete Calac, a Mission Indian from California, and Joe Guyan, a Chippewa from Minnesota, were eventually inducted into the professional football Hall of Fame. It was the only time in history three players from the same college team made the Hall. That good.

and got spending money from the coach—just like at a real college. Downtown, at Mose Blumenthal's store, Jim could get a fancy suit on Pop's account, and some extra cash from Mose, who like many merchants in town was a team booster. The school's fame brought business to their stores, hotels and restaurants.

But Carlisle was not so easy for its academic honor students. Jack Newcombe, in his book about Jim Thorpe, *The Best of the Athletic Boys*, quotes a letter from Emma Newashe, a Sac and Fox girl, to her Indian agent requesting money for

a dress: ". . . As I am President of the society I certainly will have to look decent. If I am not dressed as if I was at a reception why what will they think of their President? Mr. Kohlenberg just you put yourself in my place, having no parents to look after you, to send you no clothing. . . ."

It was her own money she was asking for, from the account the local Indian agent had set up for each Sac and Fox as part of the payoff for the government taking their land. The agent had control of the account, and Emma Newashe probably did not get her dress. But the athletes got all the perks they wanted, and some they may not have even known about. Pop paid off the local police to keep his boys out of jail when they sneaked off school grounds and went carousing downtown.

Jim enjoyed that winter after his first football season. He'd stroll the campus with his team-mates, basking in the adulation, or go into town for drinks on the house. Pop bent school rules on alcohol for his athletes. Perhaps he felt they deserved to let off steam, they worked so hard; perhaps it was a way of keeping them—many were in their twenties—in school, another ex-

ample of white men using firewater.

In spring, Jim trained hard for track. Although he never cared as much about setting records as he did about winning his event and scoring points for the team, he set a school hurdle record, the first of many.

Track teammates of Jim's included quarterback Mt. Pleasant, who was a master at the broad jump, and long-distance running champion Louis Tewanima, a Hopi from the Southwest. That summer, not long after putting on his first pair of running shoes, Tewanima placed ninth in the marathon at the 1908 Olympic Games in London.

Jim went home to Oklahoma for the summer. Ed and Adaline, his younger brother and sister, were still mourning Hiram. Jim entertained them with stories of his long leap from overalls to a varsity uniform. Jim's older half-brother, Frank, took him hunting and fishing. They shared memories of their father. Jim was twenty-one years old, and he began to find comfort in his family.

Then it was time to head back to Carlisle and suit up for his first big season.

6

Tall and sinewy, as quick as a flash and as powerful as a turbine engine . . .
—THE PITTSBURGH DISPATCH

By 1908, Jim's name dominated school cheers, press clippings and football award lists. Many of the eleven games Carlisle won that season were decided at the last minute by Jim's clutch kicking.

There were bitter defeats, too; The 17–0 loss to Harvard, that training school for millionaires and presidents, was seen by Carlisle as another humiliation at the hands of the privileged white establishment.

In the grueling 6–6 tie with Pennsylvania that Jim would later call the toughest game of his life, he missed several easy field goals before breaking loose for a long run at the very end. Such heroics led to Jim's selection as a third-team All-America.

There wasn't much time for classes. As they do today, major college teams practiced and traveled with the intensity of professionals. Jim and his friends tried to catch up on their schoolwork during the winter, but they knew that so long as they won, teachers and administrators would never flunk them out.

Jim became even more valuable to Carlisle that spring, when he won nearly every track and field event he entered and, in his first start for the Carlisle baseball team, pitched a no-hitter.

When the school year ended, hungry for a change of scene, Jim followed Carlisle classmates Possum Powell and Jesse Young Deer down to the North Carolina tobacco country, a hotbed of semipro ball. Jim signed on as an infielder with Rocky Mount of the East Carolina League. Although playing for money violated college and amateur athletic rules, it was common practice, and officials looked the other way. Many college athletes played under false names—including, the story goes, future President Dwight D. Eisenhower, a West Point halfback who roamed minor-league outfields as "Wilson."

For reasons that have never been fully explained, Jim played under his own name. Did he think he'd never be caught? Was he too honest to lie? Or, most likely, did he think it didn't matter because he had decided not to return to Carlisle? In any case, Jim's speed alone made him famous in semipro ball. One Fayetteville shortstop remembered bending down to field a hard grounder only to see Jim already blazing past first base.

The league was a mix of journeymen and college boys. Jim earned about twenty-five dollars a week, not a luxurious salary but enough to live comfortably. Local kids often gathered outside the hotels of their favorite players and carried their mitts and bats to the park. Jim was a favorite, and he loved the friendly, small-town attention and the free time without schoolwork, assemblies, chores, rules. After a while, he wired Carlisle to say he wouldn't be back. He asked his local Indian agent for some of the money in his account. It was grudgingly sent. When the baseball season ended, Jim went home to Oklahoma and found work as a hired hand. He was twenty-two years old.

Meanwhile, the Carlisle football team struggled through the 1909 season. When Jim visited the school for Christmas, Pop begged him to stay for the track season, but Jim refused; as much as he enjoyed the comradeship and the attention, he was tired of school and rules. Out in the world, he was a gifted athlete being paid for his skills, who could live the way he wanted, come and go as he pleased. In the late spring of 1910 he signed up for another season with the Rocky Mount team. Again he returned to Oklahoma for the winter. He began to feel as though he was drifting aimlessly through his life. He worked hard and he drank hard. He began to miss the security and order of school life.

And Oklahoma was changing, booming with more white settlers, more new businesses, and more hostility toward Indians, who were viewed as being in the way of progress. There was discrimination in jobs, and nasty remarks on the street.

Motion pictures were the newest craze, and one of their major action subjects was the West. The "good" cowboys almost always won. The prevailing movie attitude was "the only good Indian is a dead Indian."

That year a Chippewa delegation sent a letter to President Taft protesting the depiction of Indians by Hollywood as drunks, fools, cannibals, rapists and savages. Long after the battle for territory had ended, the battle for human rights and ethnic identity raged on. And still does.

Maybe Jim began yearning for a place where Indians were treated with dignity, even if they were being de-Indianized; a place where he was a hero, even in the downtown stores. He seemed ready to leave Oklahoma one afternoon when he bumped into Albert Exendine, in town visiting friends. Jim's old track mentor had earned a law degree after leaving Carlisle and was now coaching at a small college. When Jim admitted he hadn't been up to much lately, Ex suggested he go back and finish school. Play some more football. He noticed how much bigger Jim was now, more muscular.

"They wouldn't want me there now," said Jim, according to Jack Newcombe's book.

"You bet they would," said Ex. He dragged Jim to a telegraph office, and they sent Carlisle a wire requesting Jim's readmission.

Academic officials weren't sure if he was

"worthy" of an education. Jim's dropping out had disappointed them. And he was, after all, twenty-four years old.

But Coach Pop Warner was thrilled at the chance for another powerhouse football team, and maybe even a trip to the Stockholm Olympics that summer with Jim and Louis Tewanima. Warner convinced the administration that Carlisle could not *afford* to refuse Jim. After all, hadn't he always been "worthy" enough to sell tickets?

Pop was not only an innovative coach but a pioneer in the field of sports public relations. His staff hyped the team into a national powerhouse, and during the 1911 season it dubbed Jim "greatest all-around athlete in the world." The label stuck even before it was proven true.

In football, he was a wonder. Jim's most feared tactic during those games was a punt kicked so high that he could race downfield before the ball landed, in plenty of time for a bone-crushing tackle or even a recovery and touchdown. After one of the mighty Thorpe exhibitions that fans came to expect every time he played, *The Pittsburgh Dispatch* wrote: "This person was a host in himself. Tall and sinewy, as

Pop Warner was a model for the modern king-coach, who often has more power than the college president. But then as now, the coach needed "the horses," the blue-chip athletes who actually do the work. Pop's horses were Jim and Louis Tewanima, the Hopi long-distance runner.

quick as a flash and as powerful as a turbine engine, he appeared to be impervious to injury."

Quick and powerful, yes, but not impervious. An ankle sprain put him out of action for two weeks, and though not quite healed, he suited up for the game against Harvard, a chance to avenge the 1908 loss. The media buildup was intense, and nearly thirty thousand people attended the game in Cambridge.

The arrogant Harvard coach was so convinced that Carlisle was no match for his team that he didn't even bother to show up for the game, and he ordered his assistant to play only the substitutes.

By the end of the first half, Harvard led by

three points. Carlisle, losing to scrubs, got mad, got even and then got ahead on a spectacular breakaway touchdown and a couple of those towering kicks by Jim. Disobeying their absent coach, the frantic Harvard captains brought out the varsity team—the cavalry charging to save the day.

But it was too late. Nobody could bring Jim down. When his ankle finally gave out and he hobbled off the field, a stadium filled with Harvard fans let out a wild cheer. Later, the Harvard coach was quoted as saying, "I realized that he was the theoretical superplayer in flesh and blood."

Jim was a superstar. The next morning's papers hailed him as a future Hall of Famer. The team returned to Carlisle for days of dances, banquets and speeches.

It was sometime during those happy days of celebration that Jim discovered another reason to be glad he had come back to school. Her name was Iva Miller. She was eighteen years old, a pretty, popular honor student. While Jim loved to laugh and to dance, he was no social smoothy. In fact, according to Newcombe, he

Looking at this scrubby football field and these smallish young men in their old-fashioned uniforms, second-rate even for the time, one can only imagine how talented they were and how hard they worked to beat the best college teams in the country.

was considered a tacky dresser who was awkward around women. His first words to Iva were supposedly, "You're a cute little thing." But by Christmas of that year, people noticed that Jim was dressing more carefully and trying to act more suave. He was falling in love.

7

Thanks, King.
—JIM THORPE

The U.S.S. *Finland*, decorated in red, white and blue, set sail from New York on June 14, 1912, for Stockholm. It was Jim's first ocean ride, a joyous, rowdy trip, the best part of the Olympics, he would say later. With Pop coaching, Jim and Louis Tewanima trained on deck with their 150 American Olympic teammates. They spent hours every day on the cork track that circled the jumping mats and the swimming pool. There were newspaper stories that Jim snoozed in a hammock for most of the voyage. His teammates said that no one trained harder.

The Stockholm Olympics were the fifth Games, and the first that Americans took seriously. Women competed for the first time in 1912. From 1896 through 1908, rich young men from club teams were the core of the U.S.

Jim jogs on the deck of the ship that carried the American squad to the 1912 Olympic Games. Teammates said he trained as hard as anyone, but sportswriters, who preferred their fantasy of the "natural athlete," claimed he spent most of the trip snoozing in a hammock.

squad. But by 1912, Americans saw the Olympics as another way of flexing their muscles in the world arena.

The original Olympics in ancient Greece were also a stage for nationalistic muscle flexing—Athenians versus Spartans versus Macedonians—and sleazy practices. There were fixed races, performance-enhancing drugs (strychnine was used as a stimulant) and sexism—women were banned from even watching under pain of death, for the men competed naked.

When Baron de Coubertin of France reintroduced the Olympic Games in 1896, he announced his intentions of inspiring better international understanding through sport. Some historians believe his real motivation was to whip his own countrymen into better physical shape for their next war: They had recently lost the Franco-Prussian War to Germany.

Whatever the original purpose, there was no mistaking the elitism of the modern Games. Millionaires and aristocrats ran the Olympics, and only amateurs (the word is from the Latin meaning "to love," in this case, playing for love of sport rather than money) were allowed to compete. Olympic leaders wanted their event "pure" of the professionalism and commercialism of soccer, baseball and football. An athlete who had ever taken money to play sports or advertise products was barred from the Olympics for life. If it was discovered that an Olympic athlete had ever "played for pay," he or she would be stripped of medals and records.

It's doubtful if Jim was even thinking of such distinctions as amateur and professional. For him, the Olympics was a big, exciting track

meet in another country, all expenses paid. There was no money for competing or even winning.

Pop had entered Jim in the two most difficult Olympic competitions: the pentathlon, which in those days consisted of the running broad jump, the javelin throw, the 200-meter dash, the discus toss and the 1500-meter run; and the decathlon, which was the pentathlon plus the 100-meter

As the U.S. Olympic track team lines up for a group picture, Jim, in a turtleneck, stares off in another direction. What is he seeing, thinking about? At 5 feet 11 inches tall, he's one of the shorter athletes.

The field events of the Olympic pentathlon and decathlon were not Jim's best, but he was strong and graceful, and was a fast learner.

dash, the pole vault, the high jump, the 110-meter hurdles, the shot put and the 400-meter run.

Although some people say the decathlon is for athletes who aren't really good enough in any one event, most people think the decathlon

winner is the best all-around athlete in the world. The decathlon is the ultimate test of speed, strength and stamina.

Not only did Jim win gold medals in both events, he set a decathlon record that lasted for sixteen years. Because training has advanced enormously through the twentieth century, there is no truly objective way of comparing Jim to today's athletes; but remember that neither Bo Jackson nor Deion Sanders, among versatile modern stars, won the Olympic decathlon.

Jim was humble about his accomplishments but not surprised. "I had trained well and hard and had confidence in my ability," he said.

Along with the gold medals, King Gustav V of Sweden presented Jim with a valuable royal bronze bust. Czar Nicholas II of Russia presented him with a jewel-encrusted silver chalice in the shape of a Viking ship.

The attention Jim received was overwhelming, from the thousands on hand and the millions worldwide who followed his triumphs in the press. Louis Tewanima's triumph, a silver medal in the 10,000 meters against the strongest

Jim may or may not really have said "Thanks, King," when Gustav of Sweden called him the world's greatest athlete. But what would you say to a starchy old gent like this?

field ever assembled, was lost in the excitement over Jim.

Jim Thorpe was the first global sports star, the sporting ancestor of Pelé and Muhammad Ali and Michael Jordan. But he wasn't as good as his successors at controlling his image. When King Gustav placed a laurel wreath on Jim's head and the medal around his neck, the king said, "Sir, you are the greatest athlete in the world."

"Thanks, King," Jim is said to have replied. People who read that chuckled at the stereotype of the barely civilized native and the sophisticated royal. But historians are not convinced that such a conversation ever took place. It might be just another story, like the one about Jim training in a hammock on the transatlantic trip.

After exhibitions in Europe, the U.S. team returned to a ticker-tape parade in New York City. Jim rode in his own car and waved to millions of cheering fans. President Taft wrote him a letter. Owners of pro sports teams begged him to play football or baseball for them. Theater impresarios offered him big contracts to go on their stages; he could sing a few songs, dance, tell jokes, anything. Just his name on the marquee outside the theater would mean a full house inside.

But Pop convinced Jim to come back to Carlisle for one more year. Maybe he stressed loyalty to coach and school, reminded him that Iva was waiting or told him that after another good year in college football, he'd be worth even more.

**I hope I will be partly
excused by the fact that I
was simply an Indian
schoolboy. . . .**

—JIM THORPE

A friend of Thorpe's, Pete Calac, who played at Carlisle and later in the pros, recalled: "Jim never acted like he was better than any of us, in spite of his great fame. He always tried to be just one of the guys."

But it was Jim who made "the guys" the team to beat. He was a blur, kicking goals from outlandish distances, crunching and juking his way through entire defenses, taking daring, crowd-pleasing, calculated risks. Like all great athletes, he knew exactly what his body could do.

Pop would have benched anyone else foolish enough not to down the ball in the Lehigh end zone, but there wasn't much he could say when Jim shook loose from the half dozen tacklers

swarming over him and bolted 110 yards for a touchdown. Jim was twenty-five years old at that time, and probably at the peak of his speed and conditioning. While he was good sized for a running back of his era—just under 6 feet tall, about 180 pounds—his rocket-burst runs were powered by muscles developed in track and field.

The most anticipated game that 1912 season was against West Point. It was billed as the classic match of Indian speed and savvy against Army size and power. Looking back now, it seems like a metaphor: a team of future Army officers, symbolic sons of Custer and all the Indian fighters, against the symbolic sons of the warrior Chiefs, doing battle with a football instead of a cannonball. But that might not have been in any of the players' minds. On both sides they were jocks getting a free education at a government school and playing their hearts out for coach and teammates.

There was no doubt football filled Jim's head that day. Jim set up touchdowns for his teammates and scored one himself on a brilliant run, only to have it called back on an offside penalty.

Two cadets tried to take Jim out with a high-low tackle, but Jim pulled up in time to watch them knock each other into a daze and stagger out of the game. One of them was "Ike" Eisenhower, the future president.

Tired from a hard win, the Carlisle Indians lost their next game against a mediocre University of Pennsylvania team, but they won the rest. After a game against the YMCA eleven of Worcester, Massachusetts, Pop decided to let his team stay in the New England town for a few days of recuperation and training.

One day, a young editor for *The Worcester Telegram*, Roy Johnson, came by to watch Carlisle work out. He was chatting on the sidelines with Charley Clancy, a baseball manager. When Jim jogged by, Clancy pointed excitedly: "Hey, I know that guy!"

"Of course you do," Johnson probably said. "That's Jim Thorpe."

Clancy explained that he had known Jim a few years back, when he'd managed a club down in the Carolinas. Jim was that fast kid on the Rocky Mount team.

Johnson's heart skipped a beat. This was hot

news. He could imagine the headline: "Greatest Amateur Athlete in the World Played for Money!" It was the kind of scoop that makes a reporter's career.

Johnson was in a dilemma. He didn't want to hurt Jim. He believed the amateur rules were hypocritical; they favored rich athletes who didn't need to make a living. And, like many people, he felt the rules were unfairly strict. (Today, when most major Olympic athletes get paid, it's hard to understand what agony Roy Johnson must have gone through, weighing the pros and cons of breaking his big story.)

Meanwhile, Jim announced that the Thanksgiving game against Brown University, the last of the season, would also be his final college football appearance. Jim's teammates and fans wanted him to go out with a bang, and he obliged with three touchdowns and two field goals in a swirling blizzard. When the 32–0 victory ended, even the referee was flabbergasted.

"The greatest football player, ever" was all the referee could manage to say. Every newspaper agreed. Jim was selected first team All-America for the second year in a row.

Jim went back to Oklahoma for the holidays and returned to Carlisle, as he had so many times before, a modest and casual hero who tried to take seriously his role as a model. He gave inspirational speeches to the younger students in a pleasant, straightforward style. He made an effort to catch up on some schoolwork; the poet Marianne Moore, who taught at Carlisle early in her career, remembered him that last year as polite and intelligent, but because of the demands of sports usually unprepared in class and often absent.

He even won a school dance contest. He brought the first prize, a chocolate cake, back to the dorm. Jim was always generous with his possessions and his money.

And then everything changed. Roy Johnson, who believed it was his journalistic duty, broke his big story in January 1913, using the information from Charley Clancy. At a hearing before the Amateur Athletic Union (AAU), Clancy denied everything he had said to Johnson, and Pop, desperate to cover for himself, lied and said he never knew his athletes played summer ball. Later, when players from the Carolina

leagues confirmed the truth, Jim was left dangling to take all the blame.

Pop wrote a letter and persuaded Jim to copy it over in his own hand. Warner read it as Jim's words at the AAU hearing.

> *I hope I will be partly excused by the fact that I was simply an Indian schoolboy and I did not know all about such things. In fact I did not know I was doing wrong because I was doing what I knew several other college men had done. . . . I have always liked sport and only played or ran races for the fun of things and never to earn money.*

The letter was an admission of guilt and got everyone off the hook except Jim. The U.S. Olympic Committee, Carlisle and Pop Warner were all cleared of charges that they had known Jim played pro ball and yet had still allowed him to compete as an amateur. The bust of King Gustav and the Russian czar's chalice were returned to the International Olympic Committee, and the gold medals, which Jim had given to Pop for safekeeping, were awarded to

The gold medals Jim had to return after the 1912 Olympics weren't gold-plated, as they are today, but he had cherished them as priceless souvenirs of the time when he was the best in the world.

the second-place finishers. The name James Thorpe was stricken from Olympic record books. It was as if the flashing cameras, the cheering fans, the astonished athletes, were all an Indian fable and Jim had never been in Stockholm at all.

Was justice served? Even at the time, many people didn't think so. The fact that Jim had played baseball under his own name, whether out of honesty or stupidity, further fueled their outrage: Jim had never tried to be dishonest, yet he became a scapegoat for a system that was itself dishonest. In the years to come there would be many examples of countries that actually paid their athletes—against the rules—to play in

This bust of the Swedish king was Jim's trophy for winning the Olympic pentathlon. Not only was it taken back after he was stripped of his Olympic championships, but it disappeared. When one of his daughters, Grace, tried to reclaim the bust, along with the model of the Viking ship he had received from the czar of Russia for winning the decathlon, she was told they were "traveling" trophies that went to each new champion after each Olympics. But no one could tell her why no one else had ever gotten the trophies, or even where they were. Grace had hoped to place them in the Jim Thorpe Museum she was planning in Yale, Oklahoma.

the Olympics. But the millionaires and the aristocrats never cracked down on them.

Perhaps the main reason the AAU didn't deepen its investigation of professionalism was

its fear that many others of America's most talented amateur athletes would also have been disqualified.

On the other hand, Jim did break the rules of his time. Maybe he was naive, but shouldn't he have gotten better advice from Pop Warner, who was pretty slick? Should Pop have been punished too? Even today, when sports rules are broken, the athletes usually are punished more severely than the coaches or administrators.

Jim was lucky to have close friends at Carlisle who reminded him that he had proven to the world he was the greatest athlete, with or without the medals. But they shared a deeper sorrow: To the Indians this was another story of broken treaties. They felt that no matter how shiny their buttons or perfect their diction or how many touchdowns they scored, Indians would never be treated fairly by whites.

It seemed to them that after Jim had bested the whites at every game they taught him, he was being punished for being too good.

Jim always tried to keep his pain private, but those closest to him saw it. Years later, while on the road with the New York Giants baseball

team, John ("Chief") Meyers, a catcher who was also a Native American, awoke in the hotel room he shared with Jim to find him sitting in the dark, weeping.

"You know, Chief," Jim whispered, "I won those trophies. Fair and square."

9

Young and old loved him for
what he was—a big, warm,
fun-loving boy-man.

—CHARLOTTE THORPE

Pop Warner tried to make up for letting Jim
take all the heat by helping him negotiate a rich
baseball contract. Football was Jim's best sport,
but those early pro football teams were small
and unstable, nowhere near as popular as major
college teams, while baseball was exploding into
the national pastime. Several baseball teams
made offers, figuring that Jim's fame would
bring fans.

He joined the New York Giants. They offered a $6,000 annual salary plus a $5,000 signing bonus, an enormous amount in those days
for an untested rookie. The day Jim signed the
contract, he officially withdrew from Carlisle.
He was going on twenty-six years old, ancient
for a "student-athlete."

Jim's wedding to Iva Miller was the Carlisle social event of 1913. He stands behind his twenty-year-old bride, an honor student from Oklahoma. It is thought she had little if any Indian ancestry, one of the few whites to be educated in Indian schools.

In October, after the baseball season, he married Iva Miller in a ceremony at Carlisle that kicked off days of dances, banquets and parties. Their honeymoon was spent on a good-will tour of Giant and Chicago White Sox players to Europe, Hawaii and Egypt. They returned to an apartment in Manhattan near

the Giants' ballpark, the Polo Grounds.

John McGraw, the Giants' manager, was nearly as famous as Jim. Like Pop Warner, McGraw was a tough, cocky celebrity coach, but unlike Pop, he didn't give players the room to develop their own styles and express their own personalities. He was a strict disciplinarian, and his traditional, textbook approach to baseball quickly clashed with Jim's freewheeling ways.

Pop may have been too loud and profane, often sleazy and even cowardly, but he always appreciated Jim as an athlete and a person. McGraw was jealous of Jim's fame and mocked him for his unpolished skills. He made no real effort to make use of Jim's enormous natural gifts or his willingness and ability to learn quickly and work hard.

The relationship between McGraw and Jim became even more strained because of the manager's abuse. Once, after Jim missed a signal to steal, McGraw called him a "dumb Indian." Jim chased McGraw around the field until other Giants tackled and restrained him.

McGraw insulted Jim publicly, suggesting he was not smart enough for the complexities of

Jim's baseball skills were major league, but he was hired by the New York Giants more for his fame than his hitting. Because the manager was jealous of his stardom, Jim never got good coaching or the chance to play enough to improve.

the game and that he "couldn't hit the curve-ball," an old baseball put-down. He accused Jim of drinking too much and risking injury to other players by challenging them to wrestling matches. Actually, it was usually other Giants who challenged Jim, eager to boast of pinning the world's greatest athlete.

Jim spent most of his six seasons in the major leagues (he also played for the Cincinnati Reds and the Boston Braves) warming the bench. He said he felt "like a sitting hen, not a ballplayer."

Jim was a favorite among his teammates because he was fun to be around, and because he helped anyone in need. Later, Jim admitted that his desire for a good time and his willingness to share his wealth was the reason he was usually broke.

Jim was also famous for his appetite.

"Boy, could that guy ever eat!" John Meyers once exclaimed. "He'd order a beefsteak smothered in pork chops. And corned beef and cabbage, that was his favorite. He could down four servings in one sitting!"

Teammates respected Jim as an athlete, and some wondered how good he might have be-

come with patient coaching. By the time Jim left the game, baseball was buzzing over a new young phenom, Babe Ruth.

Jim played baseball for the money, but he got his real athletic kicks from football, which he played and coached into his forties. During the baseball off-season, he would volunteer as an assistant to Pop, at Carlisle and later at the University of Pittsburgh. Pop became more and more famous in his day, and he's still known because of the Pop Warner Leagues for young football beginners throughout America.

When the American Professional Football Association, which later became the National Football League, was created, Jim became player-coach-owner of the Canton (Ohio) Bulldogs. In 1920, he was elected president of the association. Pro football was a raucous game played by former All-Americas of varying ages. Fan loyalty and betting were fierce, the only similarity to today's high-tech game.

Jim was slower now but still a star. He never lost his kicking leg, and when it came to running and tackling, even an over-the-hill Jim could still dominate most players in their prime. Ernie

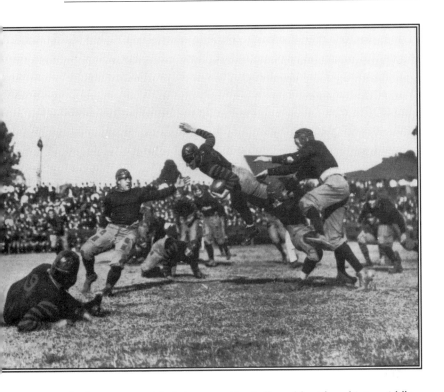

Jim's greatest athletic love was football, and he played into middle age. As a member of the Canton (Ohio) Bulldogs, he was an early player, owner and official of what would become the National Football League.

Nevers, a football star in his own right, was tackled by thirty-nine-year-old Jim and said he had never been hit so hard in his life. Jim's love for the game increased as he packed the Bulldogs with old Carlisle teammates. The postgame

parties were pretty wild, too.

Later he formed an all-Indian football team called the Oorang Indians, named for its sponsor, a dog kennel. The players hammed it up with costumes and war dances as well as dog tricks and lasted two seasons before disbanding.

"Dad did not try to set himself up as an example for others to follow," wrote his daughter Charlotte in her book *Thorpe's Gold*, written with Brad Steiger. "Young and old loved him for what he was—a big, warm, fun-loving boy-man."

Jim returned to Oklahoma with Iva and their children and bought a house in a little town called Yale, where he would hunt and fish and see old friends. At times, though, he seemed closest to his dogs, according to Charlotte: "I think my father loved his coon dogs more than anything. He loved hunting and fishing the Indian way."

Jim was not the most responsible husband and father. His seven children always remembered him with affection, but few of them knew him very well. He had begun drinking even more heavily after his first son, James Jr., died in the 1918 influenza epidemic. Perhaps he was reminded of his brother Charlie's death. He would later say that Jim Jr.'s death was the worst time of his life, that the Olympic disappointment wasn't even in the same league. The stress of the tragedy probably was the main reason he and Iva divorced.

Newspaper stories about Jim Thorpe in later life portrayed him as a pathetic, broken spirit, as "Poor Jim," especially when he turned up broke or drunk or bar brawling or digging ditches. In 1932, when he couldn't afford a ticket to the Los Angeles Olympic Games, U.S. Vice-President Charles Curtis, who was part Indian, invited him to sit in his box. They watched Babe Didrikson, perhaps the greatest all-around female athlete in American history, and a lacrosse exhibition starring a young Mohawk who would be spotted by a Hollywood talent scout. Renamed Jay Silverheels, he was to play the Lone Ranger's sidekick, Tonto.

Jim sold the film rights to his life story for a mere $1,500. The movie that was made in 1953 starring Burt Lancaster, *Jim Thorpe—All-American*, was a box-office hit, but Jim didn't share in the profits.

His own children regarded him as a big kid—more an older brother or jolly uncle than a responsible, day-to-day father. He was happy around kids, and liked to romp and laugh and hand out candy.

Don't cry for Jim. He had his good times and he made his points and he left an important legacy. He went on to speak out against the abuses of the Bureau of Indian Affairs and the government control of Indians, and he lectured to thousands of schoolchildren about the richness and dignity of native life and culture.

His own children (three daughters with Iva— Gail, Charlotte and Grace; four sons—Carl Phillip, William, Richard and John—with his second wife, Freeda Kirkpatrick) remember him as a loving, caring man, sometimes more big brother than father, but a man who was proud of them and tried his best to make a living and give them a happy life.

In 1950, the Associated Press voted him the Male Athlete of the Half-Century. He was way ahead of runner-up Babe Ruth.

On March 28, 1953, in the Lomita, Califor- nia, trailer in which he lived with his third wife, Patricia Askew, Jim Thorpe died of a heart at- tack. He was not quite sixty-six years old. It was the same year that Ike Eisenhower, the West Point football player who knocked himself out trying to tackle Jim, took office as President of the United States.

10

He is a great
symbol to us.
—CHIEF OREN LYONS

"I met Jim Thorpe when I was growing up,"
said Chief Oren Lyons, Faithkeeper of the
Onondaga Nation. "He knew my uncle, Ike
Lyons, from Carlisle. He'd hang out here with
his friends, and come watch our lacrosse games.
I'd be trying to keep my eye on the ball, but I'd
sneak glances at him. Powerful-looking man.
Friendly. He is a great symbol to us."

For generations of Native Americans, the
story of Jim Thorpe was both sad and inspiring.
He was treated shabbily, they felt, cheated out
of his medals and his prestige in the white world
because he was an Indian; yet his accomplishments proved that an Indian could be the best
in the world.

For Chief Lyons, a former All-America lacrosse goalie at Syracuse University, an artist and a world-renowned leader of the Haudenosaunee (Iroquois) Confederacy, the symbolism of Jim Thorpe was clear: The white world had to beat him down because he was so strong.

"Jim Thorpe showed up the white world," said Chief Lyons. "They were trying to prove we were savages, how else could they justify stealing our land and killing us? But here was Jim Thorpe and this raggedy group of savages from Carlisle, who just recently had their hair cut, just recently got shoes, and they're whipping West Point and Harvard. The white world took it as an insult. They had a respect for us in a way, but they had to beat us down."

Thirty years after his death, and mainly because of relentless pressure from his children, the International Olympic Committee reinstated Jim Thorpe. His name was returned to the rolls of the 1912 Olympic champions, and duplicate gold medals were struck and awarded to his children. (The IOC never gave back the bronze bust and the jewel-encrusted silver chalice, now said to be worth millions.)

It was a year after that, 1984, that forty male and female runners set out from the Onondaga Reservation near Syracuse, New York, to California, site of the Olympics, on a two-month, 3,600-mile journey called "The Great Jim Thorpe Longest Run."

So much had happened since Jim's death: The militant American Indian Movement had brought natives into the national struggle for civil rights; tribal colleges, teaching self-respect for natives' Indian identity, had sprung up; Indians had successfully used the legal system to win back land rights, fishing rights, mineral rights; Indian scholars were revealing the truth of their many Nations' histories. And white Americans were beginning to understand that Columbus' "discovery" of America was really an invasion, that the Indian reverence for nature was a starting point in saving the earth, even that there was something wrong in calling a team the "Redskins."

These were the messages the young people carried in the spring of 1984, messages worthy of a Runner for the Nation. They carried it through the late spring and early summer along

Two of the grandchildren of the great American Olympians Jim Thorpe and Jesse Owens carry the torch through New York City en route to the 1984 Games in Los Angeles. Bill Thorpe Jr. shares the honor with Gina Hemphill.

the northern rim of the United States, from the Onondaga Nation through the lands of the Oneida, the Winnebago, the Anishinabe, the Dakota, the Lakota, the Arapahoe, the Northern Cheyenne, the Ute, the Ouray, the Western Shoshone, to the lands of the California Indians and a four-day festival of art, dancing and lacrosse, the Jim Thorpe Memorial Powwow and Games. Two of Jim Thorpe's children, Gail and Grace, were there to meet the runners and thank them for keeping his spirit alive.

For the lacrosse players, the event had special significance; Jim Thorpe's story was also the story of their sport. In 1880, after more than a century of teaching Europeans how to play "bump hips," the Iroquois national team was charged with taking money in violation of amateur rules, even though they used the money to travel to overseas tournaments. Indians saw it as another white scheme to push them out of the way; they were winning too much. They were banned from international play for more than a hundred years, until the year of the Jim Thorpe Run, and then only because of a fierce campaign for reinstatement led by Chief Lyons.

Chief Oren Lyons (standing) of the Onondaga Nation, a leading Runner of the Haudenosaunee (Iroquois) Confederacy, remembers Thorpe as friendly and inspiring when Jim visited his reservation in the 1940s and '50s. Lyons went on to become one of the great college and club lacrosse players of his time, and a coach of the Iroquois national team. The player is Jimmy Bissell, Jr.

On the day before the runners set out, the
old lacrosse star himself studied the determined
faces of the young women and men as medicine
men burned leaves at their feet and an elder
chief reminded them to let nothing distract
them from their mission.

Chief Lyons smiled and nodded and said:
"Jim Thorpe was beaten, but he was never
tamed. He was too strong an individual for that.
He suffered, but he survived. And that is the
story of our people."

FURTHER READING

Brown, Dee. *Bury My Heart at Wounded Knee*. New York: Holt, Rinehart & Winston, Inc., 1970.

Deloria, Vine, Jr. *Custer Died for Your Sins*. New York: Macmillan, 1969.

Levine, Peter. *American Sport: A Documentary History*. New Jersey: Prentice-Hall, Inc., 1989.

Lyons, Oren and John Mohawk, et al. *Exiled in the Land of the Free*. Santa Fe, NM: Clear Light Publishers, 1992.

Nabokov, Peter. *Indian Running*. Santa Barbara, CA: Capra Press, 1981.
———. *Native American Testimony*. New York: Penguin Books, 1991.

Newcombe, Jack. *The Best of the Athletic Boys*. New York: Doubleday, 1975.

Steiger, Brad and Charlotte Thorpe. *Thorpe's Gold*. New York: Dee/Quicksilver, 1984.

Wheeler, Robert W. *Pathway to Glory*. New York: Carlton Press, Inc., 1975.

INDEX